12 MSC   S79887

A Life Spent for Ireland

A LIFE SPENT
FOR IRELAND

Selections from the Journals of
W. J. O'Neill Daunt
Edited by his daughter

Introduction by
DAVID THORNLEY

IRISH UNIVERSITY PRESS
Shannon · Ireland

First edition London 1896

This IUP reprint is a photolithographic facsimile of the first edition and is unabridged, retaining the original printer's imprint.

PRINTED IN THE REPUBLIC OF IRELAND AT SHANNON
BY ROBERT HOGG PRINTER TO IRISH UNIVERSITY PRESS

INTRODUCTION

William J. O'Neill Daunt is one of the most neglected figures in nineteenth-century history. His importance does not derive from his presence at the centre of dramatic events; an amiable if somewhat misanthropic hypochondriac, he spent most of his life in semi-retirement at Kilcascan, County Cork. But he was in many ways much more representative of the mainstream of Irish Catholic nationalism than some of the more heroic figures immortalized in history. In addition, he was an avid correspondent and meticulous diarist. Deprived of the telephone and the rapid transport which are going to make the writing of contemporary biography and much of contemporary history almost impossible, he corresponded voluminously with every leading Irish constitutional nationalist (except Parnell) and almost every leading Catholic thinker from Newman downwards, from the 1840s to the 1880s. He was also, like John Martin, an indefatigable despatcher of letters to the press.

The details of his life are simply told: he was born in 1807 and died at the age of eighty-seven, thereby outliving all the contemporaries whom, from the age of sixty onwards, he had assured of his total feebleness and imminent demise (28 April 1868: 'I am sixty-one years old today, and I feel the debility of age'). The coffin he notes his decision to buy in July 1870 consequently had to wait twenty-four years to receive its owner. He came from a Protestant conservative family in Tullamore but was converted to both Catholicism and nationalism in his early twenties. He was returned as a repealer in Mallow in 1832, and though critical of O'Connell for personal reasons, supported him up to his death. For the Irish Confederation he had little time, and O'Brien's venture at Ballingarry he describes, rather neatly, as 'a driftless and unaccountable affray with the police' (28 July 1848). In the mid-forties he rather drops out of politics, partly owing to a second spell in Edinburgh where he had lived for a time as a young man. (1 February 1869: 'Received Holy Communion at first Mass, and experienced something like a return of my feelings when a frequent communicant in 1832 at Edinburgh'). He had however resumed his diary by 1845, and writes sympathetically of the plight of the people in the famine. January 23, 1847: 'Reached Cork after a stormy passage. Dined with my dear old friend Father Mathew, who gave me potatoes at dinner, a rare luxury as times go now.'

The journal as published here becomes chatty rather than political for some years after 1849, and although Daunt was a close friend of Gavan Duffy's, one does not get the impression that he had the same political enthusiasm in this period as in the thirties and forties, and he possessed too strongly nationalist and too irreverent a nature to revel in the episcopal politics of the early 1860's. Political interest revives in the late 1860's with disestablishment and the birth of the home rule movement. He admired Isaac Butt, and allowed himself to be used by him as the principal channel of communication between the Home Government Association (and later the Home Rule League) and the Irish Catholic hierarchy in the early 1870's. He was offered a nomination for Wexford by Dr Furlong, Bishop of Ferns, in the 1868 election, but declined it ('I am too old, too poor, too infirm') as he was to decline many subsequent invitations to stand for parliament.

However when Butt and the other leaders of the Home Government Association, realizing that the initial membership base of the movement had been too Dublin orientated and too heavily loaded with Protestant and ex-conservative names, attempted to broaden its appeal to the traditional Catholic liberal voters, Daunt agreed to come to Dublin for four months in the first half of 1873 to act as what would now be called public relations officer to the Association. In this capacity he continued, with some relative success, to lobby the Catholic hierarchy on behalf of the home rule cause, writing to amongst others, the Bishops of Cloyne, Meath, Ross, Clonfert, the Archbishops of Cashel and Tuam (Dr MacHale) and numerous priests. He admitted that he found the results disappointing: 'It is curious that while the Orange party oppose Home Rule as been identical with Rome Rule, the Protestant Home Rulers are accused by certain stupid Catholics as intending by their movement to upset Rome' (3 April 1871). Nor did the hasty conversion of many Catholic liberals to home rule cause him to build any illusions. 'Gladstone's Education Bill unsatisfactory to the bishops—"Serve 'em right". I long ago prophesied that a good Catholic education bill could never be extracted from the English parliament; and it is discreditable that our prelates should be imposed on by the agents of Whiggery instead of throwing their weight into the nationalist movement' (15 January 1873). And again, on hearing a (false) rumour that Cardinal Cullen had been converted to home rule: 'If he be indeed converted, I don't ascribe his conversion to any patriotic feeling, or to anything better than his having discovered that his hopes of a good educational measure are *nil*...' (15 May 1873). With characteristic shrewdness he saw through the insincerity of the converts to home rule from Gladstonian liberalism in 1873–74—an insincerity which was more than anything else to destroy the effectiveness of Butt's party between 1874–79. Daunt, although socially conservative, had the rabid Irish nationalist's detestation of Gladstone. During the 1874 election campaign he wrote: 'Gladstone has dissolved parliament and hurried on a general election in order to take the Home Rulers at a disadvantage. He promises to abolish the income tax. This sounds well, but I shall not wonder if so expert a twister imposes a worse tax in place of it' (29 January 1874). And on hearing the final figures: 'The English election results in a Tory majority. Gladstone goes out; Disraeli goes in. L'un vaut bien l'autre.' (20 February 1874).

In June 1874 Daunt returned to Kilcascan, and rarely quitted it again. But he maintained his interest in politics, and the flood of letters and diary entries continues. Butt's extremely mild Land Bill of 1876 disquieted him: 'Butt sends me his Land Bill, which gives too much too [crossed out], which deals very liberally with the tenants. As I have nothing to live on but the land I have some fellow feeling for the landlords; which how-ever is greatly weakened by their unnatural anti-national pol-itics' (March 1876). Such crossing-outs are a feature of Daunt's diaries, and bear amusing witness to his charitable nature. So also was this ambivalence between social conservatism and innate nationalism, which was a common characteristic amongst the middle-class Catholics of the time. 'Cardinal Cullen refuses to allow the corpse of the Head Centre Fenian O'Mahony to lie in state in any of the Dublin Churches. I cannot blame the Cardinal for this. Fenianism is a mischievous burlesque of patriotism and the defunct Fenian was one of its leaders' (21 February 1877). Nevertheless Daunt's hatred of the English parliament caused him to side with Bigger and Parnell in the obstruction controversy of the same year: 'Parnell, M.P. for Meath, and Biggar, M.P. for Cavan, have been using the rules of the foreign house of commons to obstruct the business of that unfriendly institution. They are quite right to give it all the annoyance they *prudently* can. If the English insist on dragging Irish members over to London against the will of the Irish nation, it is surely the duty of our members to render their enforced presence there as great a nuisance as is possible to the English enemy. Obstruction, truly! Why the foreign parliament is in itself an obstruction to Irish prosperity . . .' (2 July 1877). Again, on 10 December 1878, he describes the House of Commons as a 'foreign club of robbers'. But the Land League was foreign to his socially cautious nature: 'I don't like Parnell's agitation of a peasant proprietary—not from any objection to a peasant proprietary if it grew up naturally and gradually. But to make it a prominent topic can serve no other purpose but to scare the landlords from Home Rule . . . ' (11 December 1879).

These brief excerpts from Daunt's journals will, I hope, demonstrate the relevance of his lengthy career to the understanding of nineteenth-century Irish nationalism, and the appropriateness of republishing this book today. One word of warning must, however, be sounded. Edited by his daughter, and published within two years of his death, this version of his journals inevitably presents him as an eminent, pious, Victorian Catholic. This he was. But he was also mordantly witty, iconoclastic, and if not actually anti-clerical, highly irreverent where clerical authority was concerned. A very few examples from the unpublished sections of his journals show this immediately. On the result of the famous Kerry by-election of 1872, in which the Protestant home ruler Blennerhassett defeated the clerically supported candidate: 'Hurray for Kerry! The black mass of Catholic rottenness, Dease, O'Donoghue, Kenmare, and the O'Connells have been beaten by a majority of 829.[1]

1 It was in fact 839.

I wonder has Bishop Moriarty the grace to be ashamed of having brandished his crozier in the ranks of the English enemy' (10 February 1874).

On the Catholic clergy, 7 May 1874: 'Our parish priest, Father Hurley died this day, R.I.P.—I have not spoken to him ever since he borrowed money from the government under the Glebe Loans Act'. And on hearing that two Glasgow priests had warned their parishioners against the Home Rule League on account of its alleged Protestant leadership (19 August 1875): 'These precious miscreants must be men after Cullen's heart.' On the declaration of papal infallibility, he commented with typical common sense (4 August 1870): 'For my own part I cannot see the use of it; but I am modest enough to admit that there may be some use, though I can't see it.'

With this irreverence, there went however great personal devoutness and prudishness. 'Holyoake, Bradlaugh and their gang' he denounces as 'apostles of atheism' (30 May 1871), the Communards are 'revolutionary scoundrels' (12 August 1870), 'red republicanism' is a scourge' (24 April 1871) and his reaction to reading Ouida's novel *Cigarette* was one of outrage: 'the hero is the quintessence of vicious frivolity, and the authoress seems to be a w————' (14 January 1875).

Not surprisingly, Daunt's liberal views inspired in him a great admiration for Newman: 'Here is *one* Englishman, at any rate, for whom, in spite of his country, I entertain the most profound veneration and very strong regard' (12 August 1870). But Newman *was* just about the only one: 'there never existed a more thoroughly profligate, conscienceless horde of political scoundrels than the majority of Englishmen in all cases affecting their national aggrandisement' (19 December 1878). Gladstone, that 'expert twister' was a particular object of his detestation, partly because of Daunt's nationalism, but partly also because of his conviction of the iniquity of taxation, which he associated with Gladstone, and which, with nationalism and the prospect of dying, was one of his three lifelong obsessions. But Disraeli 'the sneering Mephistopheles at the head of the government' (12 March 1879) fared no better. All pomp and ceremony irritated him, especially in connection with the awesome realities of birth and death. On the celebration by his tenants of the birth of his grandson, he wrote (1 July 1879): 'I cannot think a birth an occasion for rejoicing. There is something that jars against my feelings in associating the event with merriment.' Funerals were as bad; on the death of Joseph Ronayne, M.P., for Cork City, he wrote (9 May 1876): 'His death is a serious loss to our cause; he had honesty and ability. . . . Of course I will not go to the funeral. Funerals are foolish affairs beyond the attendance barely necessary to lower the remains to the ground and the presence of a few immediate friends and relatives.'

I have, as I said, included these further excerpts from his journals which are not printed by his daughter, to correct the slightly pompous impression which may otherwise emerge from this book. William J. O'Neill Daunt's journals and letters do not merely serve as a major source for nineteenth century historians; they also present a picture of an individual at once nationalist and conservative, irreverent and devout, morbid and humorous. His career is overdue for reassessment, and I hope that the republication of *A Life Spent for Ireland*, besides being a valuable venture in itself, will provoke the scholars of the future to look more closely at the life of this representative figure and endearing personality.

David Thornley

A LIFE SPENT FOR IRELAND

Walter L. Colls Ph.Sc.

A LIFE SPENT FOR IRELAND

Being Selections from the Journals of
THE LATE W. J. O'NEILL DAUNT
EDITED BY HIS DAUGHTER

London:
T. FISHER UNWIN
PATERNOSTER SQUARE
MDCCCXCVI

PREFACE

THE subjoined letter from that distinguished literary man, Mr Lecky, may well stand as a preface to this volume. While differing, as may be seen, in his estimate of Irish national questions, from the Diarist, Mr Lecky is sufficiently impartial and generous to comprehend the motives that underlay Mr Daunt's convictions and conduct in his long political career. While Irish Nationalists may consider Mr Lecky's championship of Pitt and Castlereagh as somewhat Quixotic and mistaken, no one can deny to him the right of holding his own opinions, and a due appreciation of his candour in the utterance of them. For the rest, his just and kindly insight into the staunch and upright character of the deceased Irish patriot is thoroughly and gratefully appreciated by the Editor.

" Dear Miss O'Neill Daunt,—You asked me
to write you a few lines, giving my impression of
your father and of his work in Irish literature and
politics. My judgment of him was not formed
from personal acquaintance, but from a tolerably
intimate knowledge of his writings, and from
a correspondence extending over many years.
My first connection with him dates from the
beginning of 1862.   In the preceding year I had
published anonymously a rather crude little volume of Irish biographies, from Swift to O'Connell,
which many years later made some noise in the
world, but which, at its first appearance, was an
utter and absolute failure.   The only exception
to the general indifference was an article from the
pen of your father, which appeared in a Cork
newspaper, and which was equally remarkable for
its kindness towards myself, and for its ample
knowledge of the period I had treated.   It was
the first public recognition that there was some
real merit in my writing, the first confident prediction that some future lay before me in
literature.   A letter of very sincere thanks which

I wrote to my unknown critic was the beginning
of a correspondence which continued, at intervals,
to near the end of his life.

" Your father, I need scarcely say, was one of
the most ardent of Irish Nationalists.   As he once
wrote to me, ' No earthly cause is so dear to my
affections as the legislative independence of
Ireland.'   He was, however, a Nationalist formed
in the school of O'Connell, and seemed to me
very unlike those of later days.   His aim was the
union, on a national basis, of all classes, creeds and
interests in Ireland, and the restoration, through
such an union, of the National Legislature.   He
believed that in one form or another the old story
of the volunteers might be renewed, and that the
gentry of Ireland might lead the people in the
path which he desired.   His dream—if it was a
dream—was at least a noble and a generous one,
and he followed it from youth to old age with a
consistency that never wavered, with a sanguine
hope that no vicissitude in Irish politics could
ever effectually quench.   He took a prominent
part in the Home Rule movement of Butt, which,
in its general lines, met his cordial approval, but

he was, I believe, profoundly disappointed when
the movement was afterwards turned into an
agrarian war, and a war of classes, and he had
no sympathy with the violence and crime that
followed. Though keenly sensible of the misdeeds of many Irish landlords, and of the abuses
in the Irish land system, he maintained, both in
public and in private, that the worst enemy of
Ireland could inflict on her no greater evil than
the agitator who was preaching among an excit-
able peasantry a war of classes. 'I wish I had
good grounds to differ from your belief,' he wrote
to me in 1880, 'that Home Rule, if now obtained,
would impart noxious power to the brawlers of
the land agitation. It is a choice of evils.
The Union is a deadly blight. A domestic par-
liment composed of —— ——, and similar
creatures, would be a very equivocal blessing.'
He, more than once, printed remonstrances
against the course which was being pursued,
risking fearlessly all the popularity he had acquired. But he disclaimed all merit in doing
so. Standing apart from active politics, he was
absolutely independent. He sought nothing

for himself, neither place, nor power, nor even popularity. As he wrote to me, ' I do not know how much or how little popularity I possess, and whatever its amount, I only value it so far as it may find acceptance for what I deem the truth.'

"Courage, consistency and hopefulness are great qualities, and your father possessed them in an eminent degree. No one, too, could come into close correspondence with him without feeling the transparent purity and disinterestedness of his motives, the honest vehemence of his convictions, and, at the same time, the essential kindliness of his nature. In his correspondence with myself, though we often differed, I never received from him one word of discourtesy or anger. He had considerable literary skill, and a remarkably wide range of knowledge of recent Irish history. His *Personal Recollections of O'Connell* is a book of much charm and vividness, and will be of use to every biographer of O'Connell. Of his many writings on the Union, and on other periods of Irish history, I cannot speak with the same praise. They are

sometimes powerfully written, and they contain
much painful truth, but they seem to me
wholly wanting in the gift of historical imparti-
ality.   The early impressions of a very vehement
nature, deepened, I believe, by a remarkably secluded life, were too strong to be modified or
effaced.   Your father's hatred of the Union, and
his antipathy to English rule in Ireland, had
become an overmastering passion, and he had
fully persuaded himself that Pitt and Castlereagh,
and indeed most past English Governments,
acted through motives of an almost demoniacal
character.   If he had possessed more power of
graduating opinions and discriminating motives,
or realising the point of view of those who
differed from him, and understanding that there
are two sides even to questions relating to
Irish Nationality; if he had accustomed himself
to judge men and actions by the moral standard
of their own age, and not by that of a later
one, your father would have been a better
writer, and would have exercised a more healthy
influence on Irish literature.

   " His knowledge, however, of the subjects he

treated was very large, and on the financial
aspects of the Union he wrote with special authority. His strong conviction that the contribution of Ireland was fixed at too high a rate,
and that her taxation was excessive, has been
supported by excellent authorities in England
as well as in Ireland. It is a subject on which
he wrote much, and he contributed largely to
bring it to the forefront. He was, I think,
rather painfully sensible of the irony of fate
which obliged him to admire, in his capacity of
Nationalist, the very statesman who, by extending the Income Tax to Ireland, had most
largely increased the burden of Irish Taxation.

" From his long personal intercourse with
O'Connell, your father perpetuated, perhaps more
faithfully than any other Irishman, the traditions of the old Repealers, and he represented a
type of Nationalist which is now rapidly passing
away. It is a type which was not without its
defects and limitations, but it was pure, honest
and disinterested, and, in my opinion, Irish life is
much the poorer for its loss.—Yours truly,

" W. E. H. LECKY."

CONTENTS

CHAPTER I

CHAPTER II

CHAPTER III

CHAPTER IV

CHAPTER V

CHAPTER VI

CHAPTER VII

CHAPTER VIII

CHAPTER IX

CHAPTER X

CHAPTER XVI

CHAPTER XVII

CHAPTER XVIII

CHAPTER XIX

CHAPTER XX

CHAPTER XXI

CHAPTER XXVI

CHAPTER XXVII

CHAPTER XXVIII

CHAPTER XXIX

CHAPTER XXX

CHAPTER XXXI

CHAPTER XXXII

CHAPTER XXXIII

CHAPTER XXXIV

CHAPTER XXXV

CHAPTER XXXVI

CHAPTER XXXVII

CHAPTER XXXVIII

CHAPTER XXXIX

CHAPTER XL

A LIFE SPENT FOR IRELAND

LEAVES FROM THE DIARY OF
W. J. O'NEILL DAUNT

CHAPTER I

Preliminary—Mr Daunt's Ancestry—Origin of 'Daunt's Rock'
—Early Aspirations—How Prince Eugene took Snuff—
Pre-Union Dublin—An Abducted Bridegroom—Spectral
Apparition—Social Life—A Fatal Duel.

THE centre of Ireland, as all the world is aware, is
covered by a large tract of peaty soil known as the
Bog of Allen. King's County, Kildare, Roscommon
and Meath each furnish a quota to the sum of the all-
pervading moorland. In this great waste of dreary
bog there are, however, many oases, and in one of these,
the pretty town of Tullamore, capital of King's County,
William Joseph O'Neill Daunt first saw the light on the
28th of April 1807.

When he was born, George the Third was king of
England and Hanover, and the Union of the Parliaments
of Ireland and England had been but seven years in
existence. Hanoverian regiments were quartered in
Tullamore along with the regiment of the Louth Militia,
of which young Daunt's father was captain, and of

which Oriel Foster, son of the last Speaker of the Irish
House of Commons, was colonel. At that period of
universal unrest, the various militia regiments did not
enjoy a repose so profound as that in which they now
rest. They were almost permanently embodied and
sent up and down the kingdom on garrison duty. The
proud boast of the Louth Militia stands recorded : 'We
volunteered for England!' Those were not days of
swift mail steamers, and some amount of courage was
needed to embark in sailing vessels, which were so much
at the mercy of every wind that Captain Daunt was, on
one occasion, eighty days on the sea between Bristol
and Cork.

Mr Daunt's family was an old one. Originally it
had migrated to England at the time of the Conquest,
and had, by marriage and otherwise, acquired estates in
Gloucestershire. The old manor of Owlpen, which still
exists in perfect repair, was the seat of the head of the
house for many centuries, until about the time of Mr
Daunt's birth, the last representative, Mary Daunt,
married Mr Staughton of Ballyhorgan, in Kerry, and
merged her name in his. Owlpen had given shelter,
according to tradition, to Margaret of Anjou, the night
before the famous battle of Tewkesbury, and a letter is
on record addressed by Edward of Lancaster, Prince of
Wales, to John Daunt, bidding him hasten 'with all
defensible array' to his assistance, and to bring with
him the rents due to the prince from an estate of his
called Mer-run-Parton, a property not satisfactorily
accounted for by antiquarians. In Elizabeth's reign,
the head of the Owlpen family, Thomas Daunt, transferred himself and his fortunes to Ireland, and acquired
on lease, from Sir Warham St Leger, the lands of

Tracton Abbey, near Kinsale, formerly a monastery of Cistercian monks, whence its name, *de Alba Tractu*. He also purchased the estate of Gortigrenane in the same county. One condition imposed on him in the Tracton lease was, that he should furnish a light horseman for Queen Elizabeth's service, when called on to serve by the Munster undertakers; and another condition was, that 'no mere Irish' should be permitted to settle on his lands, with the sole exception of a family named Healy, who, we may presume, had, for some good service rendered, found favour with the authorities. In course of time this Thomas was succeeded by another Thomas, who, in the Civil War of 1641, lost property to the value of £1562. He was succeeded by Achilles, who was conditionally attainted by King James the Second's Parliament of 1689, and fled to England. The legend exists that a fierce feud raged between this Achilles and a noted Irish chieftain and buccaneer, whose name was Philip ōge Barry, and the latter, watching his opportunity, during the period in which Achilles Daunt was fulfilling the duties of High Sheriff of the County Cork, seized and carried him off to a rock at the mouth of Cork Harbour, whence he was providentially rescued, according to one version; another account asserts his death by drowning. The rock retained his name, and is unfavourably known to seamen trading with the Port of Cork. To go back a little. The father of the man who bought Gortigrenane and Tracton married Alice Throckmorton of Tortworth, a sister of Sir Walter Raleigh's wife. His fourth son, William, was grandfather of William Daunt of Kilcascan, which property he acquired in 1712. The great-grandson of William of Kilcascan was Captain Daunt, father of William O'Neill Daunt.

Captain Daunt married Jane, daughter of the Reverend Thomas Wilson, D.D., F.T.C.D., rector of Ardstraw, County Tyrone. Dr Wilson was, next to Porson, the best Greek scholar in the kingdom. He was a staunch supporter of the Irish Parliament, and refused the bribe of a bishopric from Castlereagh in connection with the Union. When the letter containing the offer arrived, he happened to be seated at his study fire. He stooped and picked up a piece of coal, which he put on the fire, then showing his blackened hand to his wife, he remarked, 'My hand is blackened by the coal; but it shall never be stained by a bribe.' Mrs Wilson had been a Miss Crawford, whose family was an offshoot of the Crawfords of Kilbirnie, in Scotland. After her husband's death, Mrs Wilson went to live in Tullamore, and there in course of time the eldest son of her daughter, Jane Daunt, was born. And now having said so much, we will let the Diarist speak for himself.

Alluding to his early years, Mr Daunt recounts :— 'Childhood, of which I have a very distinct recollection, passed partly in my grandmother's house in Tullamore, partly at Kilcascan. . . . At Tullamore, our visiting acquaintances were chiefly the Armstrongs of Kilclare, the Curtises of Cluna, the Stepneys of Durrow, and the Turpins of Brookville. . . . I have pleasing recollections of the well-wooded domain (of Durrow), the old tumulus covered with forest trees near the mansion, the little church, of which the aisle was partly flagged with lettered gravestones, the ancient cross in the cemetery, and, above all, of the friendly, social family. The place was afterwards sold to Lord Norbury, and was the scene of an execrable and unaccountable murder, of which the perpetrator has never been discovered. . . . I had a

strange, mysterious yearning after the Catholic Church.
Fitzgerald, my Catholic tutor, knew nothing of this, so
closely did I hoard my secret. There were two rooms
of my grandmother's house containing a large number
of books. They were always kept locked, and the key
was now and then entrusted to me as a reward of good
conduct. . . . I rambled *ad libitum* through a sea of
very miscellaneous literature. Among the authors were
Swift, Dryden, Shakespeare, Milton, Rollin, Addison,
Steele, Pope, Goldsmith, Johnson, Cumberland, Molière,
Puffendorf and many others. There was a vast pile of
unbound plays which had doubtless seen their day at
the Dublin theatres during the last century, and which,
I suppose, had come into our possession while my grandfather was somehow connected with Smock Alley
Playhouse.[1]

   ' In theology I was trained to read daily a chapter
of the Old Testament and a chapter of the New. I was
taught Mann's catechism, and I privately studied the
Douay catechism, which I found in the library. . . . Her
(Mrs Wilson's) great grandfather was a Scotch officer in
King William's army, who fought at the battle of the
Boyne. He left a son Henry, who . . . served in the
campaigns of the Duke of Marlborough and Prince
Eugene of Savoy. He used to record the mode in
which Prince Eugene took snuff on the field of battle—
grasping a handful from a huge tin pocket and flinging
away all that he did not inhale.

   ' He married the granddaughter of a Lucretia Marsh
who was, through the Hydes, a cousin of Queen Anne,
who presented her with a splendid wedding-dress and a

---

[1] He had become lessee of it on the non-payment of a large
sum of money which he had lent Daly, the manager.—ED.

cabinet on her marriage. . . . My desire for the Repeal of
the Union, which I had formed in boyhood, was stimu-
lated by her (Mrs Wilson's) vivid narratives of the
splendour of Dublin during the existence of a resident
Parliament. She described the brilliant society of that
dazzling era, the magnificence of the entertainments ;
the blaze of rank and wealth that adorned the metropolis ; the gaiety of the Court ; the glories of the
memorable time when for once the Irish aristocracy
rallied at the head of the Irish democracy for the common land of both. The Dublin of that day she described with the lively touches that can only appertain
to the narrative of an eye-witness. In 1790, ninety-six
peers had town residences in Dublin. . . . Of the wealthy
commoners nearly all had town houses. Then came
the change in 1801, the black and dreary change, the
Union, the extinction of the Parliament, the decay of
the metropolis, the death-like chill that struck the
heart's core of Ireland, when Pitt and Castlereagh had
" slipped the slave's collar on, and snapped the lock." '

[Mr Daunt's great - great - grandmother, on the
maternal side, was a Scotch heiress, a certain Matilda
Liddell, who made a runaway match with a Mr
Robertson.—ED.]

In order to protect him from any penalties he might
have incurred for abduction, Miss Liddell assumed the
rôle of abductress. They eloped on horseback, the
young lady occupying the saddle, and Robertson
perched on the crupper.[1]

---

[1] A great-grandson of this romantic pair was Major-General
Sir Andrew Barnard, who was appointed military commandant of
Paris by the Duke of Wellington, during the occupation of that
capital by the allied armies.—ED.

In the spring of 1774, to quote from the diary again, Dr Wilson went to Bristol for the benefit of the hot wells. During the summer he was requested by some of the leading electors to ask the celebrated Edmund Burke, with whom he had been previously acquainted, whether he would consent to offer himself as candidate for Bristol at the next general election. Wilson's political principles were in harmony with those of that great Irishman. A correspondence followed ; Burke's letters are not forthcoming, but his friendly feelings to his correspondent appear in Wilson's second letter, published in *Burke's Correspondence*, in which the writer says :—' The particular regard you are pleased to express for me is very flattering.' Burke appeared on the hustings on the 13th October 1774 ; elections in those days were tedious affairs ; the polling continued to the 3d of November, on which day he was returned. Wilson was on intimate terms with Secretary Hutchinson. The secretary offered him much higher ecclesiastical preferment, but Wilson thought he had enough, and refused the offers of promotion. . . . These imperfect family notices would be still more imperfect if I omitted to mention the only spectral apparition that dignifies our annals. My grandfather's sister, Sarah Wilson, married in 1760 the Reverend James Crawford, rector of Killina in the County Leitrim. There is a bit of grim romance attending the mode of his death, which I shall set down exactly as I received it from his daughter Mary Crawford. He had occasion in the autumn of 1777 to cross the estuary of the Rosses on the coast of Donegal in order to avoid a round of several miles. The water was rather deep, but some men on the shore assured him that they considered it still fordable. On a pillion behind Mr Crawford sat his sister-in-law, Hannah Wilson. They advanced pretty far into the sea, until the water reached the saddle-laps, when Miss Wilson became so alarmed that she implored Crawford to turn bridle and get back as fast as possible to land. "I do not think there can be danger," said Crawford, "for I see a horseman crossing the ford not twenty yards before us." "You had better hail him," said she, "and inquire the depth of the intervening water." Crawford accordingly checked his horse and halloo'd to the other horseman to stop. He did stop, and on turning round displayed a ghastly face, grinning fiendishly at Crawford, who waited for no further parley, but faced about and returned to land as fast as the state of the rapidly-rising tide would permit. On arriving at home he told his wife of the spectral rencontre. He was settling his cravat at the mirror while he spoke, and when he described the grin of the water-fiend, she observed from the reflection of his face in the glass that he turned white as death from the terror evoked by the recollection. The popular belief was, that whenever the water-fiend became visible, the unlucky mortal to whom he exhibited himself was doomed to be drowned when he next should attempt to cross the estuary. Despite the monitory superstition, perhaps to confute it, Crawford again attempted to cross the ford of the Rosses on the 27th of September 1777, and was drowned in the attempt. His body was found about three weeks after, frightfully mutilated by the fishes.[1] . . .

I chiefly resided at Kilcascan, not quite three of these years being spent at Tullamore. The O'Connors

---

[1] In his diary Mr Daunt continues the account of his boyhood and youth, from the age of thirteen to that of twenty-one.—ED.

were thenceforth our principal companions. They were very hospitable and very amusing, indeed they were comically conscious—at least some of them—of their entertaining qualities. I have heard Feargus say, with funny self-complacency, " I am the most agreeable man I ever met, when I am dressed for it." They were anxious to impress on all a belief of their ancestral grandeur. Mary, sister of Feargus, pointing to her brother Roger, said to me, " That is one of the most high-born young men in Ireland "—a modest mode of insinuating her own patrician claims. Feargus was the only man I ever knew who could walk about the room shaving his face without cutting it. For a considerable time my father, who was a widower from 1816 till November 1822, had been wholly estranged from the rector, with whom he had a perpetual dispute about tithes. There was not just then much general society kept up in the country with the exception of an occasional fox-hunters' dinner-party. After my father's second marriage, the neighbourhood became more social. . . . Politics invaded our coterie. My father hated tithes, but was in all things else a strict Tory. He tried, by levying collusive distresses, to protect the family of one of our tenants from the inroads of the rector. He said it would be a very good thing to have a parliament in College Green, only that the Catholics would do—he could not exactly say what, but something indefinitely terrible. Arthur O'Connor was an Emancipator, and slept with a book called *The Beauties of the Press* under his pillow. It was a collection of articles selected from old Arthur O'Connor's newspaper, *The Press*, suppressed by Government a little before the Rebellion. Feargus was at that time Toryish, at least in conversation, but had written an incoherent pamphlet against the oppression of the people. The rest of our set were unmitigated wooden-headed Tories. For myself, I felt for O'Connell the same reverence in politics that I felt for Scott in the realms of imagination. While I was yet in my teens my father died.[1]

After my father's death I spent some weeks at Glanatore, which had been given to Mrs Daunt's eldest brother Richard by his father, who removed to a villa called Windsor, about two miles from Cork. Facing Glanatore, on the opposite side of the river Bride, are the picturesque ruins of Mogeely Castle, in ancient days a stronghold of the Earls of Desmond. Further down the river is Curriglass House, then the seat of my

---

[1] It may be of interest here to mention the manner of his father's death, which, to his latest days, gave Mr Daunt a thrill of horror as often as he recalled it. Captain Daunt had a dispute of a trivial nature originally, with a cousin of his, Mr Conner of Manch. Evil tongues, notably that of the rector of a neighbouring parish, the Reverend Mr K——, fanned the flame, until finally challenges to fight passed between the cousins. The duel came off at a place called Rhincrew, just within the boundaries of the County Waterford. Mr Conner's second was a Captain Beamish, whose fixed idea seemed to be that one or other of the combatants must of necessity lose his life. So that after one or two shots had passed harmlessly, and Captain Daunt's second ventured to observe that 'surely honour was now satisfied,' Captain Beamish's savage reply was : 'Put your man on his ground, sir !' The result was that Mr Conner's next shot struck his unfortunate antagonist in the forehead, killing him instantly. This happened in the year 1826. Mr Conner took refuge in France with his cousin, General Arthur O'Connor. After the lapse of a few months, Mr Daunt instituted a prosecution, which excited intense interest in Munster. The jury was packed with duellists, who gave a verdict in favour of Mr Conner. Had they been able to separate legally the second from his principal, they would gladly have hanged Beamish. Mr Conner regretted the deed very deeply. It was the last duel fought in the south of Ireland.—ED.

grand-uncle, Henry Gumbleton.   His wife was the Honourable Sarah Massey, daughter of the second Lord Massey.   She had a large dog that used to accompany the family to church, and, as I have been told, the dog occasionally created mirth by joining in the psalmody. All these people were good-natured, but they were Tories of the most pronounced type ; and as party spirit was exasperated to boiling point by the contest for the County Waterford, in which Mr Villiers Stuart was successful, I need not say that I was unable to sympathise with their enthusiasm.[1]

[1] The foregoing extracts show plainly enough that Mr Daunt had resolved to break away from class and family traditions, and to cast in his lot with the people.   He was now on the threshold of manhood, and, by his father's death rendered his own master, free to act as he pleased.—ED.

CHAPTER II

MUCH of the period from the age of twenty-one to
thirty-one was occupied with politics. I also read
some theological works, including Bossuet's *Avertisse-
ments aux Protestants* and his *Variations.* I made the
acquaintance of Father Mathew, and one of my first
acts on acquiring independence was to become openly
incorporated with the Catholic Church. I loved to
frequent Father Mathew's chapel, and often rode to
Cork for that purpose. At home Feargus was our
constant companion. He had satisfied himself that
his best road to fame lay in the adoption and advocacy
of popular views, and, when the Repeal and anti-tithe
agitations became general, he was one of the loudest
and most active agitators. I regarded the tithe system
as a monstrous injustice, and the Legislative Union as
a wicked usurpation by England of legislative power
over Ireland. I readily joined the movement when it
reached our quarters. Feargus O'Connor had made a
rattling Repeal speech at a Reform meeting held in the

Cork County Court-House in December 1831. In the following summer he addressed a great anti-tithe meeting at Macroom. . . . We had meetings at Dunmanway and Enniskeane, at the former of which my dearest brother Tom was chairman. Next came THE GREAT PUBLIC DINNER, which Feargus got up to himself at Enniskeane, and for which he was obliged to purchase the eatables and drinkables. Of that dinner 1 have given a sketch in *The Wifehunter*. THE GREAT PUBLIC DINNER TO FEARGUS O'CONNOR, ESQUIRE, came off on the 15th of August 1832, and Feargus, who had purchased the materials of conviviality, indemnified himself as best he could for his outlay by the sale of the tickets. Between eleven and twelve at night the illustrious and patriotic guest and I quitted the assembled patriots, accompanied by Mr Snow, a reporter from one of the Cork newspapers. Feargus's horse could not be found. Snow had no horse of his own; a hunter of mine was forthcoming, and all three of us mounted on his back. I occupied the saddle, Feargus bestrode the crupper, and, with Snow upon the withers, we cantered away to Fortrobert, Feargus giving vent to his delight in noisy strains that made the echoes vocal. . . . In a few days Feargus's sister Mary chanced to say that he had cleared three-and-sixpence by the dinner, meaning that to that extent the sale of the tickets had exceeded the outlay for the viands and drink. However that might be, the *débris* of the feast were carted up to Fortrobert, and formed no unwelcome addition to the domestic commissariat. Wine, whisky, and nearly a pailful of lump sugar accompanied the mutilated joints of meat. In the course of the winter he contested the county, for which he was returned at the general election, overthrowing a combination of the chief aristocratic families. He was very touchy on the subject of his own ancestral grandeur. The peers of the county he contemptuously termed the 'new families,' and he told the constituency that their choice of him demonstrated their preference for ancient blood. . . . Feargus entertained at first the expectation of superseding O'Connell in the popular leadership. In 1833 or 1834 he wrote a pamphlet against O'Connell, which he showed me in manuscript. I told him that he could only hurt himself by printing it, and I induced him to postpone its publication for a year. He, however, at length printed his pamphlet, which destroyed any remaining chance he might have had of recovering popularity in Ireland. . . . There was in his character a strain of more than romance, a sort of fancy, real or simulated, that a special guardian angel was on the watch to avenge his wrongs and to punish his assailants. Thus, when unseated for the County Cork, he emphasised the premature deaths of the witnesses against him as fulfilling his prediction of the fate which had awaited them. 'Four men,' he wrote, 'all rabid Tories, appeared to give evidence as to the value of the property out of which I qualified. . . . After they had given their evidence I met them in the lobby leading to the committee room, in the presence of Henry Noblett, when Pyne came up to me and said, " Well, O'Connor, we are very sorry to have been obliged to appear as witnesses against an old brother-sportsman." When I turned round, and in a fury exclaimed, " D—n your eyes, you perjured rascals ; you'll be everyone dead and d—d in less than a twelvemonth ! " The youngest of those four men was about twenty-three or four, the

eldest was about thirty-six, and in less than nine months after my prophecy I received a letter from Henry Noblett, telling me that my prediction was verified— that the four men were dead and buried!' . . . About this time I amused myself writing *The Wifehunter*. When the English Parliament came to the aid of the Irish parsons I was advised that my disappearance would place legal obstacles in the way of the rector of my parish, by preventing the personal service of some notices. I accordingly proceeded to the County West-meath, where, in 1836, I remained incognito for three months at the house of my Aunt Wilson's valued friend, Father Fitzgerald, parish priest of Castletown-Delvin. During my absence from home Tom made the best arrangements with the rector that the circumstances permitted, which, however, were intolerably severe.'[1]

[1] In 1832 Mr Daunt had been returned for Mallow in the popular interest, but was unseated on the petition of the Tory candidate, Sir Denham J. Norreys. With this period were connected some of the bitterest experiences of his life. The great O'Connell, for whom he entertained a profound reverence, volunteered to free him legally from the pecuniary penalties entailed on unseating on petition, and could easily have done so by handing in a formal document. But the Liberator, great as his political character was, proved himself on this and other occasions a most unreliable friend. He would not take the slight trouble of doing what he had voluntarily promised, which simply entailed the walking from one committee room to another, and so the member for Mallow, whose circum-stances were none of the most flourishing, paid the penalty of a too confiding disposition. His son, Mr John O'Connell, had often very considerable difficulty in keeping his father up to his promises to various persons. The mental anguish which this and certain other occurrences of a similar nature caused Mr Daunt, threw him into a brain fever at Darrynane, to which he very nearly succumbed. His faith in O'Connell as a man was shattered, although, with rare un-selfishness, recognising his merits as a politician, he remained true to his leadership. In a book written after that period, entitled *The*

In 1841 the Municipal Reform Bill came into operation. O'Connell was elected Lord Mayor of Dublin, and he gave me the secretaryship by way of compensation, for a pecuniary loss he had occasioned me some years before. The Repeal agitation expanded to its largest dimensions, and I went heart and soul into it. In the allocation of duties I was appointed Repeal Director for Leinster, and Head Repeal Warden of Scotland, in which kingdom I convened several meetings of the Irish who had settled there. These duties were gratuitously performed, the association merely contributing the necessary travelling expenses.

1842.—*September* 12*th*. John O'Connell and I left Dublin in the Mullingar flyboat on our mission in support of the Repeal Association ; John for the Connaught, and I for the Leinster agitation of the Repeal of the Union. Reached Mullingar in the evening, and were kindly received by the Bishop of Meath.

13*th*. We arrived at the house of the Bishop of Ardagh at Ballymahon. Good prospects of support at both places. We posted from Mullingar to Ballymahon in a miserable nutshell of a chaise, in which I could scarcely sit upright. John, being a little fellow, escaped the inconvenience of deficient space. About half-way between Mullingar and Ballymahon we got out to walk down a steep hill. Looking back at our vehicle we saw that it had broken down, and that two or three stout peasants were supporting it in an upright position by

Gentleman in Debt, he depicted O'Connell under the character of the Reverend Julius Blake, and despite this disguise he was immediately recognised by Sir C. G. Duffy. Mr Daunt was, however, very reticent in general as to these causes of discontent with the Great Tribune, and only mentioned them to the members of his own family.—ED.

their united strength. The leather braces had been jolted off the springs as soon as the wretched little carriage lost the ballast afforded by the weight of its occupants. In reply to a scolding from John, the driver defended himself by assuring us that the chaise could not possibly have given way so long as our honours were in it, as our weight would have kept the springs steady ; the springs were tied up and we resumed our journey, the driver being fully of opinion that we had not a right to complain of any disaster that might happen the carriage while we were out of it.

25*th*. We have had large and earnest meetings at Tullamore and Athlone. I have returned to Mullingar, and am now at the Bishop's house.

26*th*. The Bishop brought me to see the old Abbey of Multifarnham. Part of it is ruinous. There is, however, a large part in excellent repair, and used by the Catholics as their parish church. It derives some interest from the fact that the Catholic service was never suspended by the rage of the ' informers ' in this parish. There is a remarkable echo in the church. . . . The Bishop told us that when visiting the catacombs at Paris, the guide called his attention to the extraordinary echo at Voltaire's grave, and desired him to pronounce some words for the purpose of testing it. The words that suggested themselves were,—'Voltaire sepultus es in inferno,' which were thundered back in so many reverberations that the Bishop began to be alarmed lest his guide should perhaps understand enough of Latin to comprehend their import, and possibly possess enough of the Jacobin spirit to avenge upon him this affront to the great patriarch of infidelity.

October 2d. On Thursday last we had a meeting at

Castlepollard, the Reverend Dr Burke, D.D., in the chair. At Mr Burke's house dined a Mr Campbell, a musical enthusiast, who travels on a jaunting car with only two available seats, the rest of the vehicle being fitted up with drawers and cases containing flutes, bugle, clarionets, a violin and a bagpipe. The two seats were occupied by Mr Campbell and his piper, who usually travels with him. They duetted the whole evening, Campbell accompanying the piper on his violin. Despite the nuisance of their noise I was amused at the manifest ecstasy of Campbell as he rasped away ; the very curls of his oily brown wig keeping time with their vibrations to the movement of his bow. My host is the same Father Burke in whose parish, Castlepollard, one of the sanguinary tithe affrays occurred between the parsons and the Catholic people. The soldiers on that occasion were called to fire on the populace, and some persons were killed. Soon afterwards Father Burke received a Government circular inquiring the number of his flock, for the purpose of making up the census. He answered that as he had not yet ascertained to what extent his people were thinned out on the last shooting day, he could not furnish the required information with accuracy. Cobbett was tickled by his reverence's spirited reply, and gave it publicity in England.

16th. Thomastown, Frankford. We have had numerous and enthusiastic meetings at Clara and Banagher. The latter was indeed a noble display of patriotic zeal. The labourers engaged upon the Shannon works turned out in a body, to the number of several hundreds, to attend our gathering. . . . After the meeting I went to Ferbane. . . . Left Ferbane in the evening boat for Tullamore. Dark, cloudy sky ; the moon peeped out at intervals as we slowly passed through the dreary expanse of flat bog. I could see no scenic beauty in that bog, yet I felt that I loved it better than richer scenes in any other land, because it is my own beloved Ireland. . . . The boat stopped for a moment at Tullamore, where I bade farewell to my travelling companions. I proceeded at once to the house of my old and kind friend, Father O'Rafferty, P.P. of Tullamore, with whom I found another old and kind friend, Dr Wallace, one of the Tullamore magistrates, a Tory in politics and a Protestant in religion, but whose heart is too good to be spoiled by political or sectarian acerbities. . . .

17th. We had this day a numerous Repeal meeting on the top of Coagh hill. . . .

November 7th. Dublin. Attended a full meeting of the Repeal Association to render an account of my six weeks' mission, the meetings I had convoked and the machinery I had helped to organise. John O'Connell has been similarly occupied in Connaught, and T. M. Ray, the able secretary of the Association, is still on duty in Munster. My statement was well received. . . .

9th. Left Dublin with O'Connell, who was very amusing and full of anecdote upon the journey. What an interesting autobiography he could write! Bently, the publisher, once tried to induce him to write his life. The great Dan was willing enough to negotiate, but he has never had leisure for the task. I parted from him at the 'Royal Oak' *en route* to Kilcascan, where Mr Ray has promised to visit me. O'Connell proceeded to Waterford, where the Repealers entertain him at dinner. . . .

20th. Attended a Repeal meeting in Clonakilty.

27th. Attended a Repeal meeting in Dunmanway.

28th. Visited the Palace Anne family. . . . The stately old mansion wears a desolate and poverty-stricken aspect. During the darkest of the penal days, the Palace Anne Bernards were benevolent enough to conceal a priest who had become obnoxious to the ruling powers.

30th. To-day, Ray has gone to Skibbereen to arrange for a Repeal meeting to be held there next Sunday, and I stay at home to sow my acorn and horse-chestnut seeds. The old oak woods that sheltered this place were cut down by my great-grandfather, Joseph Daunt, about 1751. I have heard the trees then sold for only £1500, which perhaps was a good price as timber and money then rated in this district. An old retainer of ours, named Ahern, who remembered seeing the woods in his childhood, described to me the even height to which the trees had reached, by saying, " You could bowl a trencher along the tops of the trees from one end of the wood to the other."

December 4th, Sunday. Dined at Father O'Sullivan's in company with Mr Ray, Mr George and Mr Arthur Bernard, and Father Sexten. Ray told us that the home manufacture of friezes was reviving at Skibbereen from the dislike to English pilot cloth caused by its inferior quality. . . .

5th. A funeral procession passes along the Shanavagh road. May God rest the soul of the deceased! There is something wild, mournful and impressive in the funeral cry of the Irish when softened by distance. . . . The Celtic tribes are jealous of funeral honours. The lavish distribution of whisky on burial occasions was in some places deemed a point of high importance. My grandmother Wilson, who resided for some time in the County

Tyrone, used to tell a story of a young Ulster peasant who was scandalised because the dole of drink at his mother's interment was so niggardly that nobody had got drunk enough to fight. "What!" he cried with filial indignation, "not a man knocked down at my mother's *soherath*" (burial). The desire of a numerous following to the grave is, in Ireland, a national foible. A young farmer once married a girl who was penniless. On being asked why he made so poor a match, he answered, "My wife has got fifty cousins, uncles and brothers. 'Pon my conscience, if I was to die to-morrow that young woman's faction could give me as long a funeral as the king of England."

13*th.* Left home *en route* to Macroom, accompanied by Tom. The harness broke in the middle of our journey, and the mare fairly kicked us out of the gig. We asked a passer-by for some twine to mend our broken traces. He turned out to be an idiot; grinned, jabbered, and shook his stick at us. Our plight was so absurd that, although we were vexed and inconvenienced, we could not help laughing immoderately.

14*th.* Left Macroom in the Killarney mail. . . . From Killarney I proceeded to Darrynane by the Sneem road, and saw the faint outline of the glorious lakes and mountains by the light of a misty moon. Arrived at Darrynane at a late hour. Liberator in bed ; Mrs Fitzsimon and her daughter in the drawing-room.[1] . . .

21*st.* This morning O'Connell rose before dawn to catch sunrise at a distant mountain. He had tolerable sport and killed three hares. The writers in *The Nation*

---

[1] Mr Daunt describes with some detail the bold and romantic character of the coast scenery in the immediate neighbourhood of the house.—ED.

have been recommending Irishmen to cultivate French rather than British sympathy. . . . I have written to C. G. Duffy recommending a more prudent mode of treating Ireland's foreign policy than his journal has heretofore adopted.[1]

He (Tom) was in the midst of a tremendous invective against Peter Purcell, the coach contractor, who had disputed with O'Connell about something. "Say no more on that subject, Tom," interrupted O'Connell; "I have forgiven Purcell from the bottom of my heart." "*You* may forgive him, Liberator," rejoined Steele; "yes, you, in the discharge of your ethereal functions as the Moral Regenerator of Ireland, may forgive him, but I also have functions of my own to perform, and I tell you that, as your Head Pacificator of Ireland, I never can forgive the diabolical villain!" Tom has great faith in the popular efficacy of emblems. When travelling on one of his missions through the County Tipperary, he was horrified by the commission of a murder in that county. On presenting the account of his travelling expenses to the finance committee of the Repeal Association, he charged us for the purchase of a large quantity of black crape. On being asked what he had made of the crape, he replied that he wished to show the assassins that their frightful crime had put the Repeal into mourning,

---

[1] *Apropos* of a discussion then being carried on in the columns of the *Newry Examiner* between the editor and Mr Tom Steele, Mr Daunt has some observations on the character of the latter, who, however wrong-headed in some respects, was thoroughly honourable, and enthusiastically devoted to O'Connell. The Liberator, with a hope of taming Steele's too fervent zeal in his cause, had named him 'Head Pacificator of Ireland,' and this high-sounding title occasionally led Tom into the commission of eccentric actions. —ED.

and he therefore had travelled through the county with his carriage thickly covered with the sable drapery; and further, to show that the spirit of peace was intensely afflicted by the outrage, he had displayed from the vehicle a laurel branch, the best substitute he could get for the peaceful olive, enfolded in black crape, whilst a banner of the same lugubrious material dangled from its extremity. . . . Another characteristic incident. One bitter frosty day, when the east wind came sharp and cutting, a large political gathering assembled in the street at Tralee. The crowd was addressed in Irish by O'Connell, who, with other orators, occupied a platform that had been erected adjoining the hotel. The platform was graced by the presence of a harper, fantastically dressed, who, with frozen fingers, twanged ancient Irish tunes during the intervals between the speeches. The poor creature was perched at a corner exposed to the influence of the icy blast, and his blue face and stiffened hands bore witness to his sufferings. He looked so wretched that when the meeting was in the act of separating, Mrs French, O'Connell's youngest daughter, could not help saying to Steele : " Pray do something for that poor fellow; he looks very miserable." " Make your mind easy about him, daughter of Ireland's Liberator," answered Steele, " I have taken care of the bard." " Oh, have you ? That's right. But," she added, with some misgiving, " what have you done for him ? " " I have made him immortal," replied Tom. " By virtue of my office of Head Pacificator of Ireland I have constituted him O'Connell's Chief Musician." " And I have given him half-a-crown," said O'Connell, with a good-humoured laugh, probably thinking that the pecuniary donation was at least as useful to the starving recipient as the historical immortality conferred on him by Tom. . . . That Steele, being such a queer personage, should enjoy so large a share of popularity may seem strange, but in truth the Irish people have good reason to love him. He is a Protestant who, prior to 1829, evinced the most eager zeal for the emancipation of the Catholics. He is brave to a degree of chivalrous hardihood. The people of Ireland believe that he would gladly sacrifice his life to obtain Repeal or to augment essentially the power of O'Connell. . . . O'Connell read out with great glee from a morning paper, "Mr M. A. Brennan next spoke at much length *in his usual happy style ;* but from the distance *we were wholly unable to catch the purport of his remarks.*"

25th. Christmas Day. This morning O'Connell called me up by candle light. The chapel was decorated with holly and ivy. Father Doyle celebrated three masses, according to the ancient discipline for Christmas Day. . . .

CHAPTER III

Feargus O'Connor's Humility — 'Autograph' Callaghan —
To Limerick with O'Connell—A Matrimonial Failure—
Paid Orators—Corporation Debate on Repeal—A Hum-
bug—The Scotch Campaign—A Perilous Voyage—Large
Meetings at Glasgow—Meetings at Airdrie and Edin-
burgh—Prince Charlie's Hair—An Audience Locked Up
—How Mr Daunt was enrolled a Repealer—Great Meet-
ing at Clontibret—A Valiant Orangeman—O'Connell and
Federalism.

1843.—*January 6th.* There is an amusing extract in
the *Dublin Evening Post* of the 3d inst. from a sermon
preached at Leicester from Daniel ii. 34, 35, by a Mr
Cooper, in eulogy, it seems, of Feargus O'Connor. " The
disciples of truth," said the preacher, " and all great men
are humble, and do not like to see others depreciated for
the purpose of exalting themselves." As instances, the
preacher noticed Sir Isaac Newton, Hadyn, Mozart, and
Feargus O'Connor ! . . . O'Connell has occasionally
taken up a copy of Feargus's newspaper, *The Northern
Star,* saying, " Let us see what poor Balderdash has to
say for himself this week." On one occasion the Great
Dan thus commented upon its contents : " Upon my
word, this paper of Feargus's is a literary curiosity. The
first page is filled with praise of Feargus ; second page,
praise of Feargus ; third page, ditto ; fourth page, ditto ;
and so on all through till we come to the printer's name.

25

What a notion of the fellow to set up a newspaper praising himself!" . . . The last time I saw him (Feargus) was in Coventry Street, London, about two years ago. We conversed for half-an-hour about old friends and past exploits. He was as usual overflowing with self-gratulation, boasting of the revenue his newspaper netted (I think he said £15,000 a year), boasting of all he had done, and of all he was to do with the Chartists.

10*th*. This day O'Connell completed the first volume of his work, entitled, *Ireland, Native and Saxon.* The bulk of the book is a series of extracts from English and Protestant writers, detailing the crimes committed by the English and Protestant party against the Irish Catholics. Whatever good the publication of the book will do, it won't convert the Orangemen. Its contents are too blistering. . . .

15*th*. I got a letter from Mr Graham of Somertown, London, asking for my autograph. . . . *Apropos* of autographs, there was a swindler, named Callaghan, who forged other people's signatures to bills and acceptances, in virtue of which practice his friends delicately nicknamed him 'Autograph Callaghan.' He ended his days in a penal colony. . . .

17*th*. O'Connell hunted all yesterday and all to-day. Yesterday we all dined with his cousin, Mr John O'Connell, who keeps the principal inn at Cahirciveen, and who gathered a numerous company to meet the Liberator. Our coterie last night were social and amusing, under the presidency of the Cahirciveen Boniface. There was, however, little to amuse in the way of conversation, the ideas of the most of the guests being limited to shooting, fishing, hunting and agriculture. . . .

18*th.* From Hillgrove to Tralee. Dined at Miss Connor's in Denny Street. She is O'Connell's niece. Some friends assembled in the evening, and O'Connell was talkative and amusing until dancing was intro-duced. . . .

19*th.* Met Miss Catherine O'Connell, of Grena, at Miss Connor's. She found me alone in the drawing-room, and asked if I wished for anything to amuse me. I said, " Yes." She then went to the adjoining room, and presently returned with two oddly-assorted articles, saying, " Here is the *Breviarum Romanum,* and here is a cup-and-ball. You must be hard to please if you cannot interest yourself between them." The first day I met this lively young lady, I was introduced to her three times, and, strange as it seems, I actually forgot on each successive introduction that I had been presented to her before.

20*th.* After breakfast, set off to Newcastle. There is a Repeal dinner here, which follows the public meet-ing. . . . Multitudes surround O'Connell as he passes up the street, in the midst of vociferous acclamations. A stranger, who surveys the scene from the inn window, exclaims, " What ! all this noise for one man ! " I know not whether the exclamation is one of pure astonish-ment or intended for a cynical snarl. . . .

21*st.* Dublin. Arrived here at 6 P.M., not much fatigued with the long journey from Newcastle.

26*th.* The week's Repeal rent yesterday was £209, and we had a very good meeting. . . . The night before we set out, last September, John O'Connell, Ray and I held a council to determine our immediate course. I said to my *confrères,* " Our adventurous independence is amusing. Here is this colossal crime, the Union, that cost in cash three millions of pounds sterling, to say nothing of the oceans of blood that were spilt to achieve it ; and here are we, three hopeful adventurers, setting out to repeal that Union with a sum of £8 sterling each " (the amount of *viaticum* given us by the Association) ; " nobody can impute want of enterprise to three gentlemen who, with four-and-twenty pounds among them, undertake to overthrow a work that cost three millions." . . .

February 1*st*. The late Judge —— was refused in succession by a whole litany of wealthy women. He had great force of character, and was firmly resolved to marry a fortune. He persevered, and was at last the possessor of a wife with a good many thousands. I never could do as he did. . . . I saw the Bude light for the first time to-night . . . in the centre of the Upper Castle Yard. . . . I remember when gas was beginning to supersede the old oil lamps in this city ; people used to flock every night to the General Post-Office, where it was first used, and the oil lights looked faint and miser-able twinklers by the contrast. Met John de Vitt, the barrister, who generally has news of Clare and Limerick people. Here is a story, whether true or false I don't well know, of the odd way in which Mr S—— of C——n has got entangled in matrimonial fetters. It would make, or at least eke out, the plot of a disagreeable romance. S—— met a lady, who passed for a Widow O'Neill, and married her. In about six months after marriage he discovered that the lady had two other husbands living. He then tried to get rid of her on the ground that his own marriage could not have been valid. But it turned out that at the period of her union with each of those two outstanding husbands a third spouse had existed, to whom she had been originally married. This gentleman's existence naturally rendered null the lady's marriages with husbands Nos. 2 and 3, and, as ill luck would have it, he was dead at the date of her marriage with S——. Consequently, no legal impediment exists to the validity of her union with S——, who can only disembarrass himself of his inconvenient bride by the payment of a separate maintenance. It reminds me of a Tullamore woman, whose name I forget. I remember, however, that when I was a child I nicknamed her Pomona for pilfering apples. Pomona married a soldier in the Suffolk Militia. The night of her wedding the regiment quitted Tullamore, and as the bridegroom gallantly assisted his wife to ascend the baggage cart, she said to him, in a tone of prudent admonition, " Mind, Bill, that you thrate me well now. It's not quite clear to me but we'll meet my first husband at Mullingar, and if you give me any crooked usage, bad luck to me but he'll thrash you within an inch of your life ! " John Gore Jones, jun., made me a long visit to-day. Talk—storms and steam packets, the Irish junior bar and English political agitation. This last is a curious affair in some of its details. In England the political leagues and societies keep constantly in pay a staff of itinerant orators who have got no other means of support, and who receive a monthly or weekly stipend, out of which they save all they can to send home to their families. At a Repeal soiree I once attended at Manchester there was a resolution about corn laws, which one of these orators, then out of employment, was very anxious to propose or second, in order to exhibit his qualifications for a permanent employment under the Anti-Corn Law League. He was disappointed by the chairman, at whom he looked daggers. "Now," said the chairman to me, " I shall be persecuted by this poor devil until he hits off something. I shall have him complaining that I have put the bread out of his mouth, and out of his children's mouths. Yet what could I do?" . . . Voluntary contributions also are occasionally offered by individual admirers. The chairman at Manchester told me that, after our morning Repeal meeting, a handloom weaver said to him, "That was a glorious speech of Mr Daunt's. Would he be affronted if I offered him five shillings?" In Ireland we have no similar class of paid orators. . . . Our only paid talker is O'Connell, whose annual tribute is no more than a fair compensation for the splendid professional emoluments he has been compelled by his political position to surrender. . . .

10*th*. Left Dublin at 7 A. M. for the Queen's County, on the renewed provincial agitation of Repeal. Weather, hard frost. A Puseyite parson and two attorneys were my coach companions. The parson looked every inch a gentleman ; the attorneys were loquacious, and told stories, of which the chief point seemed to be intolerable cursing and swearing. . . . This agitation is less than an agreeable task in piercing weather, but grumbling and growling are useless. The business must be done, and it were sin to grudge our mother Ireland the trouble of some timely exertion. I have heard of a man who drew a bill ' on the fair of Ballinasloe,' and his draft had no greater chance of being honoured than Repeal would have of succeeding if a few zealous advocates of the cause did not specially devote themselves to agitation.

13*th*. Drove to Ballinakill to make arrangements with Father Delany for a future meeting in his parish.

Passed the handsome domain of the French family. . . . There is an odd Miss French in the family who is said to have amassed £20,000 by economy. She drives a gig, and dresses in a man's hat, coat, and cravat.

14th. An excellent meeting of four parishes at the green of Castletown. Pat Lalor gave efficient help, like an honest Irishman as he is. . . .

24th. Wrote an article on the O'Connell tribute at Duffy's request, to be printed in next Saturday's *Nation.*

28th. O'Connell brought on his motion for the Repeal petition in the Corporation to-day. He spoke for four hours and ten minutes, and made out his case conclusively as regards the argument. Butt replied in a two hours' speech. He did not disappoint me, for I had expected nothing from him. He displayed good declamatory power, but scarcely attempted the shadow of a case. . . . He made an attempt to set up Spring Rice's prosperity case; but Rice's allegations of Irish prosperity were too much opposed to the practieal knowledge of Butt's own party to elicit a single cheer. . . . He is a very fluent speaker, but his action is ungraceful. O'Connell is in buoyant spirits at his triumph in the debate. " I don't think *you* could have done that quite so well," he said to me with a most amusing air of self-complacency, when we were issuing from the Assembly Rooms.

March 1st. The Corporation debate on Repeal continued all to-day, and was adjourned till to-morrow. I am asked to attend a Repeal meeting at Dungannon, the birthplace of the Volunteer movement of 1779-82. I have fixed next Sunday week.

4th. Left Dublin at 9 A.M. in the Mullingar boat. . . . Dined at Mullingar and took a chaise to Delvin, which I reached at 10 P.M. The boat company, as well as the priests and frieze coats, were all engrossed with the Repeal debate. All are agreed that O'Connell's masterly statement, and his (if possible) more masterly reply, are noble effusions of patriotic zeal and genius. That reply was a magnificent burst of eloquence. The giant grasp which he took of all the arguments of all his opponents, crushing each in succession, called forth the reluctant admiration of the Conservatives themselves. The speech was the finest oratorical effort I ever had the happiness to hear.

5*th*. Good Repeal meeting at Castletown-Delvin. I find that the march of dandyism has reached the stable. My friend Father Fitzgerald's groom uses eau - de - Cologne and plays the accordion. . . .

June 8th. I have lately had a good deal of political occupation. On the 25th of last month, my brother accompanied me to a very large meeting at Ballinakill in the Queen's County, where the Conservative *Leinster Express* computed that 70,000 persons were present. If we say 50,000 persons were present we shall perhaps be near the truth. . . . Last Saturday I posted to Newry for a similar purpose. . . . We had an excellent meeting at Camlough, attended by Captain Seaver, a recent convert from Orangeism to Repeal. Two troops of the 3d Dragoons attended to protect the Repealers in the event of any Orange outbreak. . . . There is not the least doubt that in some important points we are a much more moral nation than the English. But before an Irish orator boasts of our superiority, he should take care that he is not himself an exception to the general rule. At Camlough an eloquent patriot harangued the crowd on our glorious domestic morality, our profound sense of religion, and our national pre-eminence in sanctity. " That fellow," said one of the audience to me, " is one of the greatest scamps unhanged ; he is married, and before the end of the honeymoon he cut off all his wife's hair, tore her clothes to rags, threw the fragments into the fire, and gave her a tremendous beating.' . . .

9th. Dined yesterday with P. V. Fitzpatrick. Story of the late Chief Baron O'Grady. A refractory witness refused to answer a question put by counsel, and said, " If you ask me that question again I'll give you a kick in the face." "Does your lordship hear that language ? " said the counsel, appealing to O'Grady. " The question is essential to my client's case. What does your lordship advise me to do ? " " If you are resolved to repeat the question," replied O'Grady, " I advise you to move a little further from the witness."

26th. On board the *Arab* steamer *en route* to Scotland ; the sky clear, the sea smooth, and the breeze fair. John O'Connell was finally unable to come, much to his disappointment and mine. So we have appointed a substitute for him in the person of Mr James O'Dowd, a Mayo barrister. Mr Charles Glendonwyn Scott, a Scottish sympathiser with the Irish Repealers, is also of our party. . . .

27th. Glasgow, 10 P.M. Thank God we have escaped the peril of yesterday. Just as we were passing the South Light upon the coast of Ulster, the steersman ran the vessel on a sunken rock about twelve or thirteen feet under water, one side of which runs sheer down and is as steep as a wall. Providentially the tide was rising at the time. Had it been ebbing, the vessel must have capsized into deep water. As it was, we were stuck fast on the rock for an hour and three-quarters, until the tide had risen sufficiently high to enable us to back the engines with effect. The men at the South Lighthouse saw our distress, and three stout boats put off to take us ashore, which, with two belonging to the *Arab*, would have sufficed to carry all the passengers and crew. For some time nobody on board could tell whether the tide was rising or falling, and during the interval . . . we felt painfully anxious . . . I accompanied Alderman Boyce into the engine-room to see if any leakage had occurred, but we could not detect any. . . . Meanwhile the wind began to blow fresh, and rain-clouds scudded over the sky to the north-east. The scene was wild and impressive ; on the east the sea extended to the horizon ; on the west, the insulated lighthouse stood out from the dark water, and the sinking sun, huge and fiery, rested for an instant on the hills of Ulster. At 10 P.M. we were floated off by backing the vessel. In May 1836 I sailed in the *Arab* from Cork to Dublin. About 10 P.M., when we were steaming up the Channel, one of the passengers rushed into the cabin exclaiming, " Get up, get up ! we're all on fire ! " I was lying on a sofa near a window, and on looking out I saw a copious shower of sparks falling, whilst the surface of the sea reflected a strong, red glare. Hastening on deck, I found that they were running a race with the *Mercury*, and had put on a tremendous pressure of steam. There was a column of flame four or five feet over the top of the funnel, the upper part of which was red hot. The appearance of matters was alarming to landlubbers, but although I remonstrated with the mate, I satisfied myself by reflecting that it was very unlikely that the captain, who had ordered on the steam, would incur danger for himself and crew. . . . The poor Irish crowded the quay (at Greenock) to see me off to Glasgow, and gave three thundering cheers for Repeal when I got on board. . . .

30*th*. Edinburgh. Here I am again in Auld Reekie. The Scotch are, for the greater part, bigoted followers of Knox, and I am a Catholic; they are the most drunken nation in the empire, and I am a teetotaler, pledged by Father Mathew himself; yet, notwithstanding these points of difference, I have a strong liking for Scotland. I do not forget that the bones of hundreds of my maternal ancestors are mouldering in Scottish graveyards. We had a magnificent Repeal meeting in the City Hall at Glasgow last night. Charles Scott, who accompanied me from Ireland, made an excellent speech. He has a good deal of histrionic power, and performs the enthusiasm admirably. The Pats cheered gloriously . . . insomuch that *The Glasgow Herald* pronounces the excitement to have been 'perfectly frightful.' We did not break up until 3 o'clock A.M. Charles Scott, who is a worshipper of Byron's muse, says that the circumstance of which he is vainest is, that his cousin-german, Lady Charlotte Harley, received the poetical homage of Lord Byron, who inscribed 'Childe Harold' to her undert he classic designation of 'Ianthe.' Ianthe is the daughter of Scott's aunt, the Countess of Oxford. I believe she is now the wife of General Bacon.

July 1*st*. Repeal soiree last night at the Waterloo rooms. It would have gone off very well, only for the enormous loquacity of our chairman, who, having what O'Connell calls an unhappy determination of words to the mouth, bestowed it all on his afflicted auditors. He occupied three hours of our time, and effectually mesmerised the meeting. Several of our Scotch friends ran away in despair and disgust, and no wonder. . . .

2d. Visited Holyrood.[1] . . .

Sunday night. Charles Scott dined with me, and we afterwards spent the evening with his mother. . . . The family of Glendonwyn, to which she belongs, is said by Sir Walter Scott, in his notes to *The Abbot,* to have been a race of superior power and consequence. They fought at Bannockburn and at Otterbourne, the heavy broadsword wielded by Glendonwyn on the latter occasion being yet possessed by his descendants. He is chronicled by Froissart.

4th. Castlecary Inn. Arrived here yesterday from Edinburgh, *en route* to attend the meeting of Repealers at Airdrie. Drove to Airdrie through a pretty, undulating country. We assembled in the theatre. . . . The Pats were all life and activity. They made speeches that delighted my heart—short, terse, to the purpose, full of accurate perception of the merits of the Repeal question, and untainted by extravagance of any kind. Many Scotch were present. The only unwise thing they did was to style me 'Revered Sir' in their address. O'Connell once got an address in which he was designated 'Awful Sir.' . . .

5th. Returned to Edinburgh for the Repeal meeting

---

[1] Mr Daunt enters on a picturesque description of Edinburgh, of which the Old Town especially appealed powerfully to his imagination. He contrasts the romantic - looking houses and streets, and the imposing buildings of cut stone, with the infinite amount of poverty, misery, vice and degradation to be met with in the squalid wynds and closes, in olden days the dwelling-places of the nobility and gentry, but now the habitat alike of the honest poor and the criminal classes.—Ed.

at the Waterloo Rooms.   Charles Scott took the chair
and spoke gallantly for Ireland.   It was a good and
satisfactory meeting.   I met an old jeweller named
Fenwick, who was introduced to me 'as the oldest
Catholic in Edinburgh.'   He is a venerable old fellow
and speaks broad Scotch, which I like.   "I remember,"
said he, "when our only chapel was a miserable room
n Blackfriars Wynd; we were then only six or seven
hunder' Catholics.   Noo, thank God, we are fourteen
thoosand, and have twa grand chapels.   My school-
fellows used to hoot me through the streets, and ca'
me Papist Geordie; but I used to fecht 'em a' and
made 'em ceevil."   In 1817 there was liberality enough
in the municipal electors of Edinburgh to make 'Papist
Geordie' a Town Councillor.   This old Scotchman
deplores the Scottish Union.   The Repealers have
given me a public dinner at the Regent Hotel.   Charles
Scott made a vigorous speech. . . .

    6th. Visited Dr Maxwell Adams, who, among other
curiosities, has got what he says is a lock of Prince
Charlie's hair, given him by Captain Macdonald, the
last surviving nephew of Flora Macdonald, whose story
is familiar to all who know anything about the Civil
War of 1745. . . .   The hair is of a bright golden
brown.   It is the most golden-looking hair I ever
saw.   Dr Adams denies the antiquity of the clan
tartan patterns, and asks how any man can suppose
that the rude and simple inhabitants of the hills in
past centuries could produce colours and patterns that
might test the skill of the best modern Paisley operatives.
"Sir," continued the doctor, "the old Highland costume
was a coarse, undyed kilt, and a blanket fastened
round the shoulders with a skewer.   Clan tartans are

all fancy, sir, depend upon it." . . . Father George Rigg[1]
visited me.   Our talk naturally turned to the past
and present state of the Scotch Catholics.   He said,
among other things, "The results of the insurrections
of 1715 and 1745 did more to upset Catholicity from
Scotland than all the labours of John Knox.   Among
the overthrown Jacobites were a large number of chiefs
and gentlemen professing the Catholic religion.   Multitudes of followers were involved in their ruin.   Had
it not been for these civil wars there would now be
as many Catholics as Presbyterians in Scotland."   The
two Stuarts, who are said to be descendants of Prince
Charles Edward, have lately been in Edinburgh, kilted
and tartaned.

   11th. Greenock. Last night a Repeal meeting here
well attended. . . .   Scott spoke well and with spirit.
All our orators were not equally successful.   Mr ——
got up, and had not been more than ten minutes on
his legs, when there was a general rush to the door.
The orator was much disconcerted at seeing the effect
of his eloquence.   The chairman sympathised with
him, and jumped up to recall the fugitive audience,
exclaiming vehemently : "Sit down, sirs, sit down!
Ye ought to be ashamed to flit.   It is not every night
ye can enjoy such a treat as a councillor come all
the way from Dublin to give ye a lecture on Repeal,
and there ye are runnin' awa' from him!   Shame!
Coom back, coom back!"   Thus exhorted, some who
were *in meditatione fugæ* returned and sat down ; others,
however, still filed off, whereupon the chairman angrily
bellowed : "Lock the door!"   The audience were accordingly locked up, and the orator continued his

---

[1] Afterwards Bishop of Dunkeld.

harangue, when the gravity of the meeting was disturbed by the grotesque noises made by a man in a camlet jacket, who, at every pause in the speech, shouted out, "hurroo!" in so ludicrous a tone that the assembly were convulsed with laughter, and the orator, quite discomfited, sat down.

12th. Dublin. Sailed from Greenock in the *Eagle*, yesterday. . . .

30th. Repeal Meeting at Blanchardstown, attended by John O'Connell and Ray. I sent an apology as I also did to Castlebar, where O'Connell this day addresses a great gathering. . . . In 1832 I thought that the question would become, as Emancipation long had been, a sessional matter of discussion in Parliament. But O'Connell often said, "It is not yet time." "But," said I, "you will watch the earliest opportunity for its judicious introduction, and strike when the right time comes?" "Trust me for that, my dear fellow," was his answer. . . . On the 15th April 1840 O'Connell said to me, "Daunt, will you come to the Corn Exchange? I am going there to work in good earnest for Repeal." I readily accompanied him and had the honour of being one of the fifteen members of the Repeal Association enrolled on the first day of its existence.

August 5th. Dungannon. Left Dublin last night at 8 P.M. . . . At Dungannon, which I reached at half-past 6, P.M., I was edified by the scribblings over the parlour chimney in the inn. 'To h—l with the Pope and O'Connell!' 'To h—l with the fellow who wrote that!' and so forth; a vigorous damnatory warfare in which village bigots gave vent to their prejudices.'[1]

[1] Mr Daunt came to Dungannon to compose a dispute which had arisen among local Repealers, on a charge of misappropriating

8th. Dublin. Went to my hotel at 9 P.M. last night . . . till a quarter to twelve, when I got into a post-chaise which waited for me, not in the street, where it would have attracted the notice, and perhaps hostile violence of the Orangemen, but in the inn yard, where it was concealed by the high wooden gates from observation. The gates were opened a little before midnight, and I was driven rapidly out, approaching the Dublin road by the circuitous course of Scotch Street. . . . We had loaded pistols and there was a sort of excitement in the possibility of danger. . . . O'Farrell rehearsed the opinion of friends and foes in the neighbourhood on the leaders of the movement. " As to Dan," said he, " our love for him approaches idolatry. If the Pope and all the Cardinals desired me to go one way, and if Dan desired me to go another way, I would follow Dan's advice." . . . Of John O'Connell, he said, " We look on him here as a very steady and industrious young man, and a worthy present made to Ireland by his illustrious father." . . . Finally O'Farrell said, " There are, sir, four picked birds ; four individuals whom the northern Orangemen pre-eminently hate— O'Connell, Tom Steele, John O'Connell and yourself. They look on you as holding in the Repeal Association the same place that Richard Sheil held in the Catholic Association." . . .

15th. Castleblaney, County Monaghan. This day there has been an enormous assemblage at the hill of Tara, to which I refused an invitation in order to be present at the meeting of the people of Clontibret, and a gallant muster we have had. Mr Conway, editor of *The*

money. He dissolved the local committee, and instituted a new method of conducting the agitation.—ED.

Newry Examiner, stated their number at 300,000. I
posted from Dublin at 2 o'clock P.M., and arrived here
at midnight. The town was full of soldiers. There
were two troops of the 3d Dragoons, two companies of
the 14th Foot, and a large party of the 60th Rifles.
Thirteen officers had taken possession of the hotel,
and I was met with the pleasant intelligence that I
could not get a bed in it nor anywhere else in town.
I was going to order the postilion to drive to Clontibret
. . . when a friendly voice asked if I would sleep in
the inn parlour, an offer which I joyfully accepted.   On
entering the house I saw a drunken officer on the stairs.
He was vociferating for the waiter, and skimming boots
and shoes over the bannisters. I escaped from the
range of his projectiles into the parlour, got into my
shakedown, and was wakened this morning at seven
by the sustained treble of the landlady who was scolding her servants for allowing me to sleep in the house ;
by which objurgation, screamed at the pitch of her
voice, she probably meant to conciliate the favour of
her Tory and Anti-Repeal patrons. After breakfast
Captain Seaver took me in his carriage to the place
of meeting.   We assembled on a rising ground ; on an
opposite eminence the troops were drawn up. . . .   I
received a history of the notorious Sam Gray, an
Orange leader who was sentenced to transportation
at the last Monaghan Assizes for firing at a man named
Cunningham.   Gray originally kept an inn at Ballybay.
When Jack Lawless in 1828 went there to hold a
meeting for Catholic Emancipation, Gray mustered a
large force of armed Orangemen, and Lawless, terror-
stricken, fled.   This exploit secured for Gray the
patronage of all the Tory gentry. . . .   He caused the

death of his own son by forcing a quantity of whisky down his throat to make him drink, as it ought to be drunk, The Glorious, Pious and Immortal Memory. He borrowed £500 from one Bradshaw, who died. Thereupon Gray forged a will in Bradshaw's name, bequeathing the £500 along with other property to one of the young Grays. He next proceeded to carry off a considerable amount of the deceased man's property. With the means thus acquired he fought the rightful heirs for one assize ; but they found Bradshaw's genuine will, which had been drawn up by one Murphy, a schoolmaster, who came forward to prove its authenticity. Gray . . . fired at Murphy from behind a hedge and killed him. He was tried for the murder and acquitted on an *alibi* sworn to by a batch of his own friends. The murdered Murphy's evidence about the will had been sustained by one Cunningham. Gray, emboldened by impunity, fired at Cunningham, but his tutelary devil here deserted him. He was committed, tried, convicted and transported for the crime. . . .

28th. Dublin. This day O'Connell took the initiatory step in the foundation af his Council of Three Hundred. . . . O'Connell's great difficulty is to keep this council clear of the Irish Convention Act. He began by calling on the Repeal Wardens of Ardee to return the name of a person whom they would recommend to the office of District Repeal Warden ; in other words, member for Ardee in the Irish Parliament.

29th. Adjourned meeting of the Association. O'Connell made a speech of defiance in reply to the Anti-Repeal bravado, which Ministers have put into the Queen's Speech. O'Connell's scheme of a restored Irish Parliament gives to the landed interest preponderating influence in that assembly. He proposes that the House of Commons should consist of three hundred members, the original number, and that of these members 173 should represent the counties, and 127 the cities and boroughs. If the landlords were wise they would join him.

(The last entry, for a considerable time, is dated 29th August 1843. The journal was suspended for the remainder of that year, and for the whole of 1844, which was rendered memorable by the conviction of O'Connell. During part of this year I was busily engaged in the Repeal agitation. . . . In 1843 O'Connell seemed inclined to give a preference to Federalism over Repeal, and in this I entirely differed from him. O'Connell came to Dublin from Darrynane in October. I was sitting in the committee room of the Repeal Association as he entered it, and I rose to greet him. His irritation at the public dissent from his Federalist policy was visible in his manner. " I am quite well," said he, as we shook hands ; "that is to say, as well as a man can be who is opposed by one half of his friends and deserted by the other half." " You cannot class me," I said, " among either the opponents or the deserters." " Certainly not among my opponents," said he, " but as to the deserters—um ! I am not quite sure." The entrance of several persons put an end for the time to our colloquy ; but next day the subject was resumed as we walked together through the town. I asked him what good had resulted from his Federalist move. He answered with great bitterness, " I was deceived. I got promises that we should have had a valuable Whig accession." " You were wrong," said I, " to place any faith in private promises from such a hollow set as the Whigs. There is not in existence a party that are more destitute, taking them as a body, of national Irish feeling." In a few weeks O'Connell recanted Federalism . . . saying, as he snapped his fingers, "Federalism isn't worth *that!*" In June 1845 I went to Scotland to hold meetings of the Irish in that kingdom, the Scotch agitation of our question . . . having been specially confided to me by the Association.

CHAPTER IV

1845.—*June 22d,* Edinburgh. Arrived here at 5 p.m.
from Glasgow with Charlie Scott. . . .

25th. Dundee. . . . There was a spirited and well-
attended meeting of the Repealers to-night. . . . I made
my speech, which the hearers were good enough to
applaud, and Charlie Scott made his, which called forth
hurricanes of acclamation.

26th. We held a sort of *levée* to-day, attended by
such of our admirers of yesterday as chose to come. . . .
A man from Arbroath discussed our comparative merits,
that is, Charlie's and mine, as orators. " As for you,
Maister Daunt, we were a' pleased wi' ye ; yes, that we
were. Your lecture was vara airgumentative; in short,
it was vera weel indeed. But—but—Maister Scott ! "
Here he paused, and threw up his eyes in mute rapture.
The action plainly said, " Your freend has beat you
hollow, Maister Daunt." " Dinna ye think sae yersel' ? "
he inquired by way of climax. . . .

July 1st. Repeal meeting last evening at the Waterloo Rooms. Excellent, spirited, numerous and re-spectable.

7th. On Saturday we had our second Repeal meet-ing at Glasgow. . . . Both have been eminently satisfactory.

17th. Aberdeen. Two days ago Scott and I arrived here from Edinburgh. . . . We visited Scott's cousin-german, Miss Helen Gordon of Letterfourie. Her brother, Sir Robert Gordon, is premier baronet of Scot-land. . . . On Tuesday night we received a sort of semi-public soiree at the Royal Hotel. On Wednesday our public Repeal meeting came off at the Concert Hall in George Street. . . .

20th. After mass to-day old Father Gordon delivered an address in broad Scotch to a party of Irish soldiers, who, I fear, lost the benefit of it from their ignorance of the dialect. . . .

22d. Edinburgh, which we reached at 8 p.m. We were instantly summoned to a public meeting that had gathered at Merchants' Hall, Hunter Square, in ex-pectation of our arrival. . . . Notwithstanding the fatigue of a fourteen hours' journey on the top of a coach, I caught the infectious spirit of the meeting, and addressed the audience, if I may judge from my recep-tion, without any symptoms of impaired vitality.

23d. I have been introduced to a rather mysterious personage, the Chevalier John Sobieski Stuart, whom I visited at his lodgings in Princes Street. He is a tall, handsome, dark-complexioned man, whose face bears a very strong resemblance to the face of King Charles I. in Vandyke's equestrian portrait of that monarch. The Chevalier talked a great deal, expressed infinite en-thusiasm for Scotland, Ireland and the Celtic race, seemed to avoid conversation on any subject that he did not himself introduce (this, I suppose, was part of his *rôle de prince*), recommended me to read *Lockhart of Carnwath's Memoirs*, and when I was taking leave he pressed my hand graciously, and said with solemn emphasis, "*Dominus dedit, Dominus abstulit !*" which words were probably allusive to certain vanished glories of the House of Stuart. . . .

25th. Dublin. . . . Charles Scott has been of essential use to the cause in our late campaign. Somebody says that the three great essentials of oratory are impudence, impudence, impudence. But this would not do un-accompanied with argument, pathos, fun, enthusiasm, etc. A speaker at one of our meetings essayed fun, and tried to tickle the audience with an anecdote that missed fire at first. I occupied a prominent seat on the front of the platform, and saw with some dismay the sea of blank and wondering faces turned towards the orator. It occurred to me to try the influence of hilarious influence on the sympathetic muscles of the audience. Accordingly, as the speaker proceeded, I thawed my countenance into a smile of admiration. Further on I improved my smile into a grin ; the audience caught the infection of my mirth, and began to grin also. When the speaker arrived at the climax of his joke, I flung myself back in my chair in a paroxysm of delighted merriment. The sympathetic audience apparently concluded that what I found so intensely diverting ought to divert them also, and the hall rang with peals of laughter. . . .

August. Darrynane. Travelled hither from Dublin, in the beginning of the month, by the canal boat to Shannon Harbour, and thence by the Shannon Lakes to Limerick. . . . I recollect on a cold, frosty morning a few winters since, the driver of Her Majesty's mail from Killarney to Cork stopped his horses, attracted by the sight of wild geese feeding in a morass. Her Majesty's guard got down and clapped his hands and shouted to startle the geese, I presume in the hope of getting a shot at them from Her Majesty's blunderbuss. . . .

O'Connell told an anecdote, if it can be called one, of an old priest in this neighbourhood, who, in Cromwell's time, disguised himself as a cowherd. He wore a *cota mhor* girdled with a straw rope, and tended a herd of cattle, barefooted. A party of soldiers came priest-hunting, and asked the supposed herd where was the priest. "*Niel aen sassenagh agum*" (I have no English), was the answer, whereupon the soldier knocked down the disguised priest with the butt of his musket. The priest jumped up and vented his rage in a jumble of English, Irish and Latin, namely,—"*Excommunication orth ipso facto*"; words which would have betrayed him to the soldiers, only that luckily they were too ignorant to comprehend their import.

(During the winter of 1845 and the spring of 1846 I was a good deal engaged in assisting to conduct the proceedings of the Repeal Association, especially while O'Connell was absent from Dublin.)

1846.—*May 2d.* This day I entered Gray's Inn. There is a painful badge of national inferiority in being obliged to qualify for the Irish bar by eating a certain number of dinners at an English Inn of Court. . . .

4th. There is a wild Scotch student here who avows himself an infidel. He says the Decalogue is unworthy of a Divine Being. I asked him in what respect?

"Take the command," said he, "Thou shalt not steal?
Why, sir, it was that diabolical command that introduced all dishonesty into the world." I believe my
philosopher's notion is this, that if things had been
left in common then each man would have taken,
as of right, what served his needs, and nobody would
have been entitled to complain ; but as soon as a pro-
hibition was issued against stealing, then everyone
began to appropriate something as his own exclusive
property, and anyone whose needs impelled him to help
himself to what his neighbour had thus appropriated,
became guilty of the sin of theft, which was thus
created by the command. An English student named
Horsey told the following circumstance :—In the course
of a lawsuit it became vitally important to one of the
parties to procure the marriage settlement of his great-
grandfather. He ascertained that it had been drawn up
by a firm of London attorneys, whose house was still
extant in the profession, and conceiving it just possible
that it might lurk in some of their repositories, he
agreed to give them twenty-five guineas for a search,
promising to give one hundred for the document
should it be found. The attorneys took the money
and said they would search. When the applicant was
gone, one of them said, "What a pity that poor fellow
did not call here a month ago. I remember to have
seen the document at that time, but it was thrown into
a fire we made of some very old papers which were supposed to be of no possible use." I asked Mr Horsey if he
thought it honest of the attorneys to take twenty-five
guineas for pretending to search for a document which
they knew did not exist. "Oh," said he, "if they had
said, 'we have burnt your settlements,' they would have

compromised the reputation of their house." During this month I have occasionally visited Smith O'Brien in the House of Commons prison, where he is at present confined by order of the House for refusing to act on an English railway committee. . . . He is extremely dissatisfied with O'Connell for not having espoused his cause more warmly when the subject was discussed in Parliament. . . . I visited O'Connell and tried *componere litem*. He said, "It is a foolish thing to run amuck at the House of Commons." But John O'Connell did exactly the same thing last year. Can we suppose that he acted without his father's sanction? I induced O'Connell to visit the prisoner.

June. Kilcascan. Arrived here from London, *via* Dublin, on the first of this month. . . .

23d. Storm and heavy rain last night. . . . Dan Conner told me the following *jeu-de-mot* of a punning parson named Chester. A vessel struck and foundered for want of lights, and all the crew perished. " I don't know much of navigation," said the reverend gentleman, " but it strikes me that if there had been more *lights* there would have been more *livers*." [1]

August 2d, Sunday. An old countryman named Deasy accosted me before Mass, and we talked partly in Irish, partly in English. " I believe," said he, " that in the ould ancient times every grand family had a great strong garrison like this ould castle " (Ballina-carriga). " I think ours," he continued, " was in the

[1] For some time Mr Daunt resided at Kilcascan, chronicling daily events, and mingling these with reflections, historical, political and religious, which, although eloquently and interestingly written, would take up too large a space for the dimensions of this volume. He notes also the appearance of the dreaded potato blight.—ED.

County Tipperary, though I cannot exactly say in what part. But we have a tradition that it was from Tipperary we came when Cromwell knocked my ancesthors out of their estate. And another tradition is that as our very small garrison gave Cromwell's sojers such hard work to get the better of them, the Cromwellian captain, out of spite, commanded that every male Deasy should be put to death. The command was executed upon everyone of them except one little boy, who was then a babby at the breast, but the sojer who was ordered to report the babby's sex took a bribe from the mother to report it as a girl. " That babby, sir," and he looked important, " that babby was my ancesthor." [1] . . .

August 9th, Sunday. A countryman from Glaun watched the congregation coming out of the chapel at Ballinacarriga, and harangued them from the top of a ditch. He advised them to go *en masse* to Ballyneen petty sessions to-morrow, armed with their spades, and there to demand employment from the magistrates. He exhorted his audience, in the event of refusal, to seize on food wherever they could find it. The crowd listened to the speaker, and dispersed when he had done. They are a quiet set of people, and nothing but the sternest necessity will induce them to follow such counsel. Meanwhile, that necessity seems to be universally imminent throughout the kingdom. The Union, between absentee rents, taxes, the manufacture drain,

[1] Mr Daunt enters on a description of the scenes accompanying the disruption between the Old and Young Irelanders. In Ireland such events constantly repeat themselves. Mr Daunt thought O'Connell went to extremes with his peace policy 'under all circumstances,' and he considered that Smith O'Brien, although rash, had some excuse to act as he did. O'Brien was high-minded, incapable of meanness—the very soul of honour.—ED.

and various other drains, has stripped Ireland at the very least of £230,000,000. It has destroyed . . . every source of manufacturing employment, has thrown the great mass of the people on the soil for their support, and has reduced them to the lowest description of food —the potato. A deadly blight consumes this only means of sustenance, and the Government announces that the partial relief of last year is to be discontinued, and the depôts shut up. (On second thoughts Government did not act on this cruel determination. Between loans and grants they advanced about nine or ten millions, not more than a few pence in the pound of the money wrung out of Ireland by the Union, and for this Mr Gladstone took care to recoup the English treasury by adding 52 per cent. to the taxation of Ireland in 1853.)

15*th, Ladyday*. . . . In the evening Tom and I assembled the tenants to take into consideration the distressed condition of the labouring class on this estate. . . . I availed myself of the assembling of my tenants and their labourers to ascertain the number of persons living on this property. Notwithstanding large emigrations there are still 271 inhabitants. Of these there are exactly twenty Protestants, leaving a balance of 251 Catholics. The Reverend J. Doheny, P.P., receives about £12 per annum for performing the spiritual duties required by these 251 Catholics, whilst the law-established parson screws £50 a year out of me for performing spiritual duties for the twenty Protestants.—I have received an invitation to agitate Repeal in Scotland, forwarded from the Edinburgh Repealers. . . .

20*th*. Relief meeting at Ballyneen, Lord Bernard in the chair. . . . I stated my own plan of landlord aid ;

Dan Conner stated his, and matters were wound up by a resolution to apply for assistance to the Government. D. Conner's plan is not so good as ours for the labourer, for it makes the minimum of relief to each labourer 2s. a week, or £5, 4s., whereas our plan makes it £8 per annum. The Government that *gave* £20,000,000 to buy up West Indian slaves, has just now announced that they will *lend* a sum, whereof the amount is not stated, to relieve the pressure of the Irish famine.

25th. This day the landlords, priests and parsons of the West Riding met at Dunmanway to take measures to avert famine from the people. I proposed the fourth resolution censuring the Government for the niggardliness of their assistance. . . . I was well cheered, and by no persons better than by our jolly cricket club, who mustered strong at the meeting. . . . [1]

September 7th. . . . To-day we went to Ballyneen on the business of the proposed new roads, and while we were there, Mr Tracy, the county engineer, arrived, and, acting under the orders of Government, dismissed a large number of persons who have been employed on the new road to the north of the village. . . . While we sat in the Court-house some of the dismissed workmen came in, and declared in accents of agony that they had not a morsel to eat, nor a farthing to buy it. [2]

29th. . . . Hounds out, but no fox visible. . . . In the evening I walked to the top of Grillagh. There is

[1] To employ the starving people, Mr Daunt borrowed money from Government to open a new line of road. The repayment burdened him for many years. He was also a constant attendant at the relief meetings.—ED.

[2] The Relief Committee wrote a strongly-worded remonstrance to Government, and got the dismissed workmen replaced.—ED.

a hole at the side of the road which marks the spo
where a priest was murdered in the penal times by a
priest-hunter named Hawkins. The faith, or superstition, of the neighbouring crones often leads them to
select the spot as the scene of their devotions. . . .
There is a tradition annexed to the place which, as it is
universally believed by the people, and contains nothing
irrational, I see no reason to discredit. It is said that
Hawkins committed the murder with a billhook, which
he then flung into the adjacent furze brake. Afraid of
the vengeance of the peasantry if detected, he quitted
the neighbourhood for many years, and settled in a
distant part of the kingdom. He did not thrive in his
new residence. He became reduced to great poverty,
and never having heard that suspicion of the murder
attached to him, he returned to his original neighbourhood. He had taken off his shoes to cross a ford of the
Bandon at the foot of Grillagh, and passing barefooted
through the field adjoining the scene of his crime, he
trod on the billhook, the rusty edge of which was upper-
most. It had lain unnoticed among the heath or furze
ever since he had flung it there stained with the priest's
blood. The wound thus inflicted on his foot festered,
and death was the result. It was a very pretty bit of
poetical justice. To-night I received a letter from John
Sobieski Stuart, sending me 'Lines addressed to Ireland,' extracted from a political work about to be published by him and his brother Charles Edward Stuart.
There is a vague sort of rumour that these brothers are
grandsons of the real, original Charles Edward of 1745.
If so, who was their father? Or are they sons of the
lady whom Charles Edward 'legitimatised' by an exercise of royal power, and who resented the indiscretion of

some person who afflicted her father by talking of his
disastrous attempt to recover the crown ? Christie tells
a story, that the wife of Charles Edward (one of these
mysterious brothers) was asked if her husband was the
grandson of the young Pretender, to which inquiry she
replied, ' Do not ask me *who* he is—I can only tell you
what he is—the most delightful man in all Scotland ! '

October 6th. Went to Dunmanway to urge on Captain
Gordon, the Government official, the necessity of commencing the new lines of road at once. The people are
famishing. Last week Father Higgins of Ballygurteen
was summoned to administer the last sacraments to a
man and his wife, who, the messenger said, were dying.
The priest found the unfortunate couple stretched on
scanty straw, quite exhausted, not having tasted food for
two days. They seemed willing to die, and were only
anxious for the rites of the Church. The priest sent to
his house for some bread, and when it was brought, the
woman was with extreme difficulty able to taste it.
The man was stronger, and the sight of food made him
so ravenous, that the priest was obliged to give it to him
in small morsels, lest in his eagerness to devour it he
might choke himself. . . .

7th. The newspapers contain a letter from O'Connell,
highly eulogising my late address to the Irish landlords,
and recommending the Association to circulate it
through the kingdom. The great Dan, while praising
my address, dexterously tries to enlist me against the
Young Irelanders by asking, " When will any of their
party produce such a document ? " The bait to catch
my vanity is rather palpable. . . . However, I may as
well acknowledge my belief that Repeal, if achievable at
all, is achievable by no other agency than that of the

Association founded by O'Connell, and as long as the planks of that Association hold together, so long will I adhere to it. . . .

15*th.* Wrote to Smith O'Brien recommending him to make up matters with O'Connell, and return to the Association. If I can prevail with him, it will give me great pleasure. . . . The late Repeal meeting in Cork was to a great extent an anti-O'Connell meeting. A patriotic man ought surely to sacrifice his personal feelings rather than suffer our noble cause to be destroyed and our matchless organisation to be broken to pieces after all the hard struggles of the Irish people to give effective strength to the Repeal Confederacy. . .

20*th.* Cork. Left home this morning *en route* to Dublin to encounter the M'Carthys in the Court of Chancery. I spent this evening with Father Mathew, who seems to sympathise with the Young Irelanders against O'Connell. Father Mathew told me that when breakfasting one day with Lord Fortescue when Viceroy, he was told by His Excellency that the appointments then made by the Government were chiefly given on O'Connell's recommendation. Lord Fortescue must have thus spoken before he denounced Repealers as unworthy of office; for his public declaration that patronage should be withheld from them is fresh in our memories.

November 2*d.* Dublin. . . . This day, being Monday, I attended the Repeal Association at O'Connell's request, for the purpose of declaring my adhesion to the Old Irelanders in the present dispute. . . . I do not like to see our gallant old leader deserted by the frivolous and unstable, and even by those who are doubtless both able and honest. O'Connell spoke, and his speech as well as his letter to the moral force Repealers of Cork display unimpaired intellectual power . . . But his physical energies are plainly decaying. . . . Smith O'Brien has finally severed himself from the Association.

9th. I spoke (at the Association) to-day in compliance with the great Dan's request. My speech was very well received by a crowded meeting. Dan praised it, but that was a matter of course. . . .

11th. Left Dublin in the Carlow train at 4 P.M. During the journey a man died in the train, and his corpse was taken out at Sallins. The unfortunate man was drunk and got smothered.

14th. Kilcascan. At Carlow I went to bed at nine, and slept till midnight, when I was awakened by the entrance of a traveller, who got into the second bed in my dormitory. He kept me awake with a succession of most dismal groans for several hours. In the morning I discovered that my groaning friend was Mr Deasy, the Clonakilty brewer; his bedclothes were scanty, there was a severe frost, and he groaned from the cold. . . .

28th. Met parson St Lawrence, incomparably the most amusing parson of the fraternity. Speaking of the family of Lord ——, he said, " They are mighty good people, but desperately dull. They used to ask me out to dinner there ; but what with chaise hire and perquisites to servants, I found it really did not pay, so at last I said to Charles B——, I beg you may give up asking me to dinner, for dining with you is very expensive, and I don't get the worth of my money. However, if at any time you have some distinguished visitor from Paris or London to whom you wish to show that the country contains one civilised individual, why, I don't

care if in such a case you send me an invitation." All
sorts of queer stories are told of St Lawrence. One of
them (mind, I don't believe a word of it, and merely
record it as a comical calumny) is, that, being at his
wits' end for money, he raised the wind by selling to
the surgeons some corpses newly buried in his churchyard. . . .

December 14*th*. The deaths from starvation increase
frightfully in the devoted districts round Berehaven and
Skibbereen. God help the people!

15*th*. This day I received a letter from Richard
Lalor Sheil, in which he says that O'Connell has 'acted
magnanimously' in proposing an amicable conference
with the Young Irelanders. If there be magnanimity
in the proposal, I wish Dan had been thus magnanimous
some months since.

24*th*. . . . Gibbings, the surveyor, opened the first
sods of my new line of road yesterday. . . . Mr
Cummins of Cork found 200 persons near Skibbereen
in a state almost of delirium from the pangs of
hunger. . . . Yet in the midst of all this misery
there is no disturbance around us, and scarcely any
theft. May God bless and relieve our poor people! . . .

26*th, St Stephen's Day*. Spent this day in inspecting
our new road. . . . There were 108 hungry men working weakly and lazily under a hard frost. When desired
by the overseer to go to dinner, fully one-half the number sat down by the ditches, having no dinner to go
to; the other half had nothing but coarse brown bread
and water. They bear their terrible privations with
heroic fortitude. . . . Although large numbers in this
country have died of starvation, I have not heard of
any robberies. . . .

30*th*. Smith O'Brien has rejected O'Connell's proposal for a compromise. . . . O'Connell has now the advantage of having offered peace, and of having his offer rejected.

CHAPTER V

Reminiscences of Curran—O'Connell's advancing Feebleness
—The Horror deepens—Death of O'Connell

1847.—*January 4th.* Attended the Presentment Sessions at Clonakilty, and obtained an additional sum of £350 for my new road. . . . Visited my kind old friend Miss Donovan. She amused us with some personal recollections of the celebrated Curran, in whose company she once passed a week. . . . Curran shone particularly after breakfast. He used to get up from table and walk about the room with his hands behind his back, showering *bon-mots* and repartees in delightful profusion, and sometimes reciting the best parts of his best speeches, which, my informant says, he did remarkably well. . . . Curran would sometimes ask, "Did you hear my *bon-mot* on such or such an occasion ?" and he would then relate some witticism, which, notwithstanding its intrinsic pungency, seemed always rather flat when thus rehearsed for admiration by its author. Another slight drawback from the charms of his conversation was this : he fancied himself to be what he was not, a poet, and he bored his friends with dull and flippant verses of his own composition. He remarked that the Stuart family were the most execrable tyrants who ever occupied a throne . . . and that

he intended to write a history of their dynasty in order
to paint them in colours as dark as they merited,
if he ever should have leisure for such an under-
taking. . . .

18*th.* Left home for Dublin to eat two term
dinners. . . .

21*st.* Visited O'Connell. Poor Dan shows the wear
and tear of years. I asked him how he was. "Very
well,' he answered, "only that I feel the feebleness of
age upon me." . . . Tom Steele said to me, "Is it
not pitiful to witness how different is the O'Connell of
1847 from the O'Connell of 1843. The people have
gone from him ; the return of the Whigs to power and
the courtesies of the Castle have given birth to sus-
picions which, though groundless, have served as an
engine in the hands of his enemies to alienate the
people from him. And he will not believe this when
I tell it to him." . . . So speaks Tom Steele. At anyrate, if John continues blind it will not be my fault, for
I backed up Steele's remonstrances with details of my
own experience on this painful subject, advising John
and his father to *cut* the Castle as the only mode of
recovering popular confidence. . . .

22*d.* Sailed for Cork in the *Vanguard.* O'Connell
sails to-night for England.

23*d.* Reached Cork after a stormy passage. Dined
with my dear old friend Father Mathew, who gave
me potatoes at dinner, a rare luxury as times go
now.

24*th.* Breakfasted with Father Mathew. . . .

25*th.* Kilcascan. . . . We were five hours and a-half
coming from Cork to Ballyneen (30 miles), partly owing
to the starved condition of the horses, whose pace the

driver tried to accelerate by pelting them with stones he had provided for that purpose.

February 7th. . . . Within the last fortnight there have been sixty-four interments in the neighbouring graveyard of Ballymoney, and elsewhere the mortality is greater.

12*th.* Meeting at Dunmanway to consider the distress. . . . Father Doheny's details of disease and death were harrowing. The famine is slaying more people than the cholera did in 1832. Ninety-four coffins were sold on Wednesday in the small town of Dunmanway. In some cases two, and even three, corpses were packed into one coffin. . . .

25*th.* Relief Committee. The horrors of the famine are such as would almost seem fabulous if we read of them in books. The tax-collectors find houses shut up, the inmates having died. Great numbers are buried without coffins. . . . Miserable creatures crawling up the rocks on the coast in search of edible weeds . . . fall into the sea from inanition. The coffinless bodies that had been interred in kitchen gardens are rooted up by pigs and dogs and devoured. Pestilence is generated by the stench of unburied carcases. . . . The cereal crops have been very abundant; of oats, wheat, barley, and also of pigs, sheep, and cattle there are within the four seas of Ireland more than enough to feed all the inhabitants. But these commodities are not for the people whose industry produced them. . . . Speaking to a farmer the other day, I could not help expressing to him my surprise and admiration at the universal forbearance from robbery. He answered: "We do not know how soon we may die, and it is better to suffer hunger than to put our sowls in danger by thieving." . . .

March 29th. In the midst of sharp privations of various kinds, I this day rode to Clonakilty to borrow money at the bank to pay the tithes to the Protestant minister.   I have sometimes dined on Indian meal porridge and sheep's milk, sometimes on a pennyworth of rice, and gone supperless to bed.   Of this I do not complain, for it is caused by a visitation of Providence.   But of the Established Church I do complain, for it is the visitation of England, not of Providence. . . .

27th. The papers say that O'Connell is dead at Genoa.

28th. The news of Dan's death is confirmed.   It is not easy to contemplate with indifference the exit of our old familiar leader, to remember how often I have been among the band who surrounded him on Repeal platforms; to have the tones of his noble voice still ringing in my ears, and then to think that I shall hear that voice no more![1] . . .

October 23d. Received a letter from the Chevalier John Sobieski Stuart, promising to send me a German translation of my work, *Saints and Sinners*, which has been published at Augsburg.

November 8th. Thavies Inn, Holborn.   The driver of the 'bus which conveyed me here said he was too busy all Sunday to go to any place of worship, so that the family devotions devolved on his wife and children. . . .

19th. Disposed of my *Personal Recollections of*

---

[1] For several weeks after this last entry, Mr Daunt was confined to bed by a low fever, caused by his privations.   While getting no rent, or next to none, the tithes and taxes were demanded with unremitting regularity.   Mental anxiety had also a share in his illness, as a vexatious and unjust lawsuit was now resumed in the Court of Chancery, owing mainly to O'Connell's conduct in putting Mr Daunt's papers into the hands of the plaintiffs.—ED.

O'Connell to Messrs Chapman and Hall. Demurring to their terms, I urged that Lady Charlotte Bury's *Diary of the Reign of George the Fourth* had sold for one thousand pounds. Chapman replied that Lady Charlotte's book was expected to contain some immoral revelations of His Majesty's exploits, and that this expectation enhanced the marketable value. " It is, no doubt," said he, " a sort of speculation not very creditable to a publisher, but it tells well with the public." . . . Grand Day at Gray's Inn. There is an old custom, on what is termed Grand Day, of handing round a morsel of bread and a morsel of toast, and a huge silver goblet full of sack, to each guest before dinner. Everyone is expected to eat the two morsels and to take a sip from the goblet.

27th. Kilcascan. Sailed from Bristol on the 22d. We dropped down the river to the North Foreland, and anchored for twelve hours in the liquid filth of the Severn, waiting for an express from London with the Queen's speech. The passengers all mutinied, but the captain was inexorable. . . . We were driven by the delay among the storms of Wednesday and Wednesday night. . . .

December 31*st.* Flax meeting in Ballyneen. Lord B—— in the chair. . . . I moved and D. Conner seconded a resolution giving priority to drainage over the flax scheme just now. The people ask for bread and they are promised flax. . . .

CHAPTER VI

1848.—*February 7th.* Dan is gone, and his mantle has
descended on no man living. *Apropos* of him, Smith
O'Brien, in a letter I received from him not long since,
thus writes : " It may be interesting to notice the religious tendencies which, during the last two or three years
of O'Connell's life, appeared to predominate in his mind.
I have more than once heard him express a desire to
enter into some religious establishment, and I have no
doubt that he would have done so if he could have
extricated himself from the exigencies of his position as
a political leader."

April 28th. A neighbouring farmer, John Good, trying to smoke a rat out of a hole, set fire to his house.
His furniture and two lambs perished in the conflagration, but the rat escaped. . . .

July 18th. . . . St Lawrence visited me. He was
very amusing. I told him some anecdotes of old Lord
Muskerry. . . . St Lawrence said, "Lord Muskerry told
me he abstained from cursing and swearing, as those
practices gave him neither pleasure nor profit. The
most dishonest thing he ever did," continued the rector,

" was to pay his debts, for by doing so he afterwards
got double credit." His lordship was an oddity. " He
told a gentleman who was dining with him to go down
to the wine cellar for a bottle of burgundy. ' My
brother is in the cellar,' said his lordship ' but don't be
afraid of him, he won't bite you.' ' Why is your brother
there ? ' asked the guest. ' He's dead,' replied Lord
Muskerry. The fact was that, either out of eccentricity,
or to save the expense of a funeral, he had buried his
brother in the wine cellar." There is a story that, when
his lordship was dying, the parson in attendance remarked that life and its vanities would soon pass away,
and exhorted him to repent. " Repent ? for what should
I repent ? " demanded the old lord ; " why, I don't remember that during my whole life I ever denied myself
anything." We spoke of the habits of the last generation. " They were odd enough," said St Lawrence.
" When my father was ordained he joined the ladies in
the drawing-room after dinner rather tipsy—it was the
only time in his life he ever exceeded in wine. He
could not walk steadily, and as he tottered along, Lady
Meath said to him, ' Tom, you are acting very impru-
dently for a man just ordained, mimicking the Archbishop of Dublin's wife ; you hit her off to a miracle,
but it is very imprudent.' My father disclaimed the
imputed intention. ' Pooh ! nonsense ! ' said Lady
Meath, ' the imitation is perfect. We know she goes to
bed drunk every night—but you should be more cautious.' People," continued St Lawrence, " lived about a
good deal at each other's houses in those days, and my
father spent much of his time at old Lord Charlemont's.
Whenever he arrived there he found regular accommo-
dation in readiness for him, as for one of the family

One day he arrived to dinner from Timolin in the County Kildare, and Lady Charlemont said, ' Now, Tom, don't talk much to Lord Charlemont this evening. He is in one of his fits of low spirits, and cannot bear it.' My father obeyed, and, being ravenously hungry after his ride, applied himself with great assiduity to an enormous rump of beef, which he carved at the foot of the table. He cut and cut away, till at last he cut a large vista in the beef, through which the sight of his face thus revealed to Lord Charlemont, from whom the solid mountain of beef had previously hidden it, struck the latter as so ludicrous that he laughed immoderately, and got into good spirits for the rest of the evening." We talked of the arbitrary habits of the old squires and lords. " Yes," said St Lawrence, " they had things their own way. My grandfather, Lord Howth, once clapped a man who had displeased him into the dungeon at Howth Castle." Speaking of pedigrees. " Smith O'Brien's pedigree," said he, " is an older one than ours; it is all a priority of plunder." We have a horse that was foaled on the 17th March, and from that circumstance my brother Tom called it St Patrick. My sister, C——, objected to bestowing on a horse the title of *saint*. " Why," said he, " I never heard you object to calling the rector of Moragh *St* Lawrence, and if your conscience allows the application of the epithet to *him*, I don't see why you should scruple to apply it to an innocent horse."

28*th*. Disastrous news of Smith O'Brien. I had prayed him to avoid all collision with the law. . . . It seems that he has engaged in a driftless and unaccountable affray with the police, and is now hiding among the hills of Tipperary with a Government reward of £500 upon his head. My heart bleeds for him ! . .

August 6th. O'Brien has been arrested at Thurles, and taken by special train to Dublin, where he is lodged in Kilmainham Jail. But one short month ago I expected his arrival here, and promised myself some enjoyment from the visit of so valued a friend. . . .

27th, Edinburgh. I met a Miss Anderson, who, I am told, was converted to Catholicity by my book *Saints and Sinners.* Visited Monro (C. Scott's lawyer), who has a charming house in Regent Terrace, overlooking the old Palace of Holyrood. He showed me the portrait of his grandfather, a Presbyterian clergyman of Cromarty, who, he boasted, was the father of no less than twenty-seven bairns. " That was as much as any of your Irish Murphys could do!" exclaimed the prolific presbyter's descendant, with a chuckle of triumph. . . .

30th. The Repealers gave me a soiree last night. Repeal is, at the present moment, only the ghost of its former self. Yet, for old times' sake, I could not but be pleased with the speeches and the cheers. . . .

September 11*th.* Aberdeen. Strolled through some of the old streets, in which one sees here and there picturesque corner turrets with extinguisher tops. . . .

12*th.* Preshome, near Fochabers.[1] Preshome has been an episcopal residence since the reign of Charles the Second. . . . In the chapel is an altar-piece of great excellence, presented by Lord Findlater to a former bishop, about the year 1770. . . . The Bishop is hospitable, and full of curious old stories. He told me of a Scotch Catholic proprietor who, in the penal times, turned Protestant to save his estate. On being reproached for his apostacy, he answered, " Ow, mon, I had

[1] Mr Daunt arrived there on a visit to the Bishop, Dr Kyle. —ED.

rather trust my saul wi' God than my estate wi' those rascals." An instance of clan feeling. A vassal of the Duke of Hamilton prayed, on the eve of a skirmish with another clan, that God might defend the right. " What's that ye're saying?" cried his wife. " The right, indeed! God defend the Duke of Hamilton, right or wrang!" A certain Reverend Mr Fraser, who annoyed Lord Lovat by claiming his title and estates, tried to establish his pedigree, in default of other evidence, by the production of an ancestral watch, on which were engraved the letters S. F., alleged by the claimant to be the initials of his ancestor, the notorious Simon Fraser, Lord Lovat, be-headed in 1746. The letters were under the regulator, and the adverse counsel laughed the claim out of Court by showing that S. F. merely stood for Slow, Fast. The Bishop is entitled, by maternal descent, to the Viscounty of Frendraught, but has neither means nor inclination to pursue the claim. . . . He showed me some very curious manuscripts, including two holograph French letters written in 1571 by Mary Queen of Scots to the Archbishop of Glasgow. He told me he had one Irish-man among his flock, an unceremonious sort of penitent, who said, " My lord, I was so unlucky as to get among the Presbyterians, and to neglect my religion. I got careless and drunken, and dishonest and profligate—in fact, I was but very little better than a Scotsman." . . . His lordship tells me there was formerly much more social intercourse and mutual good feeling between the different ranks in his neighbourhood than at present. " The late Duke of Gordon laboured to promote that re-sult, and with success. The Duke of Richmond, who has now got the Gordon estates, would do the same if he could, but he does not know how to set about it." I met here Mr Menteith, of Carstairs, in Lanarkshire, a convert to Catholicity. . . . Speaking of Scottish nationality, Menteith remarked, "We love our country, and are proud of it. As to a Repeal of the Scotch Union, however, the only thing that could stir us up to seek for it would be the success of the Irish example. If you obtained your own Repeal, and if experience should demonstrate that it greatly benefited Ireland, we should then probably bestir ourselves to obtain a similar benefit for Scotland." We spoke of the lateness of the northern season, of the bush fruit now selling in the Aberdeen market. "I had a Cambridge friend," said Menteith, "who was passionately fond of strawberries, and he followed the strawberry season from Cambridge to our northern latitudes. As soon as the strawberries were declining at Cambridge, he shifted a little northward, and caught them in their prime, and so on, until he fairly saw the season out at Inverness."—*Scotomania*. "My friend, Lord Lyndsay," continued Menteith, "was so exclusively absorbed in Scotch history, Scotch traditions, Scotch chronicles, that all his historical epochs were referred to some Scotch event. Being asked at what period some important transaction in French history occurred, 'Let me see,' said his lordship, pausing to reflect, 'it occurred —yes—precisely at the time when the Macnabs separated from the MacGregors.' What a hegira!"

. . . 15*th*. Left Preshome this morning, and had a pleasant drive to Fochabers through the extensive firwoods appertaining to Gordon Castle. Along the road, as it passes through this region, there is a line of snow posts seven or eight feet high, with black tops, to render the line of road distinguishable in the winter snowdrifts.

16*th*. Edinburgh. In the boat from Burntisland to

Granton . . . was a tall, flashy-looking Scotch baronet, . . . who struck me as having much the air of a picturesque stage brigand. On asking who he was, I was told he was Sir R. A——r, who had succeeded to a large estate by the deaths of some relatives, and I afterwards learned that he had been formerly employed by Madame Vestris at two guineas a week in some of her theatrical enterprises.

21st. . . . Mrs Scott, among her recollections of early life at Parton, mentioned that the old Presbyterian minister of the parish, Donaldson, would, after preaching in his kirk against 'Popery,' come to dine at Parton, saying to Mr Glendonwyn with a laugh,—" I have been preaching against ye the day, and noo I've come to tak' my denner wi' ye." Donaldson was a very good man. He was on terms of brotherly intimacy with Mr Glendonwyn's chaplain, Father Fraser. When the priest died, his gloves were sent by Glendonwyn to Donaldson, such a gift being esteemed in Galloway emblematic of faithful friendship. Glendonwyn and Donaldson were, with many other persons, witnesses of a curious incident at a curling match on the Dee. A number of curlers were engaged in the pastime, and as often as they cast the stone a little bird used to alight so near it on the ice that the curlers were afraid of hurting it. This happened so often that the curlers began to regard the circumstance as ominous, and quitted the place for another frozen pool lower down the stream. They had scarcely done so, when the ice on which they had been standing gave way. When old Donaldson died his place was filled by a minister named Glen, whose wife was perpetually threatening to drown herself. The family were kept in constant alarm, until one day Miss Glen, her sister-in-law, said, " Weel, since ye are sae keen for drooning, I think it wad be a vera gude plan. Come awa, and I'll show ye an excellent part of the river to droon yersel' ; a lonely spot where ye couldna be rescued. Since ye *will* do it, the suner it's owre the better." Thenceforth no more was heard about Mrs Glen's drowning. . . . We talked of epitaphs ; " my initials will do for my epitaph," said Charlie ; " C. G. Scott—(*ci-gît* Scott)."

October 2d. Read the Reverend S. R. Maitland's excellent work on the Dark Ages. . . . He mentions that the first Concordance of the Scripture was compiled by Hugo de S. Charo, a Dominican friar, afterwards a cardinal. He was assisted in his task by 500 Dominican monks. Hugo died in 1262. Mrs Scott tells me that the late Mr Menzies of Pitfoddels entertained a strong prejudice against O'Connell, until some person placed in his way O'Connell's *Letter to Lord Shrewsbury*, the perusal of which converted Mr Menzies to O'Connellism, and he forthwith forwarded ten guineas to the O'Connell tribute.

18*th*. One hundred cases of cholera and seventy-five deaths up to last night in Edinburgh, Leith and Newhaven. . . . [Mr Daunt, *apropos* of Dr Strauss's very infidel *Life of Jesus*, which he reviews at some length, continues :] To pass from Dr Strauss's theology to his domestic history : the doctor, who is said to be a Pantheist, having (in his own opinion) mortally wounded revelation, sat down to enjoy his victory in the cheerful quiet of married felicity. The partner he selected was an opera dancer. But that circumrotatory particle of the great Pantheistic existence possessed divergent qualities, and skipped away from Dr Strauss at the end of a week.

Whether he has supplied her place I have not heard. But doubtless all will go right by-and-by, when Strauss and his centrifugal heroine shall be finally absorbed into the grand Πανθέος. . . .

CHAPTER VII

Mr Daunt asked to raise a Regiment—Protection Meeting—
Superstition—An Attorney's Trick—O'Connell outdoing
Falstaff—A Robber's Cave—The Example of Moses—
Parson's Extortions.

1849. — *January* 1*st.* Another New Year. It finds
Ireland still steeped in penury, fleeced by England,
and divided at home. Will it be thus to the end of
time ? . . .

May 8*th.* Went to Clonakilty to attend a meeting.
. . . I was painfully struck *en route* with the number of
farms lying waste and untenanted, and the number of
cabins deserted and ruinous. The advocates of the
Poor Law promised that it would promote agriculture
by giving the landlords a new motive to encourage their
tenants, and that it would prevent extermination by
taxing the landlords for the support of the ejected
people. Whatever may be the result in years to come,
it must be owned that these fair prophecies have been
hitherto fulfilled by contraries. . . .

17*th.* Parliament has passed the ' rate in aid,' by
which the extra rating for the Irish emergency is thrown
on Ireland exclusively. . . .

August 4*th.* Received a letter from John Sobieski
Stuart, who is now at Presburg, asking me to assist him
in raising an Irish brigade for the Papal service, of which

my correspondent and his brother, Charles Edward, propose to be colonel and lieutenant-colonel respectively. I anticipate that the scheme will be a failure. . . . *An excellent character.* It appears by the English papers that Rebecca Smith of Chippenham has been convicted by Judge Cresswell of poisoning her infant. She confessed to having poisoned eight children by touching her breasts with arsenic. She was sentenced to death; but some good souls at Chippenham got up a petition for mercy grounded on the culprit's ' excellent character.' . . .

November (no date). I have consulted four Catholic prelates on the subject of the proposed armament for the papal service. Three of them sanction the project, namely, the Archbishop of Tuam, and the Bishops of Meath and Ardagh. Archbishop Murray looks adversely at it. If the Chevalier Stuart can furnish the money and the means of transport, the men can be had. If, however, the Chevalier expects Ireland to furnish the pecuniary aid . . . he will be disappointed.

December 23d. . . . Meeting of landlords in Bandon to petition for protection for agriculture. I attended and pitched Repeal of the Union into the Conservative gentlemen present. . . .

1850.—*January 3d.* Attended a Protection meeting at Dunmanway. . . . I moved, and Mr Gillman of Oakmount seconded, a resolution that England had robbed us, and that we should petition for redress. Carried unanimously.

March 1st. Fort-William. . . . Gervase Bushe has put ' *optimus Patrum* ' on his father's monument in Lismore church. The ' *optimus patrum* ' had the rare fortune, or misfortune, to spend two (I think I heard three) estates in succession. . . .

22d. Cork. I have been summoned here on a special record jury to try Osborne *v.* Lord Limerick; the question being the value of racehorses sold thirty-eight years ago. . . .

April 1st. Cork again. Talked with John O'Connell about Repeal; tried to induce him to get rid of the ultra-peace pledge of 1846, but without success.

5th. Letter from Lord Bernard, denying that he is opposed to the abolition of the Viceroyalty. "Injurious possibly to Dublin," he tells me, "but good for Ireland." What good, pray? Government, in proposing to abolish the Viceroyalty, propose to abstract some £40,000 a year of our money, and they give us, in lieu of it, an assurance that—it is good for Ireland!

17th. Visited Mrs Smithwick. Talking of elegies, "Paddy O'Leary, the schoolmaster," said she, "told me some years ago that he had composed some beautiful elegiac verses on his father's death. "Dear me, Paddy," said I, " I am sorry to hear your father is dead." "Oh, he isn't dead at all," said Paddy; "only I thought whenever he should die, it would be well to have the verses ready; for you know I might not have time in the hurry of the wake and *berring.*" " That was twelve years ago," continued Mrs Smithwick, " and old Leary is alive still."

30th May, Eve. This is a famous day for *pishogues* (charms) and superstitious observances. Some of the extra-wise housewives increase their butter by throwing into the churn a small quantity of holy water heated on a *smeroidh* or ember. If this should fail, then the butter is touched with a holly branch; if this be ineffectual, a withe of rowan tree or mountain ash is bound round the churn, and the coulter of a plough is employed as a lever to tighten the ends of the twig. The pressure is then increased until the hostile witch is squeezed out of the churn. . . . I remember my old writing master, Taylor, telling me that he recollected the prosecution of a woman in the County Limerick in 1805, on a charge of increasing her butter by placing the hand of a dead man in the churn while churning. The case came before a magistrate, I think one Pritchard. . . .

May 1*st.* The country collieens go out on this festival gathering druchdheens, or little white snails, which they set crawling on a plate, and they fancy their sweethearts' initials can be traced in the track made by the little reptiles. The influence of evil *spridhs, shifris* and the whole tribe of fairies . . . in general, is guarded against by placing a branch of sloethorn over the house door. . . .

23*d.* Lord John Russell carried on last Friday the first reading of his bill for abolishing the Irish Vice-royalty, by a majority of 170 to 17. . . .

June 8*th.* . . . *How to serve a writ.* Tom had been induced to join a certain gentleman in a joint note for a rather considerable sum, in the full faith that his friend, for whose exclusive use the money was intended, would pay the amount when due. This he failed to do. Just at this time Tom chanced to travel in the same coach with a talkative and intelligent person who discussed many subjects, among others the supply of game. Tom, who did not know the name of his neighbour, said that he was trying to stock Kilcascan with hares, and that the boys around him used to bring him all the young hares they could catch. "And how do they convey the hares so as not to hurt them?" asked the talkative stranger. "In handkerchiefs," said Tom. Next day

Tom, looking from a window, saw a boy approaching the house and carrying a large handkerchief nicely puffed out. " Here is a young hare," thought Tom, who immediately descended to receive the prize from the obliging bearer. " Are you Mr Thomas Daunt?" asked the gossoon. " Yes," was the reply. Quick as light the handkerchief was unfurled, and thereout came—not a hare, but—a writ which the adroit youth handed Tom, saying, " Mr Kingston Sullivan directed me to serve you with this, sir." . . . So much for a clever professional trick. In the sequel, Tom's friend paid the amount of the bill. . . .

27th. Barking oaks. Dan Conner brought me a *Northern Star* containing some capital specimens of Feargus O'Connor's swagger. O'Connell used to say : " Feargus exaggerates so tremendously, that he destroys the effect of his statements." Dan, however, did himself occasionally exhibit symptoms of an inflated imagination. Among the stereotyped ornaments of his eloquence was a favourite reference to 'the majestic mountains and fertile valleys of green Ireland.' Once at Athlone, in the very centre of the flattest part of Ireland, he exclaimed in the peroration of a patriotic speech : " Look around, my friends, on the majestic mountains," etc., compliance with which request would have severely tested the optics of his audience. Another time, Dan, when boasting at the Corn Exchange of the great attendance at a meeting he had recently addressed at Kilkenny, outdid Falstaff's eleven men in buckram, somewhat after the following fashion : He began by stating the numbers present at the meeting at 50,000, " and who will deny," he continued, " that the cause must be important and the purpose strong that could assemble together these 50,000 men? Let no man say that they gathered merely from a feeling of personal regard or curiosity on my account. It would be absurd to suppose that 100,000 men would leave their homes to look at an elderly and rather corpulent gentleman. No, sir; when that peaceful army of 150,000 Irishmen congregated round me, their presence spoke, trumpet-tongued, their firm resolution never to desist from the struggle until Ireland should have her own Parliament again. And their multitudinous masses were as orderly and pacific as they were resolute and determined. Oh, with what unspeakable delight do I not recognise, in the conduct of those 200,000 noble fellows, etc., etc." And thus Dan sailed along, upborne upon the swelling tide of his imagination; each sentence adding at least 50,000 to the previous amount, until at last he arrived at, I think, 300,000. . . .

July 9th. The Viceroyalty has been saved for the present by an unexpected ally, the Duke of Wellington, who says that without such an officer it would be much more difficult to keep the Irish people quiet in case of a rebellion. . . .[1]

September 5th. This evening Tom returned from Fort-William, to my great delight. . . . Among the Comeragh Mountains, where he has been shooting, is the hold of a robber. The place is called Crotty's Rock; it is a cave in the face of a stupendous precipice, long the refuge of a freebooter named Crotty, who once infested that district. He robbed successfully, and secured the connivance of several farmers by giving them money to help out their rents. He kept a mistress who believed

---

[1] During the remainder of July and August Mr Daunt chronicles merely domestic and local events, mingled with the preparation of one or two books for the press.—ED.

that she monopolised his affections, and whom he sub-sidised so liberally that it was not worth her while to take any of the bribes she was offered from time to time to betray him. Once, however, the police told her that Crotty had another *chère amie*, and her jealousy was so keenly piqued by the information that she handed him over to the law. Among his exploits was the plunder of a large sum of money, which he handed in a bag to the care of a farmer. The farmer's conscience impelled him to give up the bag to Mr——, the nearest magistrate, *who kept it*.

10*th*. Cricket. On the field was the Honourable Cecil Lawless, Lord Cloncurry's son. He told me that his father (who expressed to me some years ago his belief that Arthur O'Connor had unfairly sacrificed Coigly in 1797) was in Paris two years ago, and saw Arthur, who then fully cleared himself of the imputa-tion. . . . We talked of Feargus O'Connor. "Feargus," said Lawless, "is one of the most amusing companions I have ever met."

11*th*. Old M—— L——, rector of Desertserges, has died at the age, I believe, of eighty-one. . . . One of his parishioners named Crowley, who lived at Carne-voulder, once asked me whether it would be a sin to shoot his reverence. Crowley had been reading the Bible, and he had read, in Exodus ii. 12, that Moses killed an Egyptian who oppressed an Israelite. Parson L—— oppressed Crowley in the matter of tithes, might not Crowley therefore make an Egyptian of him? I scarcely think the querist was in earnest. . . .

24*th*. Feargus O'Connor has been praising me ex-travagantly in his *Life and Adventures*. I cannot conceive why, for he never does anything without a motive. . . .

28th. The parson has sent me a pastoral requisition for tithe.   The ' Established Church ' is something of the nature of an established corn blight, or an established potato disease, or an established cattle murrain, or any other 'established' calamity that affects agricultural property.   May Heaven grant us patience under the infliction ! . . .

November 18*th.* Left home for Dublin; reached Fermoy about 8 p.m.   I met only one traveller in the coffee-room of the hotel, a talkative old gentleman, who seemed wonderfully conversant with the temporalities of the Protestant Church.   We spoke of the famine.   He had seen six cartloads of dead sent daily out of the Cork workhouse in 1846. . . . He says the great Mitchelstown estate would before now have been sold, only that the creditors can get something near the interest of their money from the annual rents, whereas they could not possibly realise the principal from the sale as lands sell at present.   This delay affords Lord Kingston time to philander a wealthy widow whose personal history is a wild romance, and whom he hopes he can induce to barter £200,000 for the coronet of a countess.   My informant spoke as if he were in the widow's confidence, and said, *de haut en bas,* ' she would be sorry to marry him.'

29th. Dublin.   Visited my old friend Charles Gavan Duffy.   Frederic Lucas came in, his portly Saxon person encased in Irish frieze.   Ryan of Bruree, the candidate for Limerick, came in.   He said that his rival, Mr Monsell of Tervoe, promised that if elected he would become a Catholic.   " Then," said Duffy, " you should have threatened that if not elected you would become a Protestant. . . ."

6th December. Kilcascan.   Travelled home on the Bandon car with Mr Herbert Gillman of Woodbrook, who, himself a Protestant, groans under the extortions of the Protestant clergy.   " God help me ! " said he, " I have eleven ministers to pay, besides vicars choral, and not one of them ever abated a single sixpence to meet the times.   As to M——, he is a hard old crust.   Just think of the man that christened me bringing an execution into my house for the tithe rent charge due last May out of lands that for the last three years have paid me no rent ! " . . .

CHAPTER VIII

An Unnatural Father—A Lawyer's Opinion of Brougham—A
Lawyer's Adventure—A Philosophic 'Bus Driver—Attempt
to get Tithe from the Queen—Making Love for a Salary—
Sauter la Coupe—The Sheriff's Face—A Thousand-Years-
Old Bible.

1851.—*January* 31*st*. For a fortnight nothing has occurred to diversify the monotony of existence. Planting, thinning, and pruning as usual, and teaching my
daughter to read, spell, etc. . . . [1]

May 10*th*. Meeting at Dunmanway against the
Ecclesiastical Titles Bill. I went and took the opportunity to make a speech against the tithes. A petition
to the House of Commons against the rector's extortions
has been signed by nearly all the Tory landlords in the
parish. I have sent it for presentation to E. B. Roche.
Fungar inani munere at present. Hereafter it may, with
perseverance, bear fruit. I have an excruciating abscess
in my left hand, which is swelled to nearly thrice its
natural size. The pain is excessive. I can scarcely
journalise. . . .

June 30*th*. Sent off the last proofs of *The Gentleman in Debt* to the printers. . . . The story in its lead-

---

[1] The months of February, March and April passed in the same
manner, with occasional preparation of the *Wifehunter* for the
press.—ED.

ing features is founded on a family tragedy I learned from an old gardener, named Carroll, who lived near Castletown-Delvin in the County Westmeath. . . . Mitchelstown (near Castletown-Delvin) was remarkable for the great size of the beech and oak trees in the domain. Yet, notwithstanding the abundance and magnificence of the timber, the place was pervaded with the dismal air that attaches to deserted residences, increased in this instance by the dark tradition of unnatural guilt imputed to a former member of the Tighe family. Tighe of Southhill quarrelled with his wife, falsely accused her of unfaithfulness and broke her heart. She died leaving an only daughter, who was heiress of the estate under her parents' marriage settlements. Tighe proposed marriage to a Miss F——n, who refused to marry him unless he could get rid of the claims of his daughter. There was no mode of doing this unless by getting rid of the young lady herself. He accordingly drowned her in a lake, and married Miss F——n. I think my informant said that he got into pecuniary embarrassments and died in great penury in a garret in Thomas Street, Dublin, with no other bed than an old horse sheet.

August 7th. Left home for Scotland. . . .

12*th.* London. After several failures to secure apartments . . . we got lodgings at 11 Spring Gardens, at a rate that must be considered moderate at a time when such crowds are drawn to London from all corners of the world by this Great Exhibition.'[1]

14*th.* Visited Mr Turner. He says " There's a bad

[1] Mr Daunt and his friend, Mr Scott, had come to London to attend a law case which the latter had before the House of Lords. —ED.

House of Lords just now.   Appeals are heard by the Lord
Chancellor, one or two bishops, and a lay lord, three out
of four knowing nothing of law, and the Chancellor knowing nothing of Scotch law.   If Brougham were able to
attend, which he is not, the appellants would have a better
chance, as Brougham's instincts are to knock about
everything, and if there be any grounds at all for de-
molishing the Scotch decision, his propensity to disturb
and subvert would lead him to demolish it."   Mr Turner
told me the following adventure, which occurred in his
professional career.   He was engaged in a case in which
it was sought to confine a man of some fortune on the
plea of his insanity.   Turner went to see the man.
The house in which he lived was a tolerably good one,
but filthy and neglected.   The windows were defended
with strong wooden crossbars.   The front garden was
overgrown with weeds.   No servant appeared.   Turner
pushed open the door, and after peeping into two or
three empty and dirty apartments, he got at last into
a gloomy, darkened room in which sat the master of
the house.   Turner was shocked at his appearance.
His long, col black, matted hair was begrimed with
dirt.   He had neither shirt, coat nor waistcoat.   A
sheet pulled round his shoulders and a pair of tattered
drawers were his only attire.   He accosted Turner with
the ease of a well-bred gentleman, asked him to be
seated, regretted he had not a better chair to offer him,
began to complain that nobody would 'let him alone.'
"My fortune," said he, "is no object to me, I cannot
enjoy it.   All I want is to be let alone, but they won't
leave me at peace."   So saying, he suddenly locked the
door, and placed a pair of pistols before him on a
table in the middle of the room.   "I hope you don't feel

afraid," he said to Turner. " Oh, not at all," answered the latter, feeling wofully afraid all the while. The crazy man seemed pacified by the appearance of fearlessness in his visitor, whose inward tremors were greatly at variance with his confident exterior. But deeming the bold game the best, he continued to converse, apparently unembarrassed, and carefully noting the mental symptoms of his eccentric companion, whom he dexterously induced on some pretext to open the door. It need not be added that he speedily vanished from the dangerous premises. . . .

22*d*. Went with Scott to Amory's, 25 Throgmorton Street. . . . He protested that, according to English law, the case for the appeal was irresistible. ' I wish Brougham were Chancellor,' said I ; ' his instinct is to upset everything that has not been arranged by himself.' " Ah, Harry ! poor Harry ! " said Amory, " he is my personal friend. If he could be got to give his mind to this case he would sift the truth out of it better than any man living. I'll tell you what I've known him do. I have known him request the adjournment of a heavy appeal case on a Saturday evening, take home all the papers in a cab from the House of Lords, sit up the whole of Saturday night and all Sunday studying the case ; come down to the House as fresh as a daisy on Monday, and deliver a most luminous judgment in opposition to the opinions formed by three out of four of his brethren. But it was a mere toss-up whether he would have studied the question or not. The whim took him, and then he went heart and soul into it."

31*st*, *Sunday*. Mass at the Sardinian Ambassador's. . . . During the greatest heat of the Anti-Wiseman excitement, Major Scott was one day going through town on the box of an omnibus. Everyone was talking of the 'Papal aggression.' " In my mind," said the driver, "it's all a precious piece of fudge. ' Archbishop of Westminster,' well, and what harm in that ? " says I. " We've got an omnibus that's called the Marquis of Westminster."

September 2d. . . . Charlie is making inquiries to ascertain if his mother's estate in the Isle of Wight is tithe free. Manisty's opinion is interesting. Romance lurks in black-letter law. . . . The Vicar of Whippenham has instituted claims for tithe on various spots that had long been exempt, among others on a tithe-free portion of the Queen's estate at Osborne ; but the Head of the Church defeated the subordinate officer, Hewlett of Gray's Inn having established Her Majesty's exemption by his researches.

3d. . . . Dr Augustine Fitzgerald told us of an eccentric lady under his medical care ; her name, of course, was not mentioned. She astonished and perplexed him by seizing his hand, and assuring him of her enthusiastic admiration. As it did not suit his views to marry her, and as her malady (a mental one) required to be amused with declarations of a sentimental nature, he introduced an accomplished young gentleman, the son of a clergyman, who was employed at a salary to tell her she was fascinating and to play the piano for her. Between his music and his assiduities the lady became convalescent ; but still continues under the medical care of Fitzgerald, who receives £200 for his management.

4th. York. . . . One of my fellow-travellers was a stout, farmer-looking man. . . . He had got strong anti-clerical tendencies. " The Irish parsons," he said, " are damnable scoundrels. I consider them as bad as the priests." . . .

8*th.* Edinburgh. . . . Frederic Scott said to me at breakfast : " You and Captain M'Cann are the only two Irishmen I was ever acquainted with. M'Cann once did me a considerable service. I had lost £110 at *écarté* to an English sharper named Theobald, to whom I gave my note for the money. I felt I had been cheated, but could not exactly point out how. " Oh," said M'Cann, " I'll arrange that matter. Ask the rascal to dine at your hotel ; I'll go too. You may be sure he will propose *écarté*. I know something of the game ; I'll watch him closely, and if I catch him tripping we'll have him on the hip." " But how will this all terminate ? " said I ; " will not pistolling be apt to come of it ? " " Oh, as to that," said M'Cann, " we are two to one, so the odds are two to one that one of us shoots him." I asked the fellow to dinner, and in the evening, as M'Cann had predicted, he proposed *écarté*. M'Cann assented, and they played away till M'Cann detected him in the act of *sauter la coupe*. He jumped up, saying, " Stop, sir, that's foul play." " What do you mean ? " exclaimed Theobald. " I mean," said M'Cann, " that I saw you *sauter la coupe*. Now, sir, if you do not immediately restore to my friend Scott his note which you hold, you must abide the consequences." Theobald gave up the note. M'Cann rang the bell ; " Waiter, show that gentleman downstairs." And downstairs walked Theobald, doubtless much dissatisfied with his adventure. Frederic told a story of a sheriff of Edinburgh who forgot a twopenny ticket, whether of a railway or turnpike I don't recollect. The cash-

taker asked him for the fare. " I have already paid it,"
said the dignitary. "Then where's your ticket?" "I
have lost it." "Then you must pay again." "Come
now, friend," said the sheriff; "just look into my face
and tell me do I look like a man who would tell you
a lie for such a trifle as twopence?" The cash-taker
inspected the countenance thus offered as a guarantee
for its owner's integrity, and then drily said : "I'll just
thank you for the twopence." Story of a Frenchman
who wanted eggs for breakfast and forgot the English
for *œuf.* "Vaitere, vat is dat valking in de yard?" "A
cock, sir." "Ah! and vat you call de cock's vife?"
"The hen, sir." " And vat you call de shildrens of de
cock and his vife?" "Chickens, sir." "But vat you
call de shicken before dey are shicken?" "Eggs, sir."
"Bring me two." After breakfast Miss Glendonwyn
took me in her carriage to Craigmillar Castle, once the
residence of Queen Mary. . . . Having satisfied our
curiosity at Craigmillar we went on to Roslin, which
has often been described. The guide is the very *bijou*
of a guide . . . loquacious and intelligent . . . an enthusiast about the beautiful old chapel committed to
his keeping. . . . He quoted Sir Walter Scott, whom
he accused of inaccuracy in stating that—

> 'Twenty of Roslin's barons bold
> Lie buried in that proud chapelle.'

The real number, according to our *cicerone,* being only
ten. They are buried in their armour without coffins.
He spoke with pride of the notice he had received from
French and British royalties. "For a poor man," he
said, "I have been perhaps the most honoured man in
Europe. I have conversed with two queens and five

princes, and nobility innumerable. Queen Victoria
and Prince Albert were here and asked about everything. Her Majesty the Queen of the French, and
some of the princes were here. The old Queen tapped
me on the shoulder, and said, ' It is very beautiful.' "   . .

14*th*. Charles and I drove to Lord Traquair's in
Peebleshire. . . . The mansion is a very old baronial
edifice with thick walls and small windows. Lord
Traquair was in England, but we were received by
Father Wallace, his chaplain, who showed us the library
in which the most remarkable books were a folio black-
letter Bible, one of the earliest printed, and a manuscript
Bible one thousand years old, exquisitely written on
vellum by some ancient monk. . . . Having spent a
couple of hours agreeably enough, we recrossed the
Tweed to Peebles, where we dined, and thence returned
to Edinburgh.

October 1*st*. Kilcascan. Left Edinburgh last week;
crossed from Ardrossan to Belfast, where I spent two
days with Major Scott, whose regiment is quartered
there. . . .

CHAPTER IX

A Reminiscence of Sir Walter Scott—Mr Daunt at
Macaulay's Election—Macaulay returned for Edinburgh
—'Your Billy Shakespeare.'

1852.—*January* 15*th*. Edinburgh. Arrived here last
night with my little daughter. . . .

28*th*. Meeting of Anti-State Church Society at the
Music Hall. Charles and I went. . . . The meeting
was opened with prayer, and peppered all over with
attacks on the Catholic Church. Charles moved, and
I seconded, an amendment on the subject of Maynooth,
which was lost in an uproar of discordant noises.

March 29*th*. Leslie (of Fetternear and Balquhain)
came here. He says Jacobitism is not yet extinct as a
sentiment, and that he could find you Jacobites in Lord
Lovat's country. A Greek Catholic priest named
Gibara dined with Charles. I attended his Mass on the
14th inst. The part called the Mass of the Catechumens
precedes the Mass of the Eucharist, and is celebrated at
a separate altar ; this distinction having been derived
from the early times when ' the discipline of the Secret '
prevailed. . . .

13*th*. Met Mr Aitchison, the landlord of Mrs Scott's
new house. . . . He is a W.S. and wealthy brewer.
Knowing that we are Catholics, he makes a point of

parading a sort of patronising liberality, which one would excuse once or twice, but which, when incessantly repeated, becomes tiresome. We talked of Sir Walter Scott. " I knew him well," said he ; "his manners were simple and unassuming as a child's. He was one of the clerks of the Court of Session, and the worst of them all. Whenever I asked him a question he would put his arm round my neck and hirple along the Outer House, telling me what he thought about the matter, but always adding, ' I can't be sure about it ; go and ask Beveridge.' "

June 10*th*. Procession of the Blessed Sacrament at St Margaret's Convent. Mention was made of Mr Henry Stewart, a convert to Catholicity, whose wife displayed a queer sort of vanity. Becoming reduced in circumstances, she found it necessary to give music lessons, and in her advertisements announced that they were to be given by 'the wife of Henry Stewart, Esq., who was descended from King Robert the Second, and nearly related to the Lord Advocate of Scotland and the Marquis of ——.'[1]

July 11*th, Sunday*. Meeting of Catholic electors at St Mary's Schoolroom to arrange for the support of Macaulay at next Tuesday's election. A universal feeling in his favour ; but at a meeting at Ireland's room a few nights ago, one elector opposed Macaulay on the wise ground of his having written something in disparagement of the Catholic religion. Just as if a non-Catholic could be expected to write like a Catholic about Catholicity. Charles Scott defended Macaulay against the objector. " Why," said he, " although

---

[1] In July, Mr Daunt and his friend Mr Scott, took a somewhat active part in Macaulay's election for Edinburgh.—ED.

Macaulay is an infidel he terms our religion 'an august and fascinating superstition,' which, coming from an infidel, I take as a high compliment." Charles blundered here. Macaulay is not an infidel. It is easier to tell from his writings what he is not than what he is. He is not a Catholic, he is not a Puritan, he is not a Calvinist. Venturing a very diffident guess, I should surmise that he is some sort of Presbyterian . . . one of those whom O'Connell happily termed 'honorary members of Christianity.' . . . I knew a literary man in London whose writings had some success. One of his novels, founded on a well-known criminal trial, was written in a spirit of piety. You would say that the author must be a High Church Anglican with a deep feeling of reverence for sacred things. Yet that man said to me, " I no more believe in the Incarnation than in ———." I suppress the comparison he used. It was too abominable to be repeated.

12th. Hustings, confusion, speech-making, shouting and hooting.

13th. Macaulay is returned for Edinburgh ; a better member certainly than Duncan M'Laren. The return is creditable to the electors, as Macaulay is by no means such a bigot as M'Laren.

September 3d. . . . Major Scott tells a story of a disconsolate widower in Brazil, who, to save the expense of his wife's funeral, put her body into a barrel of brandy (aquardiente). In a few weeks a thirsty thief tapped the barrel and imbibed the brandy through a quill. He got so sick that concealment was impossible, and he complained to the owner that the brandy had a very queer taste. " I don't wonder at it," replied the widower, " for my wife has been in it for more than a month." . . .

Dined on Monday with Mr Clark of Queen Street. In talking of various matters connected with Scottish juris-prudence, he said that the lower orders of Scotch, when giving evidence in courts of law, seemed to have little or no notion of the sanctity of an oath, and that you could scarcely get the truth out of them if they had any in-terest in concealing it. . . . I wish I could acquit my own poor country of all share in this offence of perjury. I may at least say with truth that our nation is no worse than its more pretentious British neighbours. . . .

October 20th. . . . Charlie told me one or two de-tached stories of his father. Mr Scott, who was an Englishman, accompanied a Scotch friend to the Edinburgh theatre, where Home's tragedy of 'Douglas' was performed. The Scot enjoyed the performance with true national zest, and triumphing in the superi-ority of his countryman's dramatic talent, he turned to his English companion, saying, "What do you think of your Billy Shakespeare noo?" . . .

13th. I spent yesterday with Leslie, hunting out anti-quities. . . . To the Parliament Hall, where a lawyer-looking man said to my companion, "Did your mother get the estates along with the peerage?" "Both the estates," answered Leslie ; "and may leave them to anyone she likes." His step-mother was Dorothy, Countess of Newburgh, which title she assumed on the death of her brother, s.p., in the belief that a branch of the family settled in Italy was disqualified, under the Alien Act, from inheriting a Scottish peerage. But the Italian branch, as represented by Princess Giustini-ani, afterwards established their claim to the honours of the Scottish earldom. . . .

CHAPTER X.

Lord John —— and His Parents—Mr Daunt's Account of His Conversion—The Sultan's Intended Generosity—O'Connell and His Earldom—Sir R. Peel and Feargus O'Connor—At a Lunatic's Ball—Brougham and the Litigant—An Estate won by the Cudgel—Income Tax carried—A Writ of Rebellion—How Mr Brown got £15,000.

1853.—*January 1st*. When going to Mass this morning we had a specimen of Edinburgh jollity. Crowds had thronged the streets last night to welcome 1853 with alcoholic orgies. 'First foot' is the name they give this custom. . . . This morning, a little after eight o'clock, I saw crowds gathered, like swarms of bees, round the doors of the dram-shops in the Canongate. I was told they had been up all night engaged in the duties of 'first foot.' But this is scarcely credible, for if they had been, I don't think they could stand. . . .

10*th*. Walked up to Dunsappie. Some years ago, when Lord John —— was on his deathbed here from the effects of a surfeit, he was asked if he would wish for a visit from his parents, the Duke and Duchess of ——. He answered, "No; they never taught me anything good, and I don't want to see them now." He died shortly after. And just before then he had seduced a Highland girl whom he was bringing to London.

11*th*. Walked with Leslie. . . . Story of a Writer to

the Signet so formidable to his clients that one poor gentleman who employed him used to escape into a shop, or some other harbour of refuge, whenever he espied him in the street. "Why do you run away from Mr —— ?" asked a friend. "To save my pocket," was the answer. "I never can shake hands with him but I find it duly charged in the bill as an interview on business."

16th. Story of an old gentleman who was addicted to drunkenness, and who, when returning home at night from the scene of his potations, generally passed through an old kirkyard. His son, a Presbyterian minister, having long and vainly tried to reclaim the old toper by remonstrance, at last resolved to assail him through the medium of his superstitious feelings. Accordingly the reverend gentleman dressed himself in a white sheet, and suddenly confronted his father, from behind a tomb, as the latter reeled home one night through the kirkyard exceedingly drunk. "Oh, man," exclaimed the minister, in a sepulchral voice, "I have been sent to warn ye—" "Stop!" interrupted the jovial old gentleman, nothing daunted, and familiarly laying his hand on the ghost's shoulder, "tell us first, is this gaun to be a general upreesing, or are ye only takin' a wee bit daunder by yersel'?" Charlie was visited by a philosophic German, who introduced the subject of theology. I gave him the history of my own conversion to the Catholic faith. The first place of worship to which, in early childhood, I was brought was the Catholic church in Tullamore, the servant who attended me being herself a Catholic. Born of Protestant parents, and nurtured in the house of a Protestant grandmother, I had scarcely passed the years of infancy when I felt the strongest desire to be a member of the Catholic Church. I do not remember when this desire began; but of this I am sure, that it was not produced by any external influences, such as the solicitations of Catholic servants or friends. When I was about eight I was brought one night to the Catholic church to hear a Mr Wilman, a Dublin musician, perform sacred music on the organ. With our party was a Protestant boy, named William Dawson, whom I had a great desire to impress with the belief that I was a Catholic. . . . "Why," he said, surprised, "are you a Catholic?" "Yes," said I; and so I truly was in affection and desire. . . . My teachers had represented the Catholic religion as perfectly unscriptural. I found in the book-room of my grandmother's house an old Douai catechism printed by Flynn, at Cork, in 1776, and I eagerly read it. I shall never forget the pleasure with which I verified the scriptural quotations in the catechism. I was then about ten or eleven years old. Meanwhile, my desire to be incorporated into the Catholic Church became a passion. It absorbed nearly all my thoughts. I used to look with a feeling like envy at the peasantry around me who could go to Mass, and possessed a privilege from which I was debarred by family influences. . . . I instinctively rejected the figment that the ancient Church of Ireland was Protestant. The State Church, in the interest of which that figment was invented, and which assumes to itself the title of 'Church of Ireland,' is an institution originating in England, and forced, by English power, on this kingdom. In 1826 my father died, and his death removed one obstacle to the public avowal of my religious predilections. But other obstacles remained. I used to shut myself up in my room, praying to God to remove them.   I loved to haunt the Catholic chapels. I have gone into Father Mathew's old chapel in Cork in the dusk of a summer evening, and sat there when not a worshipper except myself was present.   Whence came this resistless impulse? this rushing tide of enthusiastic love for the Catholic Church? In boyhood I had learned the Hail Mary from the old Douai catechism already mentioned, and, unknown to all around me, I habitually associated that touching prayer with my ordinary devotions.   I was finally received into the Catholic Church in Cork by my dear and venerated friend Father Mathew, and soon afterwards I received the sacrament of Confirmation from the Bishop of Cork, Dr Murphy, in the chapel of the Blackrock Convent.

17*th*. . . . A Mr M'Carthy came.   His father is physician to the Sultan. . . .   We asked him if he had ever known a Turk become a Catholic? 'Never.' Had he known a Turk become a Protestant? 'Yes, one. It was a man who originally had been a Protestant, who became a Turk, and who then became a Protestant again.'

18*th*. M'Carthy (the Turk) dined with Charles to-day. He told me that the Sultan had intended to give £10,000 to the famine-stricken Irish, but was deterred by the English Ambassador, Lord Cowley, as Her Majesty, who had only subscribed £1000, would have been annoyed had a foreign sovereign given a larger sum. . . .

21*st*. Read extracts in the papers from Lord John Russell's sketch of Moore the poet. I was once offered an introduction to Moore, on, I think, the last occasion of his visiting Dublin, which I very stupidly refused, chiefly from a feeling of indifference to poetry. . . .   I recollect hearing O'Connell account for Moore's absence from the Repeal agitation by saying that he was very jealous of the popular talents of the leaders. " Before we appeared so much upon the public stage," said Dan, " Tom Moore was considered the foremost Catholic lay intellect of the day. He was jealous of losing that pre-eminence." O'Connell had a keen nose for scenting out jealousy and enmity, so keen as sometimes to scent them out where they did not exist. For instance, he fancied that Miss Edgeworth intended to insult him by making Connal the name of the rascal in her story of *Ormonde*. The Presbyterian minister of Aberdour, Mr Campbell, who recently visited me, seemed curious to know how some of our Irish political celebrities acquitted themselves in conversation. He was inquisitive about Sheil. Before I met him, John Gumbleton described him to me as illuminating every topic which he touched. I suppose I never saw him in his happier moods. In private he was sociable, full of *bonhomie*, awake to all that went forward, and all he said had the advantage of a very lively manner. His eyes were sparkling and piercing, the eyes of genius. But I don't recollect his saying anything pungent or witty or odd—anything, in short, worth remembering. Among O'Connell's best qualities in private were his great hospitality, his friendly manners, and his immovable good - humour. It was nearly impossible to put him out of temper. . . . His professional practice supplied him with many odd stories of the bench and the bar. Some of these I have pre-served in my *Personal Recollections of O'Connell.*[1] He had aristocratic aspirings. He once said to me, " If I

---

[1] A book now out of print, and unscrupulously plagiarised by T. C. Luby, C. M. O'Keefe and others.—ED.

ever took a title, it should be Earl of Glencara." It was
possibly with the thought of such a contingency that he
had a seal engraved showing his arms, surmounted by
an earl's coronet. He was sanguine of the ultimate success of Repeal. He used to say, " The timid man increases his own difficulties, the coward increases his own
dangers;" and again, " There is no impossibility to combined millions.' . . . Feargus O'Connor was in his best
days the most entertaining of companions. . . . He
was unencumbered with any superfluous diffidence.
When Chartism, under his leadership, had become
pretty widely diffused, its modest chief thus spoke : " I
have *made* the mind of England, and it is now my duty
to *guide* it." . . . An Englishman, named Steele, said
publicly, "I adore Feargus O'Connor." Another Englishman . . . bequeathed to him a house and chattels, worth
£2000, at Halifax, declaring in his will that he had long
been on the outlook for an honest man to whom he
should leave his property, and as nobody but Feargus
came up to his standard of integrity, he gladly rewarded
the patriot's merits with the legacy. . . . Feargus once
received a delicate and humorous chastisement from Sir
Robert Peel. He had declared at a Chartist meeting
his readiness to welcome to the throne any sovereign
who should grant the Charter. " If," said he, " the people
had the Charter, they need not care although the throne
was occupied by the devil." Shortly afterwards he was
making earnest declarations in the House of Commons
of his loyalty and that of the Chartists. " I am glad,"
said Peel, " to learn, on the excellent authority of the
honourable gentleman, that he is a loyal subject of the
Queen. The intelligence of his loyalty is the more
gratifying as it is rather unexpected. Very lately he

told a large assembly of his usual followers that if certain political views which he entertains were realised, the throne of England might not disadvantageously be occupied by the devil. I feel sure, sir, that if ever the throne shall be possessed by the monarch of his choice, *the honourable gentleman will enjoy the entire confidence of the Crown."* . . .

28*th.* Charlie's cousin-german, the Earl of Oxford, has died childless, or left no heirs-male, and the title is said to be extinct. Charlie's aunt, the late Countess, *née* Jane Elizabeth Scott, once formed with Lady Holland a plot in the interests of Bonaparte against the English Government. The particulars of their scheme I do not know ; but the Government got some intimation of the matter, and suspected Lord Oxford, who, as he was wholly ignorant of the project, easily exonerated himself. No suspicion fell upon her ladyship, the real culprit.

February 13*th.* M'Carthy (the Turk) came and told two incidents of the madhouse at Morningside. One . . . is this : Every Wednesday a ball is given at the asylum, at which visitors dance with the harmless lunatics. Mr Doyle, brother of the celebrated Doyle of *Punch,*[1] danced with a young madwoman, who, during the evening, grew confidential, and assured him that her relations had placed her in the establishment against her will. " I observed," said she, " there were some ladies of your party. When you are going away I can slip out unnoticed among them, and accompany you home." Doyle, who did not relish the proposal, tried to escape from her by mingling in the crowd, but she kept her eye on him all night, and when at last she saw him about to

[1] And father of Dr Conan Doyle.—ED.

go off without her, she rushed at him, clung to his arm, and succeeded in getting up a very disagreeable scene, which ended in her being forcibly removed to her cell.

March 1st. Major Scott and his wife arrived. . . . The former accompanied me to Mr Clark, W.S., and asked him if Lord Brougham's personal friend Amory could be of any use in inducing Lord B. to bestow particular attention on the Munches appeal case. "Better not try," said Clark. "There was a litigant engaged in an appeal who called on Brougham, stated his case to him, was civilly listened to, and desired by his lordship to attend next day at the House, when he promised to see what could be done. The man went off in high spirits, thinking he had made a favourable impression, and attended punctually the next day when the House sat to hear appeals. Brougham was there, and called out, 'Is Mr —— in attendance?' 'Yes, my lord,' said the man, delighted at being inquired after. 'Stand at the bar, sir,' said Brougham, sternly. 'My lords,' he continued, 'I have to complain that the person at the bar has committed a gross breach of privilege. He attempted, by a private application, to prejudice me, one of the judges in his case, and if I am thus satisfied with publicly reprimanding him instead of pressing for the infliction of the appropriate punishment, it is because I am disposed to believe that his offence arose from ignorance only, and not from a deliberate desire to infringe upon your lordships' privileges.' The culprit was then obliged to beg pardon, after which he was ordered to withdraw." William Scott tells the following story of his uncle, the Reverend James Scott, formerly rector of Otterbourne, near Winchester. The parson, when chaplain to a regiment, was summoned from his wine, after dinner, to attend a dying Protestant soldier in the hospital. He went, not relishing the interruption, and on approaching the sick man, said, "Well, my good fellow, you are not afraid to die, I hope?" "Oh, no, your reverence." "Ah, that's right, old fellow; I thought you wouldn't. Good-evening," and he returned to his wine. The gentleman who could thus economise his religious ministrations had an orthodox horror of dissent, and a practical way of repressing it. There was a strolling Methodist preacher who attracted large crowds, and thinned the congregations of the neigh-bouring rectors. "I'll take care he shall not thin mine," said the Reverend James Scott, who was very popular with his parishioners. He accordingly instructed two or three stout young men to get good oak sticks and to thrash the Methodist soundly if he dared to poach upon the spiritual preserves of Otterbourne. The preacher was duly apprised of the preparation made for his welcome, and wisely kept away. . . . . Charlie Scott records the exhortation of a Scotch democratic enthusiast to his *confrères*. "Persevere in your resistance to your tyrants; let no terrors of punishment deter you. To be sure, you may be hanged, but has not the sacred cause of freedom always had its martyrs? Even if you adorn the gallows you will be illustrious. Your bones may whiten on the gibbet—*heed it not!* for the crown of the patriot martyr will be yours,' etc. Certainly this was treating the affair *en philosophe.* . . .

April 23d. Kilcascan. Tom told me the history of a clan of Briens or Bryans in this vicinage. They were big, able-bodied fellows, who, in the palmy days of faction-fighting, formed a sort of Swiss force, and earned a good deal of money by fighting at fairs. Mr French, a neighbouring proprietor, hearing of their pugnacious renown, selected the wickedest cudgel-player of the clan as his agent to fight the rents out of his tenants, who seem to have been an intractable set. The cudgel-player acquitted himself well in his new capacity, and in time fought himself into an excellent farm. Being thrifty and industrious, he saved up means in some years to buy a fee-simple estate, of which he has now the enjoyment. . . .

May 16*th*. The third reading of the Irish Income Tax has been carried by a Government majority of seventy-one. . . . Observe here the way in which the Union defeats the constitutional principle that the people are not to be taxed unless by a majority of their representatives in Parliament. More than two-thirds of the Irish members opposed the tax. Yet the voice of a British majority has saddled us with it . . . One of Mr Gladstone's arguments is curious from its dishonest ingenuity. He extracts from our poverty a pretext for taxing us. Pitt and Castlereagh promised at the Union that Irish taxation should not be approximated to British until our increased prosperity should enable us to bear the increased burden. The prosperity has not come, but the tax must be got. If, says Gladstone, you haven't got wealth to be mulcted, your poverty will answer me quite as well. For the purchasing power of £150 is greater in a poor country than in a rich one; whence he argues that, as Ireland is poor, an Irish income of £150 is a fitter subject for taxation than an income of equal amount in England. The peculiar beauty of this reasoning is, that the poorer the country the stronger is the force of argument for taxing it. [1] . . .

June 23d. This is St John's Eve; fires blaze on all the hills, and the people are in sufficient spirits to halloo and blow horns for the *Beal Tinne* as in days of yore. . . . D. Conner came here to-day, and styled the tithe system 'a running sore.' . . . He tells me that he, his father and Gillman, of Oakmount, had an argument recently with S——, the curate of Bally-money, about the extortion practised by the parsons, and that S—— coolly told them that if, instead of a tenth, the law had given them nine-tenths, or even a whole, they would be morally justifiable in enforcing it. This same S—— one day told me that a poor wretch who should die under the guilt of stealing a penny bun to save himself of dying of starvation would certainly be damned for the act. If this be not straining at a gnat and swallowing a camel, the Scriptural antithesis was never yet exempli-fied. . . .

August 15th. Youghal. Met Captain Davis, formerly of Kilgariff. We went to see Sir Walter's Raleigh's old house, with its ancient oak room and beautiful old mantelpiece. We talked of the days of the anti-tithe agitation. "I had obtained," said Davis, "a promise from Mr Neville, the rector of Clonpriest, to abate 5 per cent. of the tithes, of which abatement I gave my tenants the benefit. Neville employed a collector named Giles, and before a year had expired, he sent me word that he could not both pay an agent and continue the abatement. I pleaded his promise. He

[1] Several weeks passed by in the ordinary pursuits of a country gentleman, the record of which may be omitted.—Ed.

did not answer my letter. I was referred to Giles, who insisted, in an insolent manner, on full payment. I felt that I was wronged and did not comply, when, one day, I was informed that there was a writ of rebellion against me in the town of Youghal. I was then in England, or should, perhaps, have committed a fresh breach of the law; for it is most likely that if Giles, or any employé of his, had attempted to seize me under a writ of rebellion, I would have broken his head." There was something delightfully grotesque in the notion of my most loyal friend, the ex-dragoon, being arrested under a writ of rebellion.

September 27th. D. Conner visited me to-day. He tells me that the Vicars Choral of Cork, a corps of clerical sinecurists, have, since 1821, got from Fanlobbus and two adjacent parishes £33,000, out of which large sum they have only given three guineas to local charities, that trifling sum, says Dan, having been shamed out of them. . . .

November 4th. The papers announce the death of good old Lord Cloncurry, whose name is deservedly dear to Ireland. In 1846 he offered his mediation to heal the breach between the two parties in the Repeal Association. John O'Connell snarled at Lord Cloncurry instead of taking advantage of his offer. To this ill-judged return to a well-meant proposal do I ascribe in a great measure the disgust at agitators which Lord Cloncurry expressed in a letter I received from him last year in Edinburgh. He had lost all confidence in them. . . . He ended by saying that so pained was his heart at the condition of his country, he would at fourscore seek another home, 'if it were not that he loved Ireland even in dotage.'

8th. This morning's paper announces the death of Lord Cloncurry's son Cecil, and states that the event was caused by grief at the loss of his father. It was not worth Cecil's while to vote for the Irish Income Tax. . . .

19th. A letter from Mrs H—— informs me that Feargus O'Connor is believed to be near death. . . . The physicians apprehend paralysis of the brain, and when that arrives it will be fatal. . . .

21st. Young Gore-Jones arrived. . . . He tells an odd story of a Connaught barrister, named George Browne, who got a fortune of £15,000 with the daughter of his cowherd. The herd could not read, and his master was in the habit of reading the letters for him received from his emigrant brother and relations. The herd's only brother had in early youth enlisted in the army, and had been lost sight of for many years. One day a letter for the herd arrived, to the care of Mr Browne, announcing that the soldier, who had risen to the rank of General, had died intestate in India. His property was about £15,000. To this sum the herd was entitled as next-of-kin. Mr Browne sent for him, and without naming the extent of the windfall, told him that he had got news of an excellent succession. The herd's imagination figured something that would perhaps buy fifty head of cattle. After a little preliminary chaffer, George Browne began to praise the comeliness and rustic graces of one of the herd's daughters, and ended by making an offer of marriage on condition of receiving the General's succession as the girl's fortune. The guardian of Mr Browne's cows was bewildered at the honour of becoming Mr Browne's father-in-law. He readily assented, and his daughter acquiesced with

great satisfaction in the offer to make a lady of her.
Browne took care that the settlements were water-
tight, and the little romance soon ended in his marriage.
' I have dined with them,' said my informant, ' and
Mrs Browne gets on wonderfully well.   She is quiet,
good-natured and hospitable.' . . .

CHAPTER XI

Lord Eldin's Little Jokes—Mr Daunt at Abbotsford—At New-battle—A Romance of Lost Property—He had Scriptural Warrant—A Priest-hunter gives a Site for a Chapel—O'Connell in Dunmanway—Vocative case of 'Cat.'

1854.—*New Year's Day.* Visited the old parish priest of Enniskeane, who mentioned an ignorant lawyer whom the attorneys called Counsellor Necessity, because, like necessity, *he had no law.* This nickname is recorded by Sir Jonah Barrington. . . .

February 21*st.* Left home for Scotland. . . .

22d. Dublin. Richmond Barracks. In the train from Cork was the most outrageous parson I ever encountered, a Reverend Mr H—— of Killarney, a bellowing, bullying, addle-brained bigot. When he had uttered a large amount of anti-Catholic *bêtises,* "Now," said he, "I have been *faithful* to you." . . . Major Scott has two stories of Father Marshall, who is an enormous proselyte from Anglicanism, seeming to measure six feet in circumference. One story is, that Marshall being obstructed on a narrow trottoir by a brace of parsons, whose purpose apparently was to force him off the flags, confronted them steadily, and solemnly made the sign of the cross, which had quite the effect of an exorcism in scaring the parsons out of his way. The other story is, that Marshall, being rudely stared at by one of the Queen's suite at the Dublin Exhibition, good-naturedly said to the starer, "You may pass on, sir ; I am not in the catalogue."

24th. Brought Scott to visit Sir Bernard Burke . . . who goes to London next week, and obligingly takes my novel to try its chances. "Let me caution you," said Sir Bernard, 'not to give an Irish name to your novel, or its English sale will be destroyed. I knew a gentleman who submitted a work on Ireland to the Longmans. They told him it was full of ability and interest, but that one mischievous letter in the title-page would damn it with the English public . . . the letter R. 'If you could make out your book on I*c*eland instead of I*r*eland it might sell here. As it concerns Ireland it will certainly fail.'" A charming neighbour is this to shed our blood for ! . . .

March 3*d.* Edinburgh. A story of the eccentric lawyer, John Clerk, afterwards Lord Eldin. Among his odd whims was the fancy of perpetrating a practical joke of too coarse a nature to be recorded here. Sir James Craig, scandalised at this piece of indecorum, ventured to remonstrate. "Really, Mr Clerk, your friends do not like it, the appearance is so strange. Now, if I were to do such a thing—" "You?" interrupted Clerk, in accents of surpassing scorn ; "if *you* were to do it, forsooth ! And how dare *you*, a d—d, low, pettifogging writer to the signet, compare yoursel' wi' *me*, the head of the Scotch bar?" Another story of the same convivial gentleman. Reeling drunk through the streets, after a jolly debauch, and unable to find his way home, he fell into a gutter, where his hapless plight attracted the notice of a passing Samaritan. The prostrate lawyer was just able to ask the stranger's help. "Can

ye show me the way to Mr Clerk of Eldin's hoose?"
"What for do ye speer the gate to Mr Clerk's hoose?"
returned the other ; "are ye no Mr Clerk yoursel'?"
"Maybe I am," said the inebriate ; "but it's no Mr
Clerk that's wanted the noo, but his hoose." Another
story told by Charles Scott : a raw young lawyer, indignant at a decree of the Court against his client,
jumped up and said, "My lords, I am grieved and surprised at your lordships' decision." The Court instantly
stopped him with a sharp reprimand for his temerity.
John Clerk interposed on his behalf. "My lords, I
beseech you to pardon my young friend's indiscretion,
which is to be imputed to his youth and his total
inexperience of your lordships' Court. Such language,
I admit, is most improper, and on his behalf I crave
leave to apologise ; my lords, if my young freend had
kenned your lordships' Court as lang and weel as I
do he might indeed be grieved, *but he couldna' be sur-
preesed* at ony decision your lordships might make." . . .

April 22d. Went yesterday evening to Galashiels,
and slept at the monastery. At Mass this morning at
Abbotsford ; breakfasted with Mr Hope Scott. Party
at breakfast—Mr and Mrs Hope Scott, Lady Lothian,
Lady Henry Kerr, her son, Mr William Kerr, Father
Cooke and myself. A lively, animated party. Mrs
Hope Scott, grand-daughter of the illustrious novelist,
Sir Walter, is a very captivating woman—young, pretty,
conversible, and with most good-natured manners ; pale,
oval face ; slight, graceful figure. . . . After breakfast
Mr Hope Scott showed me Sir Walter's library and
study. I pleased myself by sitting in the chair of the
mighty minstrel, at the desk whence issued nearly all
the marvellous family of the Waverleys. We spoke of

the strong religious prejudices of Sir Walter, and of the Catholic chapel now existing in the house founded by the author of such books as *The Monastery* and *The Abbot*. " If he had held our faith it would have sanctified his antiquarian tastes, and the world would have been a gainer," I said. " What a pity that he, with his gigantic genius and his love for everything ancient, was not a Catholic." " Why," said Mr Hope Scott, " if he had not been a Protestant, his writings would not at that time have commanded so much attention, or acquired so much popularity. As it was, he had a strong undercurrent of feeling not unfavourable to Catholicity. He painted the Middle Ages with a warm colouring that set many people inquiring into the real character of those ages.' I was much gratified with my visit, and surveyed with great interest the different apartments of that remarkable house, which some French writer calls a romance in stone and mortar. The plantations have been carefully attended to. Close to the house are some deciduous trees of Sir Walter's planting that have already shot up to a very respectable height. . . . The whole coterie were very cordial, and Mr Hope Scott asked me to revisit him in July. . . . In the evening Lady Lothian came to Galashiels to proceed by the railway to Dalkeith. As I was going to Edinburgh, we occupied the interval before the Hawick train came up in walking up and down the platform, conversing *de multis rebus*. . . . In the carriage Lady Lothian was joined by the members of the Kerr family I had met in the morning, with the addition of Lord Henry Kerr, to whom she introduced me. . . .

May 1*st.* Mr —— has recurred to his irreligious doubts. His last speculation is that there is no such place as hell, and no such being as the devil. I told him that gentlemen who contrive to persuade themselves there is no devil, generally contrive to act as though there was no God. Read Kenelm Digby's *Compitum.* . . . In *Compitum* Mr Digby gives an account of the feelings, not the reasonings, which eventuated in his conversion to Catholicity. The narrative is tender and beautiful, and possesses a peculiar interest for me from the local descriptions it contains of scenes in the King's County, which I knew formerly in boyhood. I was then acquainted rather intimately with his relatives, the Stepneys of Durrow. One day old Mrs Smith of Durrow (aunt to the *Waterloo* Marquis of Anglesea) visited my grandmother Wilson with the news ' that Kenelm had become a papist.' This intelligence was not received with the feeling of horror which perhaps was expected by the really excellent old lady by whom it was told. . . .

21st, Sunday. . . . Breakfasted at Newbattle with the Marchioness of Lothian. In addition to the family there were Mrs Hutchinson, Miss Fullarton, and two other ladies. . . . Lord Ralph Kerr brought me to see a gigantic beech, which can scarcely be less than 200 years old. I made the circuit of it, keeping, however, at a couple of feet from the trunk, which the strangely contorted roots prevented my approaching too closely, and it took me thirteen paces to go round it. . . . Lord Ralph and his younger brother, Lord John, are converts to the Church. The former had a dangerous illness, and he told me that his conversion was accelerated by the horror he then felt of dying a Protestant. After breakfast there was High Mass celebrated by Bishop Murdoch of Glasgow. Among the

acolytes were the two young Kerrs and my dear M——,
who came from Galashiels. . . .

June 3d. Story of a Scotch W.S. named Jamieson,
who recovered stolen property in so improbable a
manner that no romancer would venture to put it into
a novel. Jamieson missed his goods, which seem to
have been of a miscellaneous nature, and ran the scent
of the robber to London, where he took up his abode
in a lodging-house, greatly at a loss how to prosecute
his inquiries. On some burnt-out coals in the fire-
grate of his sitting-room were the fragments of a letter.
From habitual curiosity he took them up and put them
together, when lo, there appeared the address of the
very person of whom he was in quest. That gentleman had occupied the identical lodging in which
Jamieson now succeeded him, and from which he had
departed only that very morning. The contents of
the letter were an invoice of the stolen goods, which
had been shipped from Leith to London; and Jamieson
was thus enabled to recover his property, and to pounce
on the rogue at the wharf and consign him to the
custody of the law.

19th. House of Lords. Rolt made an excellent speech
in support of the appeal.[1] . . . Sir R. Bethell said to
me, 'We'll make nothing of it;' but he answered the
respondent's counsel in a speech which was very unlike
the harangue of a pleader who had no faith in the
strength of his cause. His oratorical powers are magnificent. Of his legal skill Mr Hope Scott had said to
me, "Bethell has the talent of a serpent." . . . Lords

[1] Mr Daunt went to London to consult eminent counsel, such
as Sir Richard Bethell (afterwards Lord Westbury), Mr Rolt and
others, on the appeal case brought on in the House of Lords.—ED.

Cranworth and St Leonards comported themselves with judicial gravity. So did not Lord Brougham, who seemed to be in a perpetual fidget, whispering, scribbling, skipping from his seat with fantastic agility, and resuming it after a short excursion through the House, to renew his eccentric movements. . . .

July 7th. Kilcascan. On the 4th I received a letter from Catherine telling me that dear Tom had died on the morning of the 2d. I hastened home, and arrived here yesterday evening. . . . At a little after three the remains were lowered to the grave close beside my mother's tomb. . . .

September 21st. A sad accident befell Dan Conner. Through carelessness in stretching across a ditch against which his gun was resting at full cock, he disturbed the trigger. The gun went off, destroying two fingers of his left hand. . . .

October 10th. Went to Clonakilty fair, but could not find cows to match. . . . Reproved Humphrey Hennessy for the laziness of his son Joe, who did not come to work till nine in the morning. I said, "I will only enter him half-a-day in the work-book." "Then your honour won't follow the gospel," rejoined Humphrey; "for there you may read that the labourer that didn't come till the eleventh hour got the same wages as the man who came at the first." Paddy Donovan, the steward, saw no wit in this perversion of the text, and set to work to confute Humphrey, a superfluous task. When I once taxed Humphrey with having *bit* me in some transaction, he answered with the gravest face possible, "Yerra, who would I bite if it wasn't my own dear masther? Sure, the likes of your honour has always the likes of me about them to be taking bites out of them."

22d, Sunday. Dunmanway. Walked with Father Doheny after Mass. . . . Doheny told me some stories of the past. In the worst days of the penal laws, Dunmanway Catholics had no place of worship nearer than Togher, four miles off. When the penal laws relaxed they ventured to have Mass in a thatched cabin on the roadside at the west end of the long bridge near the town. One day, about 1793, the late Henry Cox was riding to Cork on business. It was Sunday, and as he rode slowly through the congregation, who, too numerous for their diminutive chapel, knelt on the road, he was deeply struck with the spectacle of men, women and children kneeling in the mire under an inclement sky, pelted by the rain that dashed heavily down. "They are my tenants," thought Cox, "and it is a shame that they should be destitute of a decent place of worship." Accordingly, as soon as he returned from Cork he sent for Father Bartholomew Coghlan, the parish priest. Coghlan attended the summons with reluctance, as Cox had acquired some celebrity as a priest-hunter. His astonishment was great when Cox expressed his sympathy with the Catholics of Dunmanway in their want of a proper chapel, and ended with an offer of land whereon to build one, and a subscription of twenty pounds for that purpose. Coghlan could not believe that Cox was in earnest, and bluntly expressed his incredulity. "Well, well," said Cox, laughing, "bring the stamps here, and see if I will not perfect the lease." Cox was as good as his word, and also presented the chapel with a handsome crucifix, which he kept in his own house during the week and sent on Sundays to the priest. . . .

The Great Dan once came with a vast cavalcade

to Dunmanway. Father Doheny, who was on the box seat of O'Connell's carriage, waved his handkerchief to the crowd. "Don't signal them," said O'Connell; "let their cheers be spontaneous." In 1822 there were parts of the south disturbed, but Dunmanway was quiet. The Orangemen were formed into corps, paid by the Government; and as their supposed utility consisted in repressing disturbance, it was their policy to represent the country in as lawless a state as possible. . . . The Government sent down an officer to investigate the facts. Fortunately for the country, the officer was General Sir John Lambert, who was met at the inn by several Tory gentlemen of the neighbourhood. Fathers Doheny and Ryan presented themselves and tendered such evidence as convinced Sir John that the surrounding district was peaceable. . . . I asked Doheny if there was any truth in the story so often told by Feargus O'Connor, that a body of Protestant clergymen having at that period assembled for some public purpose in the Catholic Chapel of Enniskean, Feargus induced them all to pass a resolution affirming the peaceable state of the country, which resolution, much to their surprise and annoyance, he immediately published in the Cork newspapers. This publicity was awkward, for some of their reverences had elsewhere represented the state of the country in a mode quite at variance with the testimony borne by their resolution. Doheny said the story was quite true. . . .

24th. Attended Bandon Quarter Sessions, where I and other proprietors of this parish had engaged an attorney to seek a reduction of the tithe rent charge. . . . We succeeded in effecting a reduction of nearly one-fifth. . . .

26th. This day's paper contains accounts of extended attempts on the part of Conservative tithe payers to reduce the tithe rent charge. Among the appellants are Lord Doneraile, and, comically enough, two parsons, the Reverend Messrs Crofts and Ruddock, who, in their capacity of landlords, have an obvious dislike to be fleeced. . . .

November 1st. Attended Board of Guardians at Dunmanway. It was proposed to strike a penny rate for the relief of the widows and orphans of the soldiers who have fallen in the present war. . . . If Russia be vanquished she will deserve her defeat, for she is on the wrong side in the present quarrel. If England be vanquished she will deserve her overthrow on account, for instance, of her enormous wickedness in inflicting the legislative union upon Ireland, and quartering the Protestant clergy on the pockets of this Catholic nation. So that whether Russia or England get the worst of the *melée*, justice will be done upon somebody.

7th. Miss Macfarlane tells a characteristic story of Archbishop Whately. Provoked at the incompetence of his clergy to solve some theological puzzle, he suddenly exclaimed, " I will wager that none of you can tell me the vocative case of cat." There was a profound silence, broken at last by a timid parson, who ventured to say, " Will your Grace tell us ? " " Puss ! " cried his Grace, abruptly departing from the conference. . . .

CHAPTER XII

Travelling Seventy-Four Years ago—Country Life Seventy
Years since—Woodcocks eating Robins—The Genus
Poet ; Their Habits—A Scripture Reader's Avowal—
A Successful Land Pirate—Dr Watkins's Grave—Bad
to be 'aye Drap-Drappin''—The Duke of York and the
Tailors—A Wide-Awake Lunatic—Evil Results of Play-
ing at Ghosts—A Canny Scot.

1855.—*January* 21*st*. This day thirty-four years Tom
and I, then young boys, arrived here from Tullamore.
The first three days we travelled only sixty miles, and
our sleeping stages were Birr, Nenagh and Limerick.
We left Limerick at 6 a.m. on the fourth day, and
reached Cork in twelve hours, a distance of fifty-seven
Irish miles performed by a heavy stage coach. On the
fifth day we left Cork long before dawn, on the top of
the Bandon coach ; breakfasted in Bandon, and proceeded thence by post-chaise to Kilcascan. . . . There
was plenty of fox-hunting, also shooting and fishing and
many jovial dinner-parties. My father was not at that
time on speaking terms with the parson, with whom he
had a standing quarrel on the subject of tithes. Of
course no priest ever came near us. My father had
three or four capital hunters, and Tom and I made the
most of our time in the way of equestrian exercise.
Days they were of wild frolic, healthy exercise on foot
and horseback, roast beef and gooseberry wine ; cours-

ing, hunting, story-telling with a touch of antiquarian interest excited by the old Castle of Ballinacarriga and its legend ; days when all enjoyments were quickened by the sharp, keen zest of boyhood ; days never to be forgotten.

26th. I gather from the war news in the papers that the alliance between France and England at present resembles the fabled alliance of the giant and the dwarf, in which the dwarf got all the knocks and the giant all the glory. . . . The officials at the head of English military matters seem mentally paralysed. . . . Read Disraeli's *Sybil.* . . . He tells us in this book that infanticide is practised as extensively and legally in England as it is upon the banks of the Ganges. When he says ' legally ' he must mean that the crime is sanctioned by the *lex moris*, for there is of course no statute law in its favour. . . .

February 20th, Shrove Tuesday. . . . Weddings are rather rare this Shrovetide. Story of a couple whose parents were disputing about the chattels ; the lady's fortune consisted partly of furniture and culinary utensils. All had been nearly settled, when her father demurred to the saucepan. " And won't you give me the skillet ? " asked the bridegroom's father. The reply was an emphatic " No ! " " Then d—l a bit of my son she'll get," cried the angry parent, and thereupon the match was broken off. The posts don't arrive, the snow having blocked up the roads. . . .

23d. . . . Here are facts for naturalists ; the crows are eating each other, their ordinary food being snowed up ; this morning Shaneen M'Carthy saw a woodcock with a robin in his bill, the woodcock having taken off the robin's head. . . . *Ups and downs of life.* Some time ago my horse was held in Clonakilty by a smart little barefooted boy, whose appearance induced me to ask his name. He turned out to be the son of a person I had known as a comfortable magistrate, and whose father's hospitality I had partaken. The poor boy was now glad to earn a few pence by holding a horse in the street. . . . Sir R. M——, a baronet of the creation of 1681, passed through this neighbourhood lately, collecting signatures to a memorial to the Queen, praying that Her Majesty might confer on him some lucrative employment, or, failing that, a pension, to enable him to support his dignity as a baronet. A letter from William Gore-Jones, who commands 2000 sailors in the Euxine fleet, confirms all the horrifying accounts of the sufferings endured by the British army at the Crimea. . . .

April 4th. This day's paper announces the elevation of Edmund Roche to the peerage as Baron Fermoy. . . This peerage explains Edmund's vote for the Irish Income Tax; and doubtless the explanation is more satisfactory to his lordship than to the public. . . .

19th. Went to Bandon to vote for somebody and came home without voting for anybody. Nobody to be trusted; nobody worth voting for.

June 5th. Youghal. John Gumbleton and Margaret at dinner. Referring to the days of O'Connell, John said that an enormous multitude had once assembled at his deer park. O'Connell harangued, and Sir Richard Musgrave was chairman. " A few days afterwards a deputation thanked me for having permitted the O'Connellites to meet at my deer park. I replied that if 200,000 ruffians came in force to my hall door with a manifest determination to enter, I would say, ' Welcome,

gentlemen! oblige me by taking seats; I am extremely honoured by your visit, and am most happy to
receive you.'"

8th. Went to the curious old collegiate church. . . .
There is . . . a stately monument erected by that
nefarious land pirate, the first Earl of Cork, to himself.
There are pillars, painted statues, kneeling and recumb-
ent, of himself, his wives and children, and an inscription surrounded by his lordship's pedigree adorned with
a large number of heraldic emblazonments.[1] . . .   To
drive the native Irish out of their possessions and to
seize their estates by the strong hand was the labour
of Lord Cork's whole life from his first arrival in the
kingdom.   He declared with fervent earnestness that
confiscation 'is the work of works.'

12th. Walked in the collegiate churchyard, where the
sexton showed me the grave of a Dr Richard Watkins
who was in the habit of fortifying his assertions with the
phrase, " If I'm not speaking truth, may the grass never
grow on my grave." Now it seems odd enough that not
a blade of grass grows on his grave, although the grass
grows well all round it.   The sexton told me that he had
scuffled the surface of the grave and sown grass seeds on
it, which shot up, but soon withered away.   The doctor
was buried there eight years ago, as a mural tablet informs us. . . .

July 21*st.* Dublin.   Henry Macfarlane, who came
from Huntstown to meet me, tells a story of the Bishop
of Exeter maliciously spoiling a speech of the Bishop of

[1] It is related that a friend once exhorted Lord Cork to be
content with what he had got, and to settle down on one of his
estates, fishing and hunting, as Mr Daunt had done at Tracton.
'Mr Daunt may hunt as *he* likes,' replied Boyle ; 'but I shall hunt
as *I* like.'—ED.

Norwich (Dr Stanley) on the education question, by a bit of clever pantomime. Exeter, who was opposed to Norwich on that question, took his seat quite close to him, and when Norwich rose to speak, kept staring in his face, and assiduously taking notes of his speech as long as he was merely engaged with preliminary matter. But as soon as Norwich began to get into the marrow of his argument, Exeter tore up his notes and flung them contemptuously aside, muttering audibly, "Pshaw! I thought we should have heard something worth replying to!" This disconcerted Norwich so effectually that he hesitated, stopped and sat down.

23*d.* On board the *Elk* steamer off Belfast. Travelled with a Presbyterian clergyman, who told me of a Scotsman's censure of intemperance. "It's a bad thing," said the temperate Scot, "to be aye drap-drappin'. Noo, it's a' vera weel to tak' a wee drap when ye rise in the morning and anither at twal' and anither at four, and anither at bedtime, but I wadna' be aye drap-drappin'; I dinna approve o' it."

August 5th. Walked the other day to Lochrin House with my daughter. One of the nuns, a Miss Leslie, mentioned the death of Lord John Kerr, who officiated last year as acolyte at the opening of Dalkeith Church. His death was rather sudden. He had resolved on becoming a Jesuit, and when he found he was dying, "Oh," cried he, "what will become of my vocation?" This young enthusiast had not, I think, completed his thirteenth year.

22*d.* Went to the printer who is engaged on my reply to the Dunmanway parsons—Collie in S. St David Street—and urged him to expedite the work. "I'll do my best," said he, "but my men are so drunken that there's no depending on them. Of my whole staff there are only two in the printing-room just now." . . .

September 5*th*. Kilcascan. Heard of the death of that unhappy Feargus O'Connor. . . .

15*th*. . . . To-night Dunmanway was illuminated and *feux-de-joie* discharged to celebrate the triumph of the French army at Sebastopol. I believe the British army was fumbling about somewhere in the neighbour-hood. . . .

October 8*th*. Trained from Cork to Bandon in com-pany with Dr Donovan of Skibbereen. He told me that a very poor girl, an inmate of the workhouse, took to Protestantism as a pecuniary speculation. She was duly tutored by her new instructors, and in course of time was confirmed by the Protestant Bishop. On the night of her confirmation she became violently ill, and begged that Dr Donovan might be sent for. He came, and found her spitting blood and in a fever of mental excitement. She was greatly alarmed lest the spitting of blood should kill her, as she said it had killed her mother. She continued to cry out, " I'll die, I'll die in the night. I never was well since that d—l put his hand on me," meaning by that epithet the Protestant Bishop. The doctor bled her and administered cooling medicines, and he told me he was certain that had he not done so the excitement of her mind would speedily have resulted in insanity.

10*th*. Arrived here Colonel Scott and his wife. Gossip on various subjects, military dress and expensive changes in it. Scott said that when the late Duke of York was Commander-in-Chief, and in pecuniary diffi-culties, the military tailors used to bribe His Royal High-ness to order frequent changes in the military costume.

12th. Scott knew a tipsy parson, named Fielding, grandson of the novelist, who, as chaplain to the navy, was required, by an order from the Admiralty, to baptise every Krooman in danger of death. . . . Fielding got fuddled, and read the burial, instead of the baptismal, service over a Krooman, insisting that it was all right. Next day the captain reprimanded the chaplain for disobedience to the orders of the Admiralty. The Krooman died unbaptised, and Fielding was in some danger of losing his commission. . . . Story of a Mr Vandeleur, who wrote an illegible hand, writing to desire his attorney not to visit him. The attorney could not read the letter and came to ask Vandeleur to decipher it. I suppose he charged him 13s. 4d. for the interview. . . . Story of a lunatic sent from Warwickshire to an asylum in London under the charge of a keeper. On the journey the keeper fell asleep. The lunatic saw a paper peeping out of his pocket, abstracted it, and discovered that it was an order consigning him to the asylum, subscribed by certain competent persons in Warwickshire. The keeper did not miss the paper. On reaching the madhouse he introduced himself and his crazy companion to the managing doctor, and stated his business. " We shall of course receive this gentleman," said the doctor, " but it is necessary first to see your credentials." The keeper felt in his pockets, but the paper was gone. The lunatic now stepped forward. " What this person has told you, doctor," said he, " is perfectly true ; only that with the usual cunning of madmen he has reversed our positions. *He* is the lunatic ; I was appointed his keeper on the journey, and here are my credentials, which will show you that I speak the truth." So saying, he handed the paper to the doctor, who was perfectly imposed on by his cool, plausible, business-like manner. The unlucky keeper was accordingly confined in the madhouse, and the lunatic escaped. Many days elapsed before the error could be rectified. We took to telling ghost stories. Story of a haunted house ; a daring visitor insisted on sleeping in the haunted chamber, but publicly declared that he would fire a brace of pistols at any ghost that should appear, by which declaration he thought he secured himself against all attempts to personate an apparition. He accordingly loaded his pistols with ball, and in due time went to bed. A lamp was left burning in the apartment. Twelve o'clock struck ; a hollow, rustling sound was heard. Our hero looked forth from his blankets and beheld a tall, thin, sheeted form issuing from an adjacent closet. Bang ! went one of the pistols. The spectre took the bullet from his mouth and contemptuously flung it back at the adventurous mortal. Bang ! went the second pistol. The spectre, unharmed by the discharge, took the second bullet from his mouth and threw it also at his assailant. The fright produced instant insanity, from which the rash adventurer never recovered. It need scarcely be told that the bullets had been drawn by the confederates of the fellow who performed the ghost.

16th. Drove among the rocks and hills to the north of Dunmanway to see Togher Castle, an interesting old tower-house or fortalice built by the MacCarthys in, I suppose, the sixteenth century. . . . After spending the day in the successful pursuit of the picturesque, my friends were regaled by Father Doheny with a 'champagne' dinner. Scott mentioned an incident that occurred at Parton during the year that the Scotch Court of Session authorised his aunt, Lady Gordon of

Letterfourie, to occupy the place. There was an Irishman named Terry Connolly, who had straggled over to Scotland when young. Old Scott took Terry into his service when at Parton, and found him tolerably faithful. When the Scotts were obliged to quit Parton, many of their followers still remained there, among others, Terry Connolly. Walking one day along the avenue, Terry saw Lady Gordon advancing in an opposite direction, in deep consultation with her agent. Knowing that he was disliked by her ladyship, Terry did not wait to confront her. Neither she nor the agent had observed him, and, as the readiest way of escaping their notice, he climbed up a neighbouring tree. They continued slowly to advance, until they reached the tree, when they sat down on a bench beneath it, still conversing. " I hate to have Scott for a foe," said her ladyship ; " he is so clever, and has such ways of acquiring information. The things I do—nay, the very words I speak—he contrives to learn. He has his spies everywhere—" Here she chanced to look up. " I vow there's one of them posted in the branches over our heads ! " . . .

December 31*st.* Letter from a friend describing the last moments of poor Feargus O'Connor and his funeral. His bodily sufferings were apparently excruciating when life was departing, but the poor imbecile was unconscious of any mental pain. The attendants left the room, unable to bear the sight of his torments or to listen to his agonising groans. The Chartists subscribed for a magnificent funeral. . . .

CHAPTER XIII

General Dundas and Roger O'Connor—How to dispose of
Old Judges—Pious Brigands—Mr Daunt gets up the First
Disendowment Meeting — Deputation from Liberation
Society to Mr Daunt—Death of Father Mathew—Character of Father Mathew.

1856. . . . *January 26th.* Dined with Mrs Smithwick.
Characteristic story of her father, the 'great' Roger
O'Connor. Roger hired a house at Southgate in England from General Dundas. The house was popularly
said to be haunted, and had for some time been untenanted. At the end of six months Roger sold off by
auction all Dundas's furniture and ornamental china,
and went to reside somewhere else. Dundas, having
heard of the sale of his property, wrote to Roger for the
half-year's rent of the house, and also for the money
realised by the sale of furniture and china. Roger replied that he owed Dundas nothing, but that, on the
contrary, Dundas was largely in *his* debt, inasmuch as
his six months' occupation of Southgate had disenchanted the house of its spectral reputation, and rendered
it easy to get a tenant for it, which, for years, Dundas
had found impossible. Whether the General admitted
the force of the plea, or, what is more likely, was tickled
with its comical impudence, he let the matter rest, and
Roger pocketed the rent and proceeds without further
molestation.

February 26th. Dan Conner came here and told me a *mot* of his uncle, Commissioner Longfield. Talking of the recent attempts to force Baron Pennefeather off the Bench, Archbishop Whately said to Longfield, " What would you do with old judges when they are past their labour ? " " I would make them bishops, my lord," answered Longfield.

27th. Finished reading Aitkin's *James the First.* O'Connell used to tell a story of Charles James Fox saying to George the Fourth, *apropos* of his relations with Mrs Fitzherbert, " I always thought that your father was the greatest liar in England ; but now I see that *you* are ! " It may well perplex the historian to decide whether James the First or his son Charles held truth in the greater disregard. . . .

May 26th. Talking over the tithe question, Dan Conner said, " I used to think you and Tom quite wrong in your hostility to the Church Establishment, but I have now become convinced that it is an evil of the first magnitude." I asked him whence his change had arisen. He said that, during the famine years, the Protestant clergy had not relaxed a farthing of their monstrous demands, and in every appeal at Quarter Sessions, to bring them down to the existing average, they had resisted the appellants. . . .

July 12th. Youghal. Left home this morning for change, having lately been ill. Lord Fermoy accosted me in Cork. I forgot his appearance, or, rather, it had been altered by the growth of a great beard, so he had to announce himself. I asked his aid for our anti-tithe movement, which he, in a sort of dubious way, seemed to promise or half promise. . . . Lord F.'s political opinions are just what they always were ; but I could not get an engagement from him to attend our meeting. . . .

14th. Charles Walsh of Mogeely visited my stepmother. He gave me the following sketch of a Protestant interview between pastor and penitent. Mr Walsh had been ill for five or six weeks, when the Reverend Pierce Drew, the rector of Youghal, visited him. " I think," said Mr Walsh, " you might have come to see me before." " This is a visit of duty, not of compliment," returned the rector. " In short, Charlie, I have come to tell you that you have been a bad boy." " If that is all you have to say," retorted the penitent, " the sooner you cut short your visit the better." " It is my duty as a clergyman," persisted the rector, " to remonstrate with you concerning your past life—" " Anne, show that gentleman down stairs," said the penitent to his servant, whom he summoned by ringing the bell. . . . I am told that the narrator is inventive. He may have meant his tale to illustrate a remark he made to me, " We Protestants do not deem the attendance of a clergyman on the sick by any means necessary." . . .

18th. Scott writes to me that the brigands in Greece, being seized with a fit of piety, have sent to offer the Archbishop of Thebes his choice of three alternatives— to send them a chaplain, to ordain one of themselves, or —to be assassinated ! . . .

Kilcascan. August 15th. A capital anti-State Church meeting at Clonakilty ; thousands present. I may congratulate myself on the result, so far, at least, as this coup d'essai is concerned. And even if no greater consequences follow, it is, at anyrate, something to utter our public protest now and then against the nefarious tithe system. . . .

September 4th. The London *Nonconformist* and *Liberator* have blown our Clonakilty speeches far and wide. I have written . . . to arouse Mullingar, Kilkenny, Tuam and Tullamore.[1] . . .

6th. Arrived here, C. J. Foster, L.S.D., from London, deputed by the Liberation Society to confer with me respecting the best mode of making an effective and combined battle against the anti-Irish State Church. Mr Miall, the member for Rochdale, desires me to consider Dr Foster as his *alter ego.* I find that our Clonakilty meeting has excited an interest in England that I had not dared to hope for. . . . They expect 200 votes in support of Mr Miall's next motion in the House of Commons. . . .

15th. Letter from my dear old friend, the Bishop of Meath, promising the co-operation of his diocese in the anti-State-Church agitation.

17th. Letter from the Archbishop of Tuam ; friendly to the movement, but disposed to combine it with the tenant-right question. Wrote to Lord Fermoy (who tells me that his spirit is with us) to beg that he would give us his body also. . . .

December 8th. The papers announce the death of my dear old friend, Father Mathew. He was the first confessor I ever had, and a most excellent one.

---

[1] To Mr Daunt belongs the distinction of having, in the anti-State Church meeting of the 15th of August, inaugurated the movement which, under his fostering care, culminated in the Disestablishment Act, nine years later. He spared no exertion of brain and pen to further this cause, in which he enlisted the Irish hierarchy, and brought them *en rapport* with the English Voluntaries. The actual measure fell far short of satisfying him, and, when all was done, others received the praise and thanks which properly belonged to him, as the originator of the movement in Ireland.—ED.

Twenty-eight or thirty years ago, his little friary chapel near Sullivan's Quay was one of my favourite haunts. . . . He told me a rather strange circumstance. In the lanes that formerly occupied the ground where Great George Street now stands, there resided a knot of bigoted Protestant freemen of Cork. When the wide street commissioners dispersed these people by forming the new street, numbers of them joined the Catholic Church . . . On Easter Sunday 1842, Father Mathew invested me with the temperance medal which he hung round my neck, and which I shall always treasure as a memorial of my revered and kind old friend. . . . Mathew was popular and influential in Cork before the commencement of his temperance campaign, simply by the force of his beautiful piety and holiness. . . .

CHAPTER XIV

Philosopher Thompson—Sound in the Faith ; Slippery in
Horseflesh—Historical Viceroys—England in India—A
Colonel of Lancers on English Missionaries—Irish Mas-
sacre of 1641 a Myth—How the Marriage Fees were paid
—Sharp Practice.

1857.—*February 14th.* Letter from Leslie, who writes
from Hassop Hall and enumerates, among the historical
relics contained in his stepmother's family, the red cloth
that received the head of James Radcliffe, Earl of Der-
wentwater, executed for his share in the civil war of 1715.
He also sent me an impression of the Earl's seal. . . .

April 17th. Rode yesterday to Skibbereen to consult Dr Donovan about my infirm health. . . . Discussing the best road to take home, he mentioned the
little turret for some years a noted landmark near the
base of Carrigfodha. . . . The mention of the turret
introduced the mention of its founder, an eccentric
man named William Thompson, usually called by his
acquaintance ' Philosopher Thompson.' I remember
hearing him spoken of by my father when I was a boy.
The philosopher was an infidel. " He bequeathed his
body to me," said Dr Donovan, " and with it his library,
on condition of my stringing up his bones together
secundum artem, and sending the skeleton as a memento
of love to a Socialist lady in England, a Mrs Wheeler,

to whom he had been attached. He was uncle to one of
the Whites of Bantry, who expected to be his heir, and
who insisted on having the body interred and the Anglican burial service performed over it before the will was
opened. The officiating parson was Jones of Drumbeg.
A poor woman became clamorous at the graveyard, insisting that no infidel should be interred among the graves
of her deceased kindred. White silenced her scruples
with a sovereign, and she had not gone three fields
away, when in crossing a ditch she sprained her wrist,
which accident she ascribed to a Divine judgment. . . .
After the funeral the will was read. The deceased had
enjoined in it that no priest, whether Christian, Mahommedan or Hindoo should meddle with his obsequies.
When parson Jones heard this, he became enraged at
having read prayers over such a reprobate. I was
anxious to obtain the library," continued the doctor,
" and to entitle myself to it under the terms of the will,
I exhumed the body and prepared the skeleton for Mrs
Wheeler, who sent to Ireland for it. The philosopher
had bequeathed his whole estate to found a Socialist
community at Cononagh, near Skibbereen, according to
certain rules laid down in a book he had published.
But the rules were so detestably immoral that no court
of law could sanction them. The will therefore was
pronounced to be void, and the testator's sister came
into possession of the estate as next-of-kin. I never
got the library, though I had earned it. . . . The philosopher had picked out a dozen or so of the most irreligious rascals he could find to act as his executors." . . .
The skeleton was an affecting *souvenir d'amour.* I remember reading of a Frenchman, who directed in his
will that his remains should be burned and a ring made

of the vitrified ashes, to be worn on the finger of a lady
to whom he was attached. . . .   Dr Donovan mentioned
having known more than twenty cases of death caused
by drunkenness, near Skibbereen.   One was the drunken
heir of a drunken father, who having early succeeded to
the inheritance, drank himself first mad, and then dead
at the age of twenty-two.   "Another case," said he, "is
old William Morris.   Morris lived so long and drank so
hard that tipplers used to point to him as a proof that
excess did not abridge life.   He inherited an estate of
about £2000 a year, and drank out the larger portion
of it. . . .   About three weeks ago he was found dead in
a ditch, having evidently been overtaken there by intoxi-
cation.   He was seventy-four." . . .

May 28th. Dan Conner came here and asked me to
write a public letter exposing the mode in which parson
G——of D—— tried to trick his parishioners about the
septennial valuation of the tithes.   Dan told me all the
particulars, a comical sample of the sharpest of sharp
practice; but I was not in a humour to write the letter.
Lately Dan censured G——'s manœuvres in the hearing
of one of the reverend gentleman's friends, who said,
"G—— however is a very good clergyman."   "Maybe
so," returned Dan, "but that reminds me of the story of
a man who had given a large sum for a foundered horse,
and was asked where he got that good-for-nothing brute.
'I bought him from our parson,' he answered, 'who
figged him up for sale.'   'That was a very unclerical
act,' observed his friend.   'Ay,' rejoined the victim;
'our parson is sound in the faith, but slippery in horseflesh. . . .'"   Some years ago a priest near this displayed
a very grasping disposition.   The parishioners nailed
up the doors of his church, and went to Mass in the

adjoining parishes. The Bishop took the hint and transferred the unpopular gentleman to a distant part of the diocese. . . .

June 12*th.* Panic at the comet which is to destroy the world to-morrow. . . .

14*th.* The world has not yet ended, notwithstanding the arrival of the comet yesterday. . . .

27*th.* Hurrah! the Cork and Bandon Company are beaten. They broke down under the weight of their own falsehoods. They took to stating what the House of Commons knew to be false, and thereby overshot the mark and got their bill thrown out.[1]

July 9*th.* Roebuck's motion for the abolition of the Irish Viceroyalty has been defeated by a good majority. There are few public questions on which more nonsense has been talked than this. . . . We are told that the Viceroy injures Dublin by leading to competition in display and expense. The same may be said of every rich and hospitable nobleman all over the world. Again, it is said that the Viceroyalty generates a servile disposition among the lieges ; but in Scotland, where there is no Viceroy, the spirit of place-hunting is as prevalent as it is here . . . it is not easy to see how the substitution of some other executive system for the Viceroyalty would diminish the number of place-hunters, or inspire them with sentiments of manly independence. . . . *Apropos* of the Viceroyalty, is it not an odd omission that no Irish *literateur* has written memoirs of the Viceroys of Ireland. There are probably abundant materials for such a work in the archives of Dublin Castle and the

---

[1] Mr Daunt was at this time engaged in a conflict with the Cork and Bandon Railway Company, resisting the guarantee which they sought to impose.—ED.

family residences of the several Viceroys. To go no further back, what a narrative of stirring and romantic interest might be written of the viceregal reigns of the bold Kildare; the chivalrous Essex; the adroit, unprincipled and daring Strafford; the crafty, double-dealing Ormonde; the proud and impetuous Tyrconnel; the fastidious Duke of Shrewsbury, who complained of being incommoded by the crowded congregation of the castle chapel; Swift's friend Carteret; the courtly and conciliating Chesterfield; the jovial and facetious Townshend, who loved to be surrounded by jesters and mimics; the treacherous Portland; the hard-drinking, dissipated Rutland, whose court was not exceedingly unlike the Court of Comus, and the memory of whose beautiful duchess is still fresh in Dublin. . . .

14*th.* Youghal. . . . The *Times*, in an article on the late trial of Madeleine Smith at Edinburgh for the alleged murder of her French admirer, gives the following account of the state of domestic morality in Great Britain :—'We are shocked with the continual recurrence of attempts by women against the lives of husbands, paramours and children. Poisoning especially has become almost a domestic institution.' . . . The *Times* curiously enough prefaces the above statement by saying that it is admitted on all sides that never at any former period were domestic manners so unexceptionable. Truly, if these be unexceptionable manners, it may well be asked to what degree of iniquity exception should be taken ? . . . When the potboy, Edward Oxford, was imprisoned for firing at the Queen, there were numerous applicants for his autograph. He was visited by some ladies of condition, who felt so much interest in the would-be regicide, that they complied with his request to patronise his mother, and money was subscribed to set her up in a tobacconist's shop. One old gentleman became so enthusiastic that he actually proposed marriage to her, attracted by the prestige attaching to her as the mother of a man who had tried to shoot Her Majesty.

August 7th. Dan Conner came, and also Mr J. O'K——, fresh from Maynooth. . . . Gossip on India. . . . England must present a curious appearance to Indian apprehension. She is, according to her Scotch parasite, Dr Cumming . . . a colossal propagandist of pure evangelical Christianity.[1] . . . Along with this, England, the evangelical propagandist, has tried to conciliate the prejudices of Indian idolators and Indian Mahommedans by subsidising an idolatrous college at Benares ; contributing £7000 a year to the support of Juggernaut. . . . Lord Auckland takes off his shoes, according to the fashion of the Indian worshippers of the idol at Benares, and lays an offering at the idol's shrine. . . . My cousin, Captain (now Colonel) Macfarlane, spent three years in India with his regiment, the 9th Lancers, and so far as his experience reached . . . he describes the English missionaries in general as lazy and profligate men, who wallow in luxury and often in vice on the funds they extort from well - meaning persons in England. . . . Macfarlane told me he had so often detected falsehoods in the statements sent home by the missionaries, that he never would again believe a missionary report from India. A few nights ago Lord Ellenborough said, in the House of Lords, that if the

[1] Mr Daunt then goes into details of tyranny and personal barbarities inflicted on the Indian population by representatives of British power.—ED.

English were now to evacuate India, they would not leave a dozen sincere converts behind them. . . .

17th. Read Lord Brougham's *Statesmen.* . . . He approvingly quotes Hume to the effect that there are three descriptions of persons who must be considered beyond the reach of argument . . . an English Whig who asserts the reality of the 'Popish Plot'; an Irish Catholic who denies the massacre in 1641 ; and a Scotch Jacobite who maintains the innocence of Mary Queen of Scots. . . . As to the alleged Irish massacre in 1641, we may fairly deny it on the ground of insufficient proof. The total silence regarding it of contemporaneous documents, in which it must have infallibly been mentioned if it really had happened, seems decisive against the Protestant accounts of it. . . . The assertors of the massacre all say that it occurred on the 23d of October 1641. Lingard points out that no mention of a massacre is made in the proclamations and despatches of the Lords Justices at Dublin Castle, dated respectively 25th October, 25th November, 27th November and 23d December in the same year. The despatches bearing these four dates accuse the Irish of various acts of turbulence and plunder ; they specify the murder of *ten* of the garrison of Lord Moore's house at Mellifont by the rebels ; but they do not contain the slightest hint of any general massacre of the Protestants by the Catholics. . . . Had a massacre really occurred, it is incredible that the men by whom at that very time the despatches were written—men who were the bitter enemies of the Irish people — should have omitted all notice of it, especially when they took pains to chronicle such minor offences as the ten homicides at Mellifont. . . .

September 10*th*. The *Times* has an article on the Mormon abomination, in which it is stated that nine-tenths of the Mormon ranks are recruited from the votaries of English Protestantism. . . . Not one convert have the Mormons gained from Irish Catholicity. . . .

October 18*th*, . . . *Sunday*. To-day we had a bit of stringent discipline. Father Bohane announced after Mass that if a certain person who has been too attentive to the wife of a man, now absent in America, did not, on or before next Sunday, cut the connection, and make a solemn promise to live morally henceforth, he and his frail friend should be publicly excommunicated. . . . The voluntary system. Story of a girl who, with her sweetheart, applied to their parish priest to marry them. The priest demanded a sum which the girl deemed excessive. The priest said he could not abate a farthing of his demand. " Well," said she, " I'll see what I can do to make it up." So saying, she walked out, took the priest's cloak from a peg on which it hung in the hall, pawned it for a sum that made up the deficiency, and returned with the full amount required by his reverence, who then married the couple. When he missed his cloak he was told he could redeem it from the pawn-office himself, for which purpose the pawn-ticket was sent to him. . . .

December 2*d*. . . . Received a letter from J. B. Gumbleton about the effigy of a knightly ancestor copied by a London artist from a brass monument in Canterbury Cathedral. The artist charged ten guineas for his alleged copy, which was purchased at that price by J. B. Gumbleton. The latter then wrote to the Dean of Canterbury to inquire respecting the brazen original.   The dean replied that there was no such monument in his Cathedral.   It looks as if the artist had hit off a clever device to obtain a purchaser for an ancestral 'relic,' which he had found unsaleable in London.

29th. Walked to the old castle of Ballyward. . . . The roads in the parish of Kilmeen were principally made by a very active parson, the Reverend Edward H. Kenny, who was rector for many years.   A story is told of one of his road contractors, who, in order to get the amount of his contract at the Cork Assizes, was obliged to swear that a certain sum had been expended on the road within a particular period.   This had not been done, and Kenny, to enable the deponent to make the required declaration, spread the money upon the macadamised surface of the unfinished highway, so that the contractor could swear that the requisite sum ' *had been laid out upon the road.*'   This story, if true, is a queer specimen of somebody's tortuous ingenuity. . . .

CHAPTER XV

1858. — *January* 12*th*. Accompanied my sisters to
Kinneigh. . . . This is the parish whose spiritualities
some time ago enlisted the pious indignation of Feargus
O'Connor, who told his English admirers that, when
attacked in the Kinneigh pulpit by the Reverend Mr
Hall, he clapped his hat on his head and walked out
of the church, followed by the whole congregation!
Feargus's charges were, firstly, the perpetual absenteeism
of the rector, who for thirty-five years had not favoured
the parish with a visit; secondly, that the clerk's salary
was raised *because* he went to reside out of the parish;
and thirdly, that the sexton kept a house of ill fame at
the churchyard gates. *Ou a changé tout cela.* . . . When
Feargus O'Connor and Garrett Standish Barry were
colleagues in the representation of the County Cork, a
large number of turkeys were stolen from Barry.
Feargus was employed for the defence, and procured

the acquittal of the accused person at the Cork
Assizes. Just then fifty-seven turkeys appeared brows-
ing at Fortrobert. The coincidence was amusing, and
'calculated to excite remark.'

February 2d. Bought a horse . . . from Curly
Crowley for £18. He told me he could have got £2
more from a sporting gentleman in our neighbourhood.
"You would have got his promise," said I, "but you
know he is not the best pay." "Och, I wouldn't care
for that," returned Crowley, "for he couldn't keep me
out of the money beyond the next quarter sessions,
and the cost of the process would be only five shillings."
There was something very 'Irish' in this notion of
selling a horse on the security of a lawsuit with the
purchaser. . . .

17th. Visit from C——, who seems to have found the
fairy cap. Recently a hamper of wine was sent to him
by an anonymous donor, and a friend, who is not a
relation, has written to offer him the gift of a large sum
of money. . . . He tells me that when his brother was
appointed rector of D——, Father Creedon, whom the
previous rector had tormented with souperism, asked
him to abstain from interference with the Catholics.
His reverence answered, "I'll get every man of them to
come to my church if I can ; but I won't give them so
much as a potato for coming." Creedon was quite
satisfied with this, well knowing that, bribery apart,
there would be no conversions.

March 2d. Spent the evening with my sister C——.
. . . Talked over old stories. Among the rest she
mentioned an attempt at abducting an heiress, a Miss
Vaughan, that occurred in Tullamore when my grandmother Wilson was a little girl, probably in or about

1760. At a late hour one dark winter evening the lover knocked at Miss Vaughan's door. On the door being opened, Miss Vaughan inadvertently walked from the parlour into the hall, and was instantly seized by her admirer. A struggle ensued, during which somebody extinguished the lights, and an elderly housemaid contrived, in the darkness, to substitute herself for her young mistress. Fully convinced that he had secured his prize, the lover placed his fair burden on the crupper of a horse he had provided, and, springing into the saddle, galloped off. . . . When about a mile out of town the housemaid said, "Musha, where does your honour want to take me?" "Oh, confound you!" cried the disappointed lover, "I thought it was Miss Vaughan I had got." He allowed the housemaid to escape unscathed.

3d. . . . Left Enniskean this morning in the early car (for Youghal). . . . Left Cork at 4 P.M. in the Youghal coach, in which I met a Cork merchant named O'Brien, who deals extensively with English houses. We spoke of Morrison of London, the millionaire, who died lately worth £4,000,000 sterling. "I know his history from a person concerned in his establishment," said O'Brien. "He began life as a street porter. Passing the shop of one Todd, a very wealthy Scotch mercer near St Paul's, some frolicsome comrades thrust him through a large pane of glass into the shop, where Todd instantly collared him, and called him a ruffian. "I'm no ruffian," said Morrison; "I did not break your window intentionally. My companions thrust me in for a lark and made off. Here's six shillings, it's all I have, to pay the damage." "Six shillings won't do," replied Todd; "the glass cost sixteen." "Well, I'm a poor man," said Morrison, "and have not the money; but if you hire me as a porter, I'll pay you the balance out of my earnings." Todd agreed; hired him for two weeks at ten shillings a week; Morrison lived on five, and handed Todd the remaining five each Saturday night. Todd, by this time, came to like him so well that he engaged him permanently as a porter. By-and-by he placed him behind the counter, where he gradually acquired more and more of his master's regard, and also that of his master's only daughter. Todd was then worth about £150,000. Morrison become his son-in-law and partner, and finally succeeded to his wealth, which he largely increased. Thus his wonderful prosperity may be said to have originated in his being shot through a window like a brickbat by a knot of frolicsome blackguards." . . .

6th. Read Macaulay's Essays on *Hallam's History.* . . . Macaulay has performed a marvellous literary feat; he has made history as amusing as a Waverley novel. . . . Speaking of the period when Johnson's literary career commenced, he says in his review of Croker's *Boswell,* "All that is squalid and miserable might now be summed up in the word 'Poet.' The word denoted a creature dressed like a scarecrow, familiar with compters and sponging-houses." Such was also the conventional meaning of the word in quarters far removed from London. O'Connell used to tell that, at a meeting of some Kerry club which was more numerous than select, a member proposed the admission of a literary friend, urging, as a recommendation, that the postulant was a poet. "A poet! then we'll blackball him," cried an old member; "there are too many poets among us already;" meaning that the club contained too many disreputable paupers, the only synonym he knew for poets. . . .

Maurice of Desmond, a Norman-Irish chief, went to war with De la Poer for calling him a poet. . . .

8*th*. The papers have an extract from Sir Archibald Alison's *History*, asserting that Father Mathew's temperance movement was an engine for the collection of the Repeal rent. ' *Voilà justement comme on écrit l'histoire !* ' This is, however, a less outrageous assertion than the accusation discharged at Father Mathew's movement by the Orange party at its outset—that it was designed to promote idolatry and murder. . . .

April 2d. Dan Conner. . . . told me two ancedotes. Mr Herbert O'D——, an attorney of no particular religion, though, if it be anything, Dan rather thinks he is a Protestant, resided with his Catholic wife in the adjacent parish of D——.   A huge Newfoundland dog of O'D——'s used to follow Mrs O'D—— to Mass, and as the Catholics were scandalised at the intrusion, they tied a kettle to the dog's tail and hunted him out of the churchyard.   O'D——, furious at this indignity, rushed off to M—— C——, the rector, complained of the affront that had been offered to his dog, and protested that he would thenceforth attend the Protestant service.   " That is as you please," said the rector ; " but if you do you must not bring the dog."   This reception cooled down O'D——'s Protestant zeal, and he looked on C—— with no friendly eye. . . .   Just then an illegitimate child, the offspring of an officer and his lady relative, emerged upon the parish, and O'D—— revenged himself for his fancied wrongs by ascribing the paternity to the rector. The latter sought redress by an action for libel, and recovered £50 damages. . . .

18*th*. Cork.   Visited the schools of the Christian Brothers.   In the cemetery are the remains of Gerald

Griffin. His pure and pious spirit found a congenial home among the Christian Brothers, in whose works of love and charity he shared for some time before his death, at the early age of thirty-six. He died in 1840. . . .

May 27th. I was grieved to hear to-day of the sudden death of my dear old friend and fellow-labourer, John O'Connell. . . . He had the very rare quality of faithful friendship. *R.I.P.* . . .

June 7th. Received a mad letter from Quebec, postage 6d. I was going to return it unopened, but ——, impelled by curiosity, broke the seal, and lo! an epistle from a lunatic, subscribing himself Lord Vincent O'Neill Daunt, informing me that he is my long-lost son, who, after spending many years in pursuit of a papa, had at length discovered that I was the parent of whom he was in search, and that he thus responded to an advertisement offering a reward of £2000 for the recovery of my missing progeny. Lord Vincent . . . claims a title and estate through me, and threatens that if his claim be resisted he will defend it in the House of Lords! . . .

July 10th. Sailed from Youghal to Camphire in a market boat. Passed Ballinatray, a noble place which has recently lost its owner, whose death is said to have been hastened by the deleterious effects of hair-dye. . . . Bessie Colthurst has a queer bit of gossip about the defunct making love to a millionaire widow who was accused of having poisoned her first husband, and tenderly insinuating a wish to hear the truth of the matter from her own fair lips. The widow fainted, at least so the story goes. . . . At Strancally I saw a small boat sculled across the river with a shovel by a little girl, the solitary occupant. The scenery is exquisitely lovely, especially passing Dromana, where the wooded heights on both sides of the broad stream rise almost from the water's edge, barely leaving room on the left bank for the road. The rich perspective is closed by the blue mountains of Clogheen. . . .

15*th*. Mrs Daunt spoke of a gentleman, in former times the occupant of Brook Park, near Dunmanway. He had been a parson, and was unfrocked ; he had been a captain, and was cashiered ; he had been a magistrate, and was dismissed from the; Bench. He then sought consolation in matrimony, and made love to a Miss ——, in whose £4000 he hoped to find balm for his misfortunes. " During the courtship," said Mrs Daunt, " he used to come to dinner with a brace of pistols in his pockets." " For what ? " asked an auditor. "To shoot the bailiffs—he was always afraid of an arrest." Speaking of Colonel Bushe she said, " They tell him he is married, and he admits it—sir, he would admit anything ! "

August 5*th*. Ballabuy Fair. The madman who wrote to me from Quebec, claiming to be my son, arrived here this morning to prefer his claim in person. I turned him out of the house, but he refused to quit the place unless compelled by the police. . . .

6*th*. He spent the night *al fresco* on the grass. Dan Conner and the police came here this morning. I swore informations before Dan. The noble lord (he claims a peerage through me) was trundled off to Dunmanway bridewell.

9*th*. I attended the sessions to-day at Dunmanway. . . . The law only imprisons for a week in a case of trespass without violence ; but as I assured the peer-expectant that he should enjoy the hospitality of Bridewell as often as he visited me, I may hope to

hear no more of him. . . . D. Conner made a pretty
fair pun. There were music books on the magistrates'
desk. "Are these the studies of the bench?" said I.
"Rather of the *bar*," returned Dan.

30*th*. More about this mysterious nobleman. To-
day I got a letter signed John Baynton, M.D., dated
from Frankfort-on-the-Maine. Dr B. says that having
seen a report of his lordship's case in *Galignani*, he is
thereby induced to acquaint me that, when in Canada in
1833, he became aware of a child, supposed to have been
abstracted from parents of condition in Ireland, and
placed in charge of a French-Canadian. . . . The absurdity is quite delicious, and recalls the scene in
Molière's comedy, in which M. de Pourçeaugnac on arriving in Paris from Limoges, is surrounded by a crowd
of young gamins who have been trained by Sbrigani to
salute the poor Limousin with cries of "Papa! Papa!"

September 3d. Colonel Scott arrived last night. He
tells two anecdotes of Catholicity at Falkirk. A Presbyterian couple lately brought a child to Father
Macdonald to be christened, alleging that the ministers
did not believe the baptismal rite to be essential, and,
at anyrate, administered it in so slovenly a way that
it could scarcely be supposed to be validly performed.
Father M. consented to baptise the child, stipulating
that the parents should hereafter allow him to study
the Catholic religion, and to embrace it, should his
studies convince him of its truth. The parents gave
this promise. The other incident is this: An old
woman who had been born and baptised in the
Catholic Church, but who had in early childhood fallen
among proselytisers, and during her long life remained
apparently a Protestant, felt, in a dangerous illness,

impelled to seek the ministry of a priest. On her
deathbed she mentioned her desire to her husband, an
Irish Orangeman, who said he would consent if his
wife could find a messenger, fully believing that she
could not find one. It chanced that a young man,
a Presbyterian, had entered the cottage to light his
pipe, and hearing the old woman's request, he offered
to be her messenger. . . . "Mind," he added, turning
to the husband, "you gave consent if your wife could
find a messenger. I see, by the way you are glowering
at me, you would rather I let the job alone. But I
ken you Irish Orangemen weel, and there isna a worse
lot on earth. If ye meddle with me, ony o' ye, I sha'n't
avoid ye; but whoever attacks me will run the risk o'
a sound threshing." The spirited envoy proceeded to
Father Macdonald, whom he summoned to the dying
woman, and who was extremely surprised that a long
life wholly spent among Protestants and out of the reach
of all Catholic influence, should terminate thus.

4*th*. Scott and I went to look at Dunmanway
Manor House. . . . Returning home at night, we be-
guiled the way with talk *de multis*. Story of the Scotch
judge, Lord Robertson, big and corpulent, who entered
a mail coach in which three big Presbyterian parsons
left scant room for his burly lordship. How to get rid
of them, and so have the coach to himself, was a question that did not long puzzle his inventive brain. "I am
happy," said he, looking around with a bland smile, "to
find three brethren of my cloth here; and I trust they
are all of the same persuasion as myself." "What may
that be?" asked a minister. "I am a Roman Catholic
priest," returned Lord Robertson, "and I trust that I address brothers in the same holy faith." "We are ministers

of the Kirk of Scotland," said a parson. "More's the pity that I should be jammed up with three infernal heretics," exclaimed his lordship, with a look of horror; "fellows who deceive their unfortunate congregations with false doctrines, and are steering right for everlasting damnation." The ministers attempted a defence, but Lord Robertson, whose long forensic practice had improved to the utmost his natural powers of vituperative eloquence, waxed so violent in his abuse that the poor ministers were fain to get outside. His lordship had then room to stretch his legs on the opposite seat. . . . Another time the same sportive judge, having, as I suppose, some spite against a parish minister, pretended to a party of fellow-travellers that he (Lord R.) was the minister in question. "There's my manse near the road, and I'll be happy to give ye all your dinner." The travellers gladly accepted the invitation, and the poor parson was besieged by a hungry troop, while the frolicsome judge kept out of the way, enjoying, with the zest of a monkey, the confusion he had caused. . . . We talked of Spanish and Portuguese morality. I said, "Father Macdonald, who spent several years at Valladolid, told me that an illegitimate birth that happened while he was there was mentioned with surprise, which seemed to him to infer the rarity of such an occurrence in that place." "With regard to female morality," said Scott, "I think the Portuguese stand higher than the Scotch. In Spain and Portugal they cannot at all realise the idea of a man claiming money damages, as the English do, in compensation for the seduction of their wives. The offence is, in those countries, deemed so deadly that blood alone can atone for it. . . . At the table of a Portuguese restaurant I heard Sir John D——

boast that he had obtained £700 damages from a person who had seduced Lady D——. He added, " If I had got as much from every *ami* of her ladyship, I should have been one of the richest men in England." A Portuguese officer said, " I cannot understand this at all. Here is a deep and deadly wound inflicted on your honour, and yet you can compound for a sum in gold, and think yourself well paid for the ignominy. In Portugal we would have the villain's life." Sir John replied, " I would rather have £700 of gold in my purse than one ounce of lead in my body." Talking of the religious feelings of the peasantry, Scott said, " An English priest in Portugal told me he was once highly edified by a conversation he overheard among a party of poor muleteers who were at supper in an apartment under his bedroom. Their whole talk was about the mode in which they heard Mass. None of them could read. One said, 'During Mass I recite my rosary.' Another said, ' During Mass I recite Paternosters in honour of the Five Wounds of Our Saviour,' and this last seemed to be the general practice of the humble party. The whole conversation was religious. . . Yet these men belonged to the most humble class in Portugal. One great fault in your national character," said Scott, "seems to be sycophancy. . . . I lately met Lord D——n at a dinner-party at the house of a very respectable gentleman, and I was perfectly disgusted at the wholesale toadying he received from men of independent means and good position, merely because he was a lord. I have often observed in Ireland similar instances. . . . This, however, is only a social fault. In the weighty matter of religion the Irish have been no sycophants." Scott told the following legend of the founding of an

old church in the County Donegal. There is somewhere on the rugged coast of that county a precipitous
bohereen or bridle-road which crosses an arm of the sea
that is at a dizzy height spanned by a narrow bridge
unprotected by parapets. One dark and stormy night
the parish priest was summoned to attend a sick parishioner. His way was along the steep path aforesaid.
When passing the bridge he was startled by the sound
of a faint wail borne on the wind as of some person in
distress. He listened ; the cry was repeated. " That is
a human voice," he said to his attendant, " we must try
to assist the sufferer." " It would be madness to attempt
it," returned the latter ; " whoever he is, he is down
among the rocks, and one false step is death." " I think
I know the path, dark or light," rejoined the priest ; " this
poor creature may be dying, and in the name of God let
us go to his assistance." The priest then shouted, and
the shout was answered from below. Guided by the
sound, he descended a steep and intricate path leading
down to the water's edge. His companion reluctantly
followed. They found a man who addressed them in
the Spanish language, which the priest, who had been
educated in Spain, fortunately understood. The man
was a shipwrecked Spaniard who had been cast ashore
from a vessel that had gone to pieces off the coast. He
was dying from the injuries he had received by dashing
on the rocks, and he expressed great joy when he found
that one of his assistants was a priest. He received the
Last Sacraments and then said, " I make you my executor. Round my body is a hollow belt containing
gold. Distribute half of it among certain relations,
whom I shall name, and keep the other half for whatever religious purpose you think fit." The priest faith-

fully executed the dying Spaniard's instructions, and with the half given to himself he erected the church of the parish where the incident occurred.

5*th*. Scott and I rode to Clonakilty . . . and thence . . . to Glandore. . . . Talking of the Duke of M——'s family, with whom old Scott had been intimately acquainted, Scott said that the Duke's son, Lord Charles C——, was for many years estranged from his father. In 1832 Lord Charles wanted to get into Parliament for the family borough of W——, which could only be effected through the Duke's permission and influence. " He asked my father," said Scott, " what he should do. ' You must go down to B——,' was the answer, ' and make up matters with the Duke.' Away went Lord Charles to B——, where the Duke was leading a criminal life with a *chère amie*. Lord Charles effected his purpose about the borough, and returned to London. There he found, to his consternation, that his maternal aunt, Lady Catherine G——, from whom he received a very convenient annuity . . . had withdrawn it, being sorely scandalised at her nephew for the visit he had paid to the Duke's immoral establishment. Lord Charles was puzzled how to act. After much cogitation he at last cried, ' I have it. Parnell,' he said to an *habitué* of his house, ' get a Bible—there must be one somewhere in the house—and copy for me all the texts you can find about the conversion of sinners.' Parnell fished out a Bible and copied the texts. Lord Charles, armed with the texts, went off to visit his aunt. She bitterly reproached him, as he expected, for allowing any temporal or political consideration to induce him to enter the polluted mansion of his father. ' My dear aunt,' said his lordship, ' you wrong me much. You are evidently not aware of the real object of my visit. I deemed it a sacred duty to try if I could lead my poor father from his evil ways, and I flattered myself he would not be insensible to the force of certain passages of Scripture which I ventured to submit to his notice; here are the texts' (presenting them to his aunt) 'that struck me as particularly calculated to impress his mind with salutary alarm at the life he leads, and I assure you I am not without hope that a good effect has been already produced. Of course one could not tell all this to the public. To canvass the burgh was a good pretext for a visit, and if I can be returned so much the better.' . . . Lord Charles looked so sanctified, and acted his part with such address, that Lady Catherine, completely imposed on, continued his annuity." Scott continued, " When that old Duke was on his deathbed, at the age of eighty-four, his last hours were disturbed by a very singular scene. His gardener asked permission to see him. The assistants consented, supposing that the man wished to take an affectionate and dutiful farewell of his dying master. He approached the bed, looked hard at the Duke, and said, ' I have come to tell you that you will be in hell in five minutes, and that the devil never got a greater blackguard into his clutches ? ' " Scott did not know the cause of the gardener's hostility to the Duke. . . .

19*th*. Cardinal Wiseman's progress through Ireland has been a continuous triumph. Trinity College has done itself great honour by the frank courtesy with which its authorities invited the Cardinal to inspect their University, and the graceful respect with which they received him. They have acted like gentlemen. . . .

December 27th. Met Dan Conner. . . . He told a

story of his grandfather Conner, who in 1798 advertised in Cork, as was not then unusual, for a companion to join him in a post-chaise to Dublin. A gentleman answered the advertisement, and when they reached Clonmel he said to Conner, " I hope it will not incommode you to rest here for an hour, and to order dinner." " Not in the least,' said Conner ; " what shall we have ? " " A roast shoulder of mutton," suggested the stranger; "and if you are kind enough to give directions I shall look about the town." Away he walked. Conner ordered dinner ; the mutton was roasted ; dinner was ready ; but the stranger did not reappear. Conner walked out to find him. The Assizes were proceeding, and Conner, approaching the courthouse, looked up at a gallows near it, from which, to his horror and astonishment, he saw his travelling companion dangling at the end of a rope. Conner, impatient to escape from such a perilous vicinage, did not wait for his shoulder of mutton, but posted on to Dublin as fast as possible. He could only conjecture how his ill-starred companion had got into his fatal scrape. The poor fellow had perhaps been out on bail, and incautiously ventured among his unfriends, under a notion that he had settled matters effectually with the witnesses. Or perhaps he was hanged in mistake for someone else. Hanging was in fashion at the time, and the Government officials were not very scrupulous. Dan told the following, " When Sir Michael O'Loghlen went circuit for the first time as judge at Ennis, the Catholic criminals expected some favour from a Catholic judge. When O'Loghlen decided the cases on their merits, the criminals were disappointed, and their friends exclaimed, ' Why, d—n it ! he hangs them like any Protestant.' "

CHAPTER XVI

1859. —*January 24th.* Letter from Scott, who has declined an invitation to preside at one of the festivals to be held all over Scotland in honour of the poet Burns. . . . I observe that Leigh Hunt praises Burns for wishing Satan penitent and released from his den. My grandmother Wilson used to tell a story of a Presbyterian divine who introduced this sentiment into the pulpit. Having expatiated on the resources of omnipotent mercy, and the duty of praying for the conversion of sinners, the preacher proceeded : "And noo my frien's, let us pray for the conversion of the puir auld de'il." The same narrator had another story of the Presbyterian pulpit. . . . A long-winded minister, named Pettigrew, was sorely scandalised at the narcotic effect produced by his eloquence upon his congregation, a large number of which he regularly preached to sleep every Sunday. Vainly he thundered his reproof at the drowsy delinquents. . . . One day Mr Pettigrew privately

asked a somnolent parishioner why the flock were so
regardless of his anxious exhortations to remain awake
during the sermons. "They think it unco strange,"
replied the person appealed to, "that you should aye
scold *them* for sleepin', and that you ne'er say ae word
anent the sleepers belonging to yersell." "Till mysell?
How mean you, Donald?" "I mean that your ain wife
sleeps ilka Sabbath amaist the haill sermon; but ye
dinna see her, for she sits close under the poopit." "Do
you tell me sae!" exclaimed the astonished minister. . . .
"Weel, and that be sae, I shall no spare Mistress Pettigrew. Keep your ee on her neist Sabbath, and when
she nods, just haud up a finger." Donald took care
not to sleep on the following Sunday. The minister
commenced his discourse, and had not proceeded far
when Donald made the appointed signal. Pettigrew
bent forward, and saw, sure enough, his consort enjoying
a snug nap on the seat beneath the pulpit. With a
thundering blow upon the desk he aroused her from her
contraband slumber, and as the lady, who, according
to the legend, was destitute of fortune or beauty, looked
up, he addressed her in accents of wrath, "Sit ye up
there, Jean Pettigrew! Ye are na bonny; I gat nae
tocher wi' ye, and gin ye ha'ena heavenly grace aboot
ye, I ha'e gotten an unco bad bairgain o' ye!"

May 14*th*. Began barking oaks to-day. . . . It is
pleasant to poke about in the glen and to hear the dash
of the waterfall some twenty yards beneath my feet:
thence to pass to the north brake marking trees, and
amuse myself with fancying a resemblance between it
and Bocaccio's tangled brake in the tale of Sigismunda
and Guiscardo.

¹ For some months Mr Daunt was laid up with illness.—ED.

25th. My pugnacious youngster came in to-day with his face streaming blood from a blow of a stone near the eye. . . . It was almost impossible to get him to tell who hit him. " It is done now," said he, "and what does it matter who did it ? " He took the matter very philosophically, saying that " in our course through life we must expect to meet accidents." . . .

August 1st. Letter from Colonel Scott defending Louis Napoleon, and he considers that English machinations, by exciting, or at least by inflaming, disaffection in Italy, are chargeable with a large share of the terrible carnage that horrifies all Christian minds. Lord Palmerston's tone is that of intervention in behalf of what he calls the oppressed Italian nationalities. Louis Napoleon is precisely as well entitled to take a similar tone in behalf of Ireland. . . .

September 10th. The panic of a French invasion of England seems rather abated of late. . . . A proffer of French troops to win Repeal was made by Ledru Rollin in the heyday of O'Connell's agitation. O'Connell publicly declined the offer in courteous terms. In private he said, " I wonder if there could have been anything real in Ledru Rollin's offer ? Those French fellows have such a lot of balderdashical vanity about them that Ledru may only have made his offer to get talked of in the newspapers." Another time O'Connell said, " Before Grattan made his last journey to England he expressed a desire to see some of the Catholic leaders. A party of us went to his house, and were shown into a parlour, where we had not chairs enough. We were obliged to sit down turn about, and were kept waiting for an hour before Grattan appeared. At last he entered the room, half dressed, as if he had just risen, and with a blanket fastened round his neck by a large pin. He immediately addressed to us a long harangue, deprecating the notion of an Irish-French alliance, and insisting on unshaken fidelity to the British crown.' Such was O'Connell's account of the interview, and I could gather from his narrative that the harangue seemed to its hearers so inapplicable to the then state of the Catholic question, that, coupled with the fantastic attire and scanty courtesy of the speaker, it helped to weaken their affection for him. But Grattan was then very old, his body was weakened by years and severe illness, and his mental powers may probably have been impaired. At the interview his physical prostration was so manifest that the gentlemen who were present entreated that he would not incur the fatigue of going over to London to plead their cause in Parliament. He, however, persisted in going, and died within less than a week after his arrival. . . .

November 1*st*. Sent off a letter on Disendowment of the State Church to the newspapers.

8*th*. The Archbishop of Tuam writes to me that my letter is well worth the deep attention of the country. Most surely it is so, unless the country is satisfied to continue hag-ridden by the Establishment. . . .

17*th*. Wrote, and sent off to Sir B. Burke, a chapter on 'The O'Connors of Connerville,' which he asked me to contribute to his forthcoming series of *The Vicissitudes of Families*. The task recalled old times and many recollections of Feargus. I think I see his big, burly, brawny, round-shouldered figure, and his long, fiery tresses. His very look was a joke. They used to call him the Red Cat. . . . He had great mimetic powers. . . . He told how he had once mimicked a man to death. The victim was a County Meath farmer, an undutiful son, whose misconduct was supposed to have helped to kill his father. Feargus, to avenge the defunct, came at night to the cottage window dressed up in a white sheet, and in tones exquisitely imitated from the injured father, reproached the son with his unfilial wickedness, and menaced awful punishments. The farmer, terrified at hearing the threats thus uttered by his sire's ghost, became ill, and died of the fright. At least, Feargus said he did. Among the more active supporters of his canvass of the County Cork in 1832 was a Macroom linen-draper named Riordan, who had many good qualities. . . . He was indefatigable in his endeavours to bring electors to the registries and the hustings. He scoured the country, night and day, on his stout horse, Devil-stick-the-Minister ; in snow, hail or tempest he never wore a good coat, but provided for the needful warmth of his person by an extra number of shirts. . . . There was an attempt in Macroom to get up a public dinner to celebrate the triumph of Reform. I arrived in the town about 5 P.M. on the day of the dinner, and was met by Riordan, who, all enthusiasm and activity, told me that about 400 guests might be confidently expected to attend. I entered the dining-room a few minutes afterwards. The viands smoked upon the tables, but the promised 400 had shrunk to 17. The word Reform had scant attractions for the Irish peasantry. Feargus read for the select few . . . a letter he had recently received from O'Connell. . . . The letter was addressed simply, ' Feargus O'Connor,' and the great Dan added in a postscript, " You see I dispense with the foolish ' Esquire.' " . . . He made himself familiarly at home with the priests. Arriving at night at the cottage of a priest who had only one bed, Feargus unceremoniously popped into it. The owner had been absent . . . and on returning, wearied with his day's labours, he found his couch preoccupied, and was fain to content himself with some sort of shake-down. Yet, with all my fiery friend's devotion to the clergy, he did not set much store by clerical ministrations. When the cholera broke out in Cork in 1832 he was greatly alarmed. I asked him by what clergyman he would choose to be attended if the epidemic should reach him. " None of them shall come here buggabooing me," was his reply. . . .

December 17th. Letter from Father Lavelle, P.P. of Partry, informing me that Bishop Plunket has served notice to quit on fifty-two heads of families because they refuse to send their children to his lordship's Protestant schools. . . .

1860.— *March* 2d. Went to the county election at Bandon. Voted for Lord Camden against the new Attorney-General, Deasy ; not that Deasy is personally objectionable, but he is now the servant of the Government.

17th. Very ill lately. . . .

April 17th. Peace has been proclaimed between the Protestant Bishop of Tuam and his Catholic tenants. His lordship has been induced to relent, and the tenants' children are not to be forced to go to the Protestant schools. *Deo gratias !*

May 4th. Read Charlotte Brontë's capital novel *Vilette.* . . . This novel about a school reminds me of Theresa Daunt's school experiences. She was for eight years *en pension* with a Scotch ogress, a Miss Hay, who kept a school in the County Durham. The ogress was a terrible tyrant. Theresa was sometimes locked up for days together in a solitary garret, sometimes confined in a cellar, sometimes fed on bread and water for a week, which she was obliged to eat standing at a table in the hall. This last penalty was imposed for an error in arithmetic. Meanwhile, she was obliged to write letters to her father, who was moving about the world with his regiment, in which her condition was described as most delightful. Her mother was dead ; and so strict was Miss Hay's surveillance that she had not an opportunity of writing a real account of her misery to any human being. Nine pupils, whose parents lived within an accessible distance, left the school to escape from Miss Hay's tyranny, and I believe that Theresa was at last the sole remaining victim. . . .

19th. Dined with L——. In the evening met W. Smithwick, who told me an anecdote of his grand-uncle, Bob Conner, of Fortrobert. Bob commanded a corps, which he always pronounced *corpse*, of cavalry yeomanry. Intending to make some martial boast, he said to Hedges Eyre, of Macroom Castle, " Hedges, did you see my *corpse* ? " " Faith, I wish I did," replied Hedges, with malicious significance. Feargus used to mimic Bob with incomparable drollery, vaunting the tremendous exploits he was to perform at the head of his *corpse* on the Continent, including the capture of Bonaparte, whom he was to hang up in an iron cage in the hall at Fortrobert. . . .

June 29th. Got a letter from the Abbé Adolphe Perraud (now Bishop of Autun) asking statistics of the property usurped by the alien church in Ireland. . . .

July 27th. Youghal. The grass *has* grown thinly on H. Watkins's grave. . . .

September 3*d.* Letter from Scott, who tells a story of Father Strickland, S.J., recently returned from India, where he learned to wear a long beard kept trimmed to a point. While preaching a few days since in Sligo, he observed that an old woman was greatly affected, and shed tears. He ascribed her emotion to his sermon, and seeing that she still retained her place when the congregation had dispersed, he went to her and . . . inquired the cause of her tears. She looked up wistfully at his beard, and sobbed out, " Och, it's bekaise your riverence reminds me powerful of my poor ould goat that died last week." Father Strickland came away more amused than flattered.

26*th.* Arthur O'Connor came here. It seems that his Uncle Feargus made a will leaving Arthur everything he had. The legatee is slightly puzzled to discover whether *everything* means anything or nothing. I incline to the latter interpretation. . . . When I was about six or seven years old, a certain countess, whom my mother took me to visit, pronounced me to be 'a handsome boy with a bad countenance.' I do not name her ladyship, who was said to have scared Lord C—— into marrying her, by threatening to stab herself in the event of his refusing to accompany her into Hymen's temple. She was a very clever woman . . . could be very captivating and very disagreeable. In old age she still clung to the vanities of youth. I have seen her, when more than fourscore, with a bare neck, an enormous sable wig, curled into multitudinous ringlets, and surmounted by a fantastic little pink satin hat, that contrasted strongly with her old, withered, wrinkled, toothless, haggard visage. . . .

December 4*th.* Dublin. Great Repeal meeting at the

Rotundo; The O'Donoghue in the chair; the round room crammed; immense enthusiasm. I moved the first resolution. It was interesting to recollect that these walls, seventy-seven years ago, echoed the declaration, by the Grand Volunteer Convention of Ireland, of the identical principles we were met to proclaim to our countrymen. . . .

20th. Arthur O'Connor called here. (Kilcascan.) He told me of an English Protestant soldier, quartered in Tullamore, who became a Catholic and married a Catholic girl. A few days after his marriage Parson Berry met him in the street, and asked him what he had done. "Oh, nothing bad, your reverence; I was married to a Catholic woman." "And I hear you have joined her Church?" "Why, yes; before we were married Father O'Rafferty made a bloody Christian of me."

25th, Christmas Day. Roads sheeted with ice. My quiet Christmas contrasts strongly with the social mirth that marked the celebration of the season a century since. At Tullamore the invitations came on Christmas Eve for twelve days in succession. Mummers, fantastic-ally dressed, and musicians, called the waits, paraded the town before dawn. One mummer personated Satan, and sang some doggerel commencing thus :—

> " Here come I, Beelzebub,
>   In my hand I carry my club,
>   And under my arm a dripping pan," etc.

. . . After Christmas the women - servants got new gowns to reward them for the extra brewing and baking of the festive season. My grandmother's recol-lection of prices in Tullamore, during her early years, was thus taken down by my Aunt Wilson : Mutton, 1½d. a pound ; beef, 1d. ; soft sugar, 4d. ; white sugar, 6d. ; green tea (which alone was used), 10s. per pound ; port, 1s. a bottle ; fine English cider, 3s. a dozen ; Irish cider, 10s. 6d. per hogshead ; beer always brewed at home. The reminiscent was born in 1753. Here are some *disjecta membra* of Dublin gossip of the last century thrown together at random. Mr Massey Dawson, a man of good property, was separated thirteen times from his wife, a beautiful woman without fortune. . . . On one of their quarrels in court the judge said to her, "What fortune did you bring Mr Dawson ? " She answered with spirit, " As much as he was promised, and more than he deserved — I brought him myself." " Confound her, how handsome she looks ! " cried Dawson. " Come home, sweetheart ! " They went home friends ; but probably soon quarrelled again. It was Massey Dawson who placed an old goat in his drawing-room, and then told his wife that Lord W—— wished to see her there. She went, and found the goat butting furiously at his own reflection in a superb and costly mirror that Dawson had lately put up, and which was soon battered to fragments. She left the goat in the room, and on the stairs met her husband. "Well, sweetheart, did you see Lord W——? " " Yes, my dear, and his lordship now wishes to see you." Dawson entered the room and found the floor strewn with the glittering fragments of his beautiful mirror. . . . Another martyred wife, Miss Theodosia Magill, a wealthy heiress, married the scampish Earl of C——, who insulted her by driving through the street in which she lived in an open carriage, accompanied by an infamous woman named Fleetwood. He spent all his wife's fortune, except her pin-money, which was £800 a year. Notwithstanding his misconduct, she supplied his wants, including a bottle of wine daily. Yet his hat was sent round to the charitable and humane. . . . Another story. At a later period, Sir M. C——, whose father had made a large fortune by grazing, opposed, at a road sessions in his county, Lord W——, whose mother had not been renowned for strict decorum. Lord W—— was indignant at the baronet's opposition, and said that it was quite too bad that he, the descendant of a long line of nobles, should be opposed, in that county where for centuries his ancestors had held great influence, by the son of a grazier who had made his own money. The baronet retorted thus: "The noble lord has reproached me with the successful industry of my father. Well, so he can, for everybody knows who *my* father was. His lordship has certainly the advantage of me there, for I believe it would not be easy to tell who *his* father was!" *Words to that effect.* At a trial at which it was sought to establish the incapacity of a simpleton, Lord Ely, to manage his own property, a witness was examined concerning an interview he had recently held with his lordship. "Did you hear Lord Ely speak?" "Yes." "Did he talk rationally? What did he say?" "His lordship said, 'bladderum boo,' or *words to that effect.*" Anne Stewart, niece and heiress of the second Viscount Mountjoy, married her footman, Luke Gardiner, in 1711. She had interest enough to get him made a privy councillor and appointed Deputy Vice-Treasurer of Ireland. Their son, Charles Gardiner, married Miss Florinda Norman, by whom he had a son, Luke, after-

wards created Viscount Mountjoy, who married, in
1773, Elizabeth, one of the beautiful Miss Montgomerys.
These sisters, three in number, produced a rage in
Dublin by their charms. . . . When Elizabeth married
Luke Gardiner, the gentlemen wore silver lace bows
in their hats, the ladies in their bosoms. The servants
had bows of white lustring ribbon, with silver buttons,
and all had white gloves. The wedding favours were
worn for about ten days. The lovely bride appeared
in the stage box of the theatre, on the Thursday after
her marriage, in a pale pink lustring *negligée*. Gardiner
came forward and bowed to the audience. Mrs Gardiner blushed, and, with apparent reluctance, rose to
curtsey her thanks for the cheers that greeted her
appearance. She obtained more confidence subsequently, for she called out one night to her spouse, from
the gallery of the House of Commons, " Luke, when
shall I send the carriage for you ? " She sailed upon
the wave of fashion, one of the leaders of *haut-ton*.
But there were sometimes ripples in the stream. It
chanced that a very exclusive ball was to be given
at the Rotundo. None but the *crême de la crême* were
admissible. Mrs Gardiner was one of the patronesses,
and concerned in the distribution of tickets. Mr
Bowles, a gentleman of good family, but who lived
much retired, applied to her for a ticket. She
haughtily answered that, as she had never met him
in society, she must decline to oblige him ; intimating,
also, that if he had been a person of any consequence,
she must have heard of him. " Madame," said Bowles,
" my grandfather went in his coach when your husband's
grandfather stood behind one." She burst into tears,
and complained of the affront to her husband, who

told her that as Bowles's uncivil retort was perfectly
true, the less said about the matter the better. . . .
The lucky footman, who was transformed into a privy
councillor, was great - grandfather of Charles John
Gardiner, second Viscount Mountjoy of the later
creation, and first Earl of Blessington. . . .   When
my mother and Aunt Catherine were children, Lord
Abercorn gave them, as a New Year's gift, two
lottery tickets in a carved ivory box.   The tickets turned
out blanks, no fault of the donor.   He also presented
them with guitars and music books.   Lord Abercorn
was odd.   The officer in command of a regiment
near Baronscourt asked permission for himself and
his brother officers to shoot in his lordship's preserves.   To which request he returned the following
curtly - written reply:—"Not a feather, by G——!
ABERCORN."

When the beautiful Lady de Vesci (Elizabeth Selina,
daughter of Sir Arthur Brooke) was married in 1769,
one Owen M'Mahon, a tenant of her husband (then
Lord Kingston), asked as a favour to be shown the
lovely bride.   Lord K. pretended to comply, and presented to Owen a tolerably good-looking lady who was
on a visit with him.   "That's not her ladyship," said
Owen, who did not consider her pretty enough.   The
true bride was then produced, and as her charms
realised the report Owen had heard of them, he was
satisfied of her identity.   A Dublin footpad partook
of Owen's admiration of Lady de Vesci.   One night,
returning from the Castle in her chair, with footmen
and flambeaux, she was attacked by a single robber,
who discomfited her attendants and plundered her of
money and jewels.   He then held a flambeau to her

face, declared she was the prettiest woman he had ever seen, and insisted on giving her a kiss. She permitted the salute, which she had no means of avoiding. . . . Among the Dublin notorieties were the Ladies Gore, daughters of the Earl of Arran, who are said to have terrified their timid brother, Lord Sudely, by personating highwaymen and attacking his carriage as he was driving home to town one night through the Phœnix Park. One of the sisters, Lady Catherine, married a certain baronet, who afterwards inherited a peerage. His lordship, saith the legend, had a natural daughter, who was brought up in ignorance of her illegitimacy. She called her father's wife 'mamma,' and her ladyship good-naturedly suffered the delusion to continue. There was an old woman about the place who occasionally accosted the young lady in her walks, and talked with her civilly, but very respectfully. The young lady asked the steward who the woman was, observing that she rather liked her. "Maybe, miss," said the steward, "you might not like to hear who she is." "Why shouldn't I like to hear it? What harm could it do me?" "Why, then, miss, that woman is your own mother." This revelation shocked Miss F—— to such an extent that she attempted to drown herself. The news flew about the place at once. The steward was instantly dismissed and his cottage burned. My informant's father saw it in flames. The young lady was rescued from the attempt to drown herself, and I think was afterwards placed in a lunatic asylum.

Well known in Dublin in the last century was the Right Hon. John Hely Hutchinson, Secretary of State. His paternal name was Hely; he descended from the very ancient Munster race of that name. He lived on terms of close friendship with my grandfather, whom he probably loved all the better because the latter not only never sought promotion, but actually refused it when offered to him.   His son Richard, afterwards Lord Donoughmore, was my mother's godfather. . . .   Of the Secretary, who was also Provost of Trinity College, his enemies said that his greed of office was insatiable. Shortly before his death, which occurred in 1795, he complained bitterly to my grandfather of the desertion of some of his former adherents. . . .   "Rats fly from a sinking ship," was Dr Wilson's reply.   "You are right, Wilson," said the dying statesman, and in his weakness he wept.   Among the gossiping memoranda of the century was the imprisonment of the Countess of Belvedere by her husband, at Gaulstown Park, in the County Westmeath.   Lord Belvedere invented a pretext for shutting her up within the confines of his park ; he pretended to be jealous, but the general belief then and since attached no weight to his imputations on his wife's fidelity.   He allowed her a carriage and horses, to be used within the precincts of the park.   On her directing the coachman to drive her to the nearest village, he refused, pleading his master's peremptory orders, which, he said, he dared not disobey.   Lady Belvedere then said that if restricted to the park she could dispense with an equipage, and accordingly she sent away the carriage.   Her imprisonment lasted thirty years, with the exception of a short interval, during which she contrived to escape, only, however, to be speedily recaptured.   She was a daughter of the third Viscount Molesworth.   The Earl died in 1774, and his death restored his wife to freedom, but with health greatly shattered, and with mind more or less impaired by the long and unmerited persecution she had suffered. Another bit of Dublin gossip was the marriage of the Earl of Lanesborough's daughter, the Lady Elizabeth Butler, with her father's footman. He was, saith the story, placing coals on the drawing-room fire when Lady Elizabeth put a note into his hand, which he transferred to his pocket, supposing that it concerned some outdoor errand. Downstairs he went; but on looking at the note he saw that it was addressed to himself, and contained strong assurances of affection, ending with an offer of marriage. The footman accepted the offer; the pair were married; her lady-ship dropped her title and called herself plain Mrs ———. They took a house on the road to Irishtown, which was shown to me many years ago by the person who told me the anecdote. My grandfather's town residence was in York Street. . . . One of his amuse-ments consisted in inventing nicknames for people he disliked. Four high officials had been styled 'the Pillars of the State.' "Ay," said he, "the *quatre* pillars (caterpillars) of the State, sure enough." A foreign military leader . . . he styled, "that Paphlagonian Pur-gopolynius, Charles Frederic Braggadocio Rhodomon-tado Swaggerero Rattlebags, lieutenant - general and commander-in-chief of the Cacadæmonio - Catilinarian Tyrannocracy"—a gigantic and sonorous description. He received at his house, in York Street, some of the *élite* of Dublin, and some who were anything but *élite* —adventurers, namely, whose only passport was their talent to amuse and their impudence. Among these was a blackleg who appeared as the 'Count de Burgh.' This man had been received at the Castle, where Wilson saw him at a drawing-room, during Lord Townshend's viceroyalty, conversing familiarly with Lady Townshend. But his means gave way, and the discovery of his real character was hastened by his own incaution.   Another visitor — not, indeed, in York Street, but at Moyle, County Tyrone—was a rather mysterious Lady Nicholson of Kenmay, usually called Lady Kenmay.   Her ladyship's history was strange.   She was the daughter of a poor laundress near Omagh.   Thence, I know not how, she found her way to Paris.   At Paris she found her way to the heart of a Scotchman, Sir Robert Nicholson, who married her.   She was obliged to fly from Paris at the Revolution.   I don't know what became of Sir Robert, who was much her senior.   She was extremely handsome and very fascinating, and had quite the manners of a *grande dame*.   It was noticed, to her credit, that she affected no secrecy about her parentage, but visited her humble mother, as a daughter should.   My grandfather met her somewhere, liked her conversation, asked her to spend a week at Moyle—she came and stayed nine months!   The question then was how to get rid of her, for she seemed to have taken firm root. At last, Mrs Wilson asked her what she meant to do. "To live and die with you!" was her ladyship's naïve reply.   "Oh! Lady Kenmay, that is impossible; you cannot reside permanently here."   Her ladyship said she had no money.   Mrs Wilson advanced her thirty guineas. . . .   She departed, having pressed her hostess to accept a diamond ring, which was, of course, refused. The family coach conveyed her to the town, where she was to take the Dublin stage.   But, in less than an hour, the coach reappeared, driven at full gallop, and containing Lady Kenmay, in a state of great excitement, flying back for refuge from a threatened arrest for some debt.

. . . She was got finally off, however. Six months passed without bringing any tidings of her movements or of the thirty guineas, when, one morning, Dr Wilson received a letter from a French gentleman, written in bad English. " Monsieur," it began, " I am very sorry to tell you of so bad a matter as the dead of Lady Kenmay." There was nothing said about the loan, and my grandfather looked on 'the dead of. Lady Kenmay' as a little apocryphal. . . . My grandmother, who went to Dublin in 1770, was a living chronicle of the fashions, which she remembered and detailed with a minuteness that seems scarcely consistent with the depth and seriousness that really belonged to her character. . . . My kind old chronicler had store of playhouse memories. She saw Macklyn as Sir Archy Macsycophant. Lord Newbattle, who was one of the audience, exclaimed, " That is the image of my grandfather ! " (the Marquis of Lothian). . . . She saw Placido, whom Louis XVI. called 'the little devil,' and who rolled or tumbled into his coat, hat and wig, which lay scattered on the stage.

There was a bow-legged lady who, one fine Sunday evening, asked my grandmother, then a girl in her teens, to accompany her to church. Away they went, and when near the church, a huge, unruly sow bolted right between the lady's legs, lifting her off her feet. She could not have kept her seat if her young companion had not held her fast by the arm, racing smartly along to keep pace with the pig. The animal, if I recollect aright, took its course through the open door, up the aisle, and in this unprecedented fashion was the rider borne to her devotions. As a record of the way in which rectors were able to live in those days, my informant described the style of a Reverend Mr Jackson's

establishment at Tullamore between 1760 and 1770 . .
His apartments were furnished expensively and with
elegance. There were paintings by foreign artists, and
ornamental china. Mrs Jackson's dressing-room was a
perfect toy-shop of *recherché* nicknackery. The domestic
staff included a butler, two footmen, a coachman, three
gardeners, a housekeeper, two housemaids and a waiting-
maid, besides the kitchen officials. Breakfast was at
nine, dinner at three, tea at six, after which cards filled
the time until ten, when supper was served. . . . The
Reverend Mr Jackson's *ménage* gives us a sample of par-
sonic life in the eighteenth century. Of episcopal life in
an earlier period of the century we have a graphic description from the pen of the lively Mrs Delany.
Among my grandmother's friends in her youth was an
old Mrs Margaret Crow, of whom I am able to record
that she wore a bell hoop. Her husband was a captain
in the Duke of Cumberland's army in 1745. He was
taken by the Highlanders and stripped to his shirt.
Escaping from his captors, he made his way to the royal
army, where he rushed into the presence of the Duke.
"What have we here?" asked Cumberland, amazed at
the entrance of his officer almost *in cuerpo*. "A bird
without feathers," replied the plucked Crow, who then
detailed his adventures. "We must get you feathers,"
said the Duke, and the next vacant majority was given
to Crow, who was known to be a brave man and a good
officer. Crow had once to fight a duel. The time fixed
was early in the morning. His wife awakened him at
cockcrow lest he should be late in the field. He fought,
killed his man, and returned to bed as if nothing particular had happened. Mrs Crow was in Scotland in
1740. While there, she heard the following story :—A

farmer's wife went to pay her husband's rent to their landlord. A neighbour, who knew she had money on her person, overtook her on a lonely road. Being on horseback he offered to take her *en croupe*, as their way was the same for some miles. She accepted his offer, though I think with some misgivings. He dashed on rapidly until they arrived at a deep quarry pit, close to the road, which here ran through an unfrequented wood. He then jumped down and lifted the terrified woman from the horse, which he tied to a tree. He plundered her of her money and commanded her to take off her clothes. She had no means of resistance, being wholly beyond the reach of human help, and entirely in the ruffian's power. She accordingly doffed her garments until she came to her chemise. They were standing on the very verge of the pit. She stepped back a couple of paces, begging that, for decency's sake, he would turn his back to her. Taken by surprise, he consented. Her movement had placed him between herself and the edge of the pit, and as soon as he turned his back, she rushed at him with all her strength and pushed him over the edge. He was killed by the fall, and the heroine, mounting the horse, made the best of her way to her landlord. Mrs Crow had a wild, unruly nephew, with whom she had not been on the best terms. After her death this scapegrace gave a guinea for his old aunt's cat, from a touch of affectionate regard for the defunct. The town of Tullamore was the property of Moore, Earl of Charleville of the first creation. It is told that when collecting funds to relieve the suffering poor in a season of severe distress, he entered the shop of a rich merchant, whom he found scolding a housemaid for wasting a remnant of candle. This indication of what seemed miserly economy discouraged him ; but on his stating the object of his visit, the merchant handed him a £50 note. Lord Charleville seemed astonished. The merchant laughed and said, " I suppose, my lord, you did not expect so much because you heard me scolding the maid for wasting a candle ; but it is by looking after every item, however trivial, and suffering no waste in the smallest particular, that I have amassed means which enable me to help the distressed with liberality." It was during the period of Mrs Wilson's sojourn in Dublin that the Volunteers became enrolled, and that Grattan, backed by their arms, carried the Declaration of Independence. Assuredly it was a time of deep and captivating memories. A brilliant metropolis inhabited by a splendid nobility and gentry ; the whole Irish people mustering to demand their liberties ; their demand rendered irresistible by the genius and virtue of one illustrious man, and Ireland raising her crowned head among imperial nations. . . .

CHAPTER XVII

Resisting Payment of Income Tax—Incident of '98—
Married *en bloc* — George Robins and the Clergy—
William Howitt—Tricking an Exciseman—Fighting the
Tithes—Acquittance in Full—Mr Lecky's *Leaders of
Public Opinion in Ireland*—Fortunate Recovery of Money
—Ghost Stories—'Warning' a Landlord.

1861.—*January* 15*th.* The Chancellor of the Exchequer
having taken the dishonest step of demanding Income
Tax upon income which will not become due to us
for more than three months. . . . Mr Conner of Manch
joins me in refusing payment and in addressing a strong
remonstrance to Gladstone. . . .

February 25*th.* Mr Conner and I having successfully
resisted the attempt to get one quarter from us in
advance of income, Mr Gladstone wrote us a long letter
in reply to our memorial, in which he did not controvert
our statements, but very coolly pleaded the necessity
England was under of raising eleven millions to fortify
herself within a certain time. The Union all over ! . . .
We thought it better to withhold payment than to
prolong a controversy with Gladstone, notwithstanding the temptation of publishing his letter with the
capital rejoinder to which he laid himself open. So we
didn't write and didn't pay—till the second quarter had
elapsed. . . .

May 6th. . . I find the following incident of 1790 in my Aunt Wilson's handwriting : " Old Jack Tarleton, a magistrate and captain of a yeomanry corps in '98, went out with his men, one night, to a farmer's house between Philipstown and Tullamore. He ordered out the eldest son, who, I think, was in bed, and who, I suppose, was suspected of being a rebel. When he appeared, Captain Tarleton commanded Elgee Boyd, son of old Boyd, curate of Killeigh, to shoot him. Elgee obeyed, and the young man fell dead. His mother, who witnessed the scene, has ever since been bereft of reason. The name of the family was Molloy. . . . Matters were hushed up; Elgee entered the Church, and is still in the north, rector of a good living." . . . More scraps. At a contested election in Connaught, a landlord named Foster sold his whole stock of votes for a good sum to each of the candidates ; having pocketed the money of both, he called all his freeholders together. Foster was too generous to keep all the traffic to himself. " Boys," he exclaimed to his expectant serfs, " I don't care a button whom you vote for. I have made the most I could of you ; go, sell your votes every man of you to the best advantage that you can." Away went the voters to profit by his honour's considerate advice . . . Four couples, all manifestly beggars, presented themselves to a clergyman to be married. His reverence naturally disliked the trouble of four several repetitions of the marriage service where douceurs could not be hoped for. He accordingly abridged time and trouble by addressing the postulants collectively : " You four beggar men, will you take these four beggar women to be your wedded wives ? " " Yes, your honour ! " burst from the four enamoured mendicants in chorus. " And

you four beggar women, will you take these four beggar
men to be your wedded husbands?" The ladies shouted
a rapturous affirmative; and thus did the clergyman,
by a happy economy of his labour, perform four nuptial
rites in quarter the time they would have occupied in
the hands of a less-gifted divine.

16th. Scott writes to say that Parton must be sold.
. . . It has been the estate of the Glendonwyns since
1458 . . . probably from an earlier period. One source
of profit . . . was the right of presentation to the parish,
a very strange right for a Catholic to possess. Miss
Glendonwyn sometimes got a douceur of £500, or even
£600, from the Presbyterian minister whom she appointed. . . . I do not think that Church preferments
are ever put up to open auction in Scotland or Ireland,
but in England there is a regular mart for this species
of traffic at 20 Tavistock Street, Covent Garden. Many
years ago, William Howitt, the Quaker author, gave me
a graphic description of the sale by auction of a Church
living, at which he was present. The celebrated George
Robins was the auctioneer, and was puffing the next
presentation with his wonted eloquence. Several clergymen were present to bid, and the company included a
lay gentleman who had brought his son, a lad of fifteen.
The auctioneer expatiated on the advantages offered
by the living. "A noble opportunity," he said, "for
the display of clerical ability, and the exhibition of
apostolic zeal. The pastoral duties of the incumbent
could, if desired, be lightened by occasional sport, for
which great facilities existed in the neighbourhood—
three packs of hounds, excellent fox-covers, etc. The
aged incumbent now in possession could not, in the
nature of things, hold out very long. The time could

not now be very distant when he would reap, in a better and happier world, the reward of his pious labours in this sublunary sphere." Here a parson broke in : "How old is he, eh?" To which George Robins answered : "He has reached the patriarchal age of seventy." Another parson exclaimed : "But is he healthy?" "Um—that is a delicate question," said Robins; "I cannot say that he has any decided complaint, but he is weak, and at his time of life. . . . Your son, sir, I presume," said the auctioneer, graciously bowing to the lay gentleman above mentioned. The gentleman bowed affirmatively. "I would recommend you to make a bid at this living for the young gentleman," said George ; "quite a clerical cast of features—intellectual forehead indicative of ability ; put him in training, get him ordained—may have him in full orders just about the time that the present venerated pastor ascends to the realms of beatitude." "Why, sir,' said the parent, " I haven't fixed on any particular profession for him yet." "Then fix upon the Church, sir, and put him in harness at once. The Church, believe me, is the very best investment for money just now. There's the army—no war now, nor likely to be ; nothing to arouse the martial spirit of British heroism ; you send a young man out to be fried like a herring on the rock of Gibraltar, or to sweat and stew and scorch under Indian suns. There's the bar—profession overdone, overstocked. . . . But the Church, the Church, sir, is a certain investment. You cannot do better for your amiable and gifted young hope, sir, than to take a bid at this most eligible lot— dead sure return for the outlay, besides the sublime associations attaching to the professional character." Howitt, whom I met many years ago, related to me the above scene in pretty nearly the foregoing words. He said that such scenes were of daily occurrence, and that he was much amused at the apparent unconsciousness of the clergy who congregated to bid for next presentations, and who discuss in the way of traffic the age and bodily condition of the existing incumbents. . . . Story of a sporting party at Ballydonellan, County Galway. All were provided with licences except one gentleman. The local excise officer encountered the party, and demanded to see their licences, which were at once produced by those who had them. The man who had no licence took a piece of paper from his pocket, put it into the muzzle of his gun, and presented the gun, cocked, at the exciseman, saying, "You may have my licence this way if you like." "Oh, all right," said the exciseman, apparently thinking the paper was the licence, and that the mode of presenting it was a piece of facetious eccentricity.

17th June. Old Smithwick lately told me a characteristic story of Feargus O'Connor. Sir Edward Temple having named Frank O'Connor with praise in his book on South America, Feargus, in an ecstasy of inflation thereat, thus unburdened his delight. "Well, Standish, we are certainly a most remarkable family. My brother Roderic is the greatest man in Van Dieman's Land; my brother Frank is the greatest man in South America, and I, as I need scarcely tell you, am the greatest man in Ireland!" . . .

July 8th. Rode to Clonakilty Quarter Sessions. Five poor men on the road, who learned that the tithe cases were to be tried, took off their hats, looked up to heaven, and solemnly prayed I might defeat the attempt of the rector on our pockets. The applications of two parsons for increase of tithe were heard and dismissed, on which the agents for our parson withdrew his case from court. . . .

20th. Left home for Scotland. Slept at Colthurst's. C. Colthurst compared modern travelling with a former mode. " I once," said he, "travelled to London with Sir Nicholas Colthurst. At Holyhead he gave his servant £50 to defray the expenses of the road, and before we reached London the money was exhausted and the servant asked for more. We posted with four horses."

25th. Arrived at Glasgow . . . trained to Edinburgh. . . .

27th. Landed on the Dublin Quay. . . . Visited Mr Fisher at the Record Tower, and had a long genealogical conversation with him. When parting he said, " I dine to-day with a Mr Gibbon who is ninety years old, and who often heard Grattan and the other great orators in our old House of Commons. He knew Sir Boyle Roche, who, he says, was a very shrewd fellow, notwithstanding his blunders. In fact, he had a genius for comical blunders, and was in the habit of inventing them in order to make the House laugh, and to divert attention from dangerous points."

22d. Letter from Scott, who tells a story of the present Bishop of Dromore, Dr Leahy. His lordship spent some weeks at Bundoran for the benefit of sea-bathing. The house where he lodged was infested with rats, and his landlady, who had great faith in the episcopal power of rat-hunting, presented him with repeated petitions to ' say an office ' for the expulsion or destruction of the vermin. To all her requests the Bishop, it need hardly be said, turned a deaf ear.

At last, when taking his departure, she handed him her bill for board and lodging, which seemed to him of such exorbitant amount that he paid it with an ungracious grumble.   He then got into his carriage and was driving off, when the landlady said, " I hope your lordship won't forget the office."   " What office ? " demanded the Bishop.   " The office for the rats, my lord."   " Here it is," returned he, handing her back her bill ; " give them *that*, and I'll warrant they won't come to you again." . . .

October 11*th*. In the face of the general distress, the parsons have revived their attempts to get increased tithe.   At Middleton Quarter Sessions some merriment was excited by a rector named Nason, who employed an attorney to get the tithe increased in the parish of which he is rector, and at the same time employed another attorney to *resist* the increase in the neighbouring parish of Ballynoe, in which he pays tithe as a landowner.

November 2*d*.   Ushaw College, Durham.   College magnificent.[1] . . .   In the evening, a gentleman who dined with the professors told the following story :—In the palmy days of Chartism, a Conservative of very violent principles, and still more violent modes of expressing them, was haranguing the company assembled at a festive gathering about the political sins of the Chartists, and especially those of Feargus O'Connor. At a card-table, near which the angry orator harangued, a red-haired gentleman whom he did not know was playing whist.   The orator declared that the Chartist leaders deserved the gallows.   " I would willingly go

---

[1] Mr Daunt records his journey to Scotland and England, to place his children at school.—ED.

twenty miles," said he, "to see that rascally Feargus O'Connor hanged ; would not you ? " he added, appealing to the red-haired whist player. " I cannot say I would," replied the foxy gentleman. "What ! " rejoined the other ; " so you would not wish to punish the ringleader ? I presume you consider yourself a loyal citizen, and, if so, what reason can you give for not being anxious to see that public disturbers get the rope ? " " The best possible reason," answered the foxy personage ; " I am Feargus O'Connor myself." . . .

December 11*th*. Home again. Read an entertaining little book, *The Leaders of Public Opinion in Ireland.* . . . The author is a Protestant, but he is also a nationalist. He worships Grattan, who, as I once said to his son, is my political patron saint. . . . There is an Irish mason's daughter in the vicinity from Wales, where her family have been long settled. She tells a story of a Welsh preacher who assured his flock that people of all nations have souls to be saved, " even the Irish ! ' Here is a slight incident concerning William Conner, of Connerville, uncle of my grandmother Daunt. Conner brought a large sum of money to lodge in a Cork bank. The place was greatly crowded, and Conner's valise containing the money, which he had just laid on the counter, suddenly vanished. With the least possible delay he set out in a chaise and four for Dublin, to stop payment of the notes at the bank which had issued them. Arrived at the Dublin bank, he found a man at the counter getting gold for notes. The man's face he at once recognised as that of a fellow he had seen at his elbow at the bank in Cork. A glance enabled him to recognise his own property. He of course recovered his money, and I hope, for the sake of poetical justice, punished the thief. . . . Conner died in 1766.

14*th*. Father Fitzgerald, P.P. of Castletown Delvin, told me that during one of the seasons for collecting the annual tribute to O'Connell, he was privately visited by Lady Chapman, of Killua Castle, who gave him £150 for O'Connell, adding that she did so to show her appreciation of his services 'in making Ireland respected.' Lady C—— was a Protestant. . . . The clever author of *The Leaders of Public Opinion in Ireland* confounds O'Connell's private tribute with the Repeal Rent.

16*th*. Read Hugh Miller's *Scenes and Legends of the North of Scotland*, a very pleasant volume of tradition, anecdote and speculation. His ghost-stories are well told. My aunt Wilson told a story of a man, a foxhunter, I believe, who was boasting to a jovial party, assembled on a snowy night in a snug inn parlour, that he was superior to the folly of superstitious terror. The hunters had passed during the day near the crumbling ruins of an ancient church in which was piled up a large number of skulls. "If you are as brave as you tell us," said one of them to the boaster, "go this instant and bring us one of the skulls." The man of valour seemed scarcely to like the proposal, but consented to go. Bets were made whether he would achieve the abstraction of the skull. The poor fellow set off on his dreary expedition, and after encountering some delay from the inclemency of the weather, he at last groped his way among the ruins to the corner where the mouldering relics of past generations were heaped, and he took up a skull. He had scarcely done so, when an unearthly voice said : "That is my skull—drop it !" Our hero accordingly dropped it, but instantly took up a second; a second voice then sounded through the gloom, "That is my skull; drop it!" but braced his nerves to seize a third skull, with which he made the best of his way through the snow-covered graveyard in spite of another ghostly voice from the dark church claiming the ownership. Away he ran much faster than he had come, surmounting the impediments of snow and darkness with an agility that surprised himself. He quickened his pace as he heard the patter of feet in pursuit; he did not venture to look back, and his nerves just sustained him till he reached the inn where his fellow-convives were eagerly watching for his arrival. "Well, did you bring the skull?" "Yes, yes," he hastily answered, "but for heaven's sake shut the door, for the owner is at my heels." A loud laugh chorused this announcement. I need scarcely say that some of his merry companions had contrived to reach the ruined church before him, and that theirs were the awe-inspiring voices he had heard there. I have an imperfect recollection of a strange, wild legend, that a solitary rambler through this parish (Ballymoney) was startled at seeing, after midnight, lights gleaming from the windows of the little old church, it may be some ninety or a hundred years since. Looking into the edifice, he saw the pews occupied by a staid congregation of cows, and the pulpit was filled by a horned preacher —the bull, I presume. We need be at no loss to conjecture the real nature of the beings that assumed this shape in a building devoted to religion. By-and-by the congregation passed out through the wall. . . . A tale of Miller's reminds me of the following. The merry widow of a farmer returned from her husband's funeral on the crupper of a neighbour's horse. On the road from the graveyard, the owner of the animal asked her to marry him. " To be sure I will," returned the widow, "*why didn't ye spake sooner ?* " *Apropos* to nothing at all, here is a story of a runaway tenant. In a year of bad crops and great distress, some of the tenants of my great-grandfather Gumbleton, like many of their neighbours, took to running away with stock and crops, leaving empty lands for their landlords. Gumbleton begged one of his tenants, in whom he had some, though perhaps not much, confidence, not to follow such an evil example. " You will solemnly promise me Jerry," said he, " that at anyrate you will not go without giving me warning." Jerry solemnly promised compliance with this moderate request. One bleak and stormy winter night, Gumbleton, while retiring to bed about midnight, was startled by the noise of gravel flung at his windows. He looked out . . . and called, " Who is there ? " " It's Jerry Hegarty, your honour," shouted a voice through the storm. " Oh, Jerry, is that yourself ? What business have you on such a night, man ? " " Just to keep my promise of giving warning to your honour. I said, you know, I wouldn't run away without letting your honour know of it; I am running away now. Good-night to your honour, and good-bye ! " So Jerry ran away, stock, crops and all being also *en route*. . . .

31*st*. Looking over some old letters to-day, I found one from Henry Grattan, in which he described an iron helmet, believed by him to have been used as an instrument of torture in Richmond Prison, Dublin. There is a characteristic paragraph : " As to the Repeal cause, I hope it will not suffer. By me it never shall. The Irish must know I will never abandon it through friendship or through fear, or through interest." . . .

CHAPTER XVIII

A Novel Visiting-Card—The Prince Regent and the Sheridans
—A Virago—The Liberation Society—Canonisations—
Bonaparte and Lady Oxford—Polemics—Address from
Berehaven—The Supernatural.

1862. — *New Year's Day.* Dined at Brook Park. Talk—historical, religious persecution, etc. No doubt the exclusion from political offices or franchises, on account of theological tenets, is supremely absurd. . . . And this was O'Connell's view also. I recollect reading a letter he addressed to the Archbishop of Tuam canvassing that prelate's support of the Repeal movement, in which he said, "There would be no Protestant ascendency over the Catholics, and no Catholic ascendency over the Protestants."

22*d.* Received a letter from John Martin, consulting me about a renewed Repeal organisation. He has also consulted Smith O'Brien. . . . These occasional movements keep the question alive till better times, till the ideal patriot—hero of my prayers and hopes—shall arise to claim the mantle of Grattan. . . .

March 17th. . . . I have found out who the author (of *Leaders of Public Opinion in Ireland*) is. He is a Mr Lecky. I reviewed the work as a labour of love in the *Cork Examiner*, being anxious that the brilliant abilities of a young Protestant nationalist should receive appreciation. . . . Full of gratitude for the review, the author writes from Naples to thank the editor. . . . He says that his national principles are neither so unknown nor unpopular in Trinity College as the reviewer appears to suppose. . . .

April 30*th.* Read Swift's journal to Stella. . . . A relative of mine, when a widower, married a lady with £4000, which was settled on the survivor for life. . . . The gentleman was a perfect Harpagon in the matter of economy, and hunted through the livery-keepers' establishments to cheapen the carriage which should take him and his bride to church. He got a very crazy chaise for a small sum, and it was considered a piece of good luck that it did not break down. He got a handsome monument erected over the grave of his first wife, and had a large drawing of the monument rolled up in a tin case. It is told of him, I know not how truly, that having occasion to visit a gentleman to whom his appearance was unknown, he got the servant to usher him into the drawing-room without announcing his name. The master of the house begged to know to whom he was indebted for the honour of his visit. An ordinary mortal would have presented his card or verbally announced himself. Not so our genius. Opening the tin case he extracted, and solemnly unrolled, the monumental drawing, which he presented to the wondering eyes of his host, pointing to the inscription, " Sacred to the memory of Mrs ——." When that gentleman had read thus far, his solemn visitor said, with a sepulchral bow, " I, sir, am the unhappy widower." When Solomon said there was nothing new under the sun, he certainly had not heard of a monumental inscription being made to do duty for a visiting-card. . . .

May 15*th*. Mrs Gore Jones, Sheridan's niece, showed me, some years ago, a curious letter she had received from her father, Charles Sheridan, in 1804, describing a dinner at Carlton House. The Prince of Wales had heard much of Charles's colloquial talents, and frequently desired 'Sherry' to bring his brother to dinner, but Sherry always contrived to evade compliance on one pretext or another. Royalty was not to be baulked, and when at last it became evident that Sherry had no wish to introduce his brother to the Prince, the latter conveyed an invitation through some other friend to Charles, at the same time inviting Sherry, from whom His Royal Highness concealed that Charles was to join the party. Sherry's astonishment was great at the unexpected rencontre. Royalty was delightful, and evidently fascinated Charles, whose letter was quite rapturous on the subject of his host's affability and powers of enchantment. . . . I think Charles ascribed Sherry's conduct to jealousy. . . . Scott, in a note, tells the old story of Swift desiring his cook to dress the overdone meat less. Parson Gouldsbury of Tullamore had a cook named Isabella, who was despotic in her department. One day Gouldsbury had some friends to dine with him, and the meat, unlike Swift's, was nearly raw. Gouldsbury sent it back to the kitchen with orders to Isabella to dress it properly. In a few moments Isabella burst into the dining-room with the joint in her hand, and angrily demanded who had ventured to say it was ill-dressed. She looked so fierce that nobody cared to identify himself with the complaint, at the risk of an altercation with the angry artist, and Isabella returned to the kitchen with the glory of having bullied the whole company in the parlour.

17th. Dined at Brook Park. Story of Victy or Victoria Sullivan, a Ballineen beggar-woman, who had begged a few sods of turf on a cold day, and asked Mrs Bullen, the apothecary's wife, for a *smeroidhe* or live coal to kindle them. The request was granted, and Victoria, in an ecstasy of gratitude, exclaimed,— "Thank ye, my lady! Fire everlasting to your sowl, Madam Bullen, alea (darling). Amin ! "

June 18*th.* Received a letter from the Secretary of the London Liberation Society, saying I had been named as one of the executive council, and asking if I would accept the office. Declined on the score of feeble health, and the inconvenience of attending the annual meetings of the council in London. I have found some of our Catholics unwilling to join forces with men so full of anti-Catholic bigotry as the English nonconformists, but I think I have tolerably well removed that unwillingness. . . .

25th. . . . Gorgeous celebration at Rome. . . . Canonisation of the Japanese martyrs. . . . Mr M——, the Protestant curate of the parish, sarcastically asked Arthur O'Connor how the Pope knew that these twenty-seven gentlemen were admitted into Heaven. . . . He forgot that he had himself canonised, not merely twenty-seven persons of resplendent and unimpeachable sanctity, but every individual Protestant over whose dead body he ever performed the burial service as set forth in the Book of Common Prayer, for that service announces 'that it hath pleased God of his great mercy *to take unto Himself* the soul of our dear brother (or sister) here departed.' And in a subsequent prayer the officiating clergyman remarks, "We give Thee hearty thanks for that it hath pleased Thee to deliver them out of the miseries of this sinful world." Now this is precisely what the Pope affirms of the Japanese martyrs. He says this of men whose lives were holy, and who were martyred for the faith. M—— and all other Anglican clergymen affirm it of every worthless scamp whose obsequies they celebrate. Yet they find fault with the Pope.

21st. Arthur O'Connor came here. Talked of the old tales of Feargus's funny humbug. Story of his coaxing one of our labourers, Shane Ruadh, to carry him across the river on his back, on a very cold day. Shane refused, till Feargus promised to reward him with a guinea. He then stripped off his nether habiliments, and after carrying Feargus across, demanded the reward. But Feargus, who had not promised to give him the guinea in specie, coolly answered, "My fee as a lawyer is a guinea. Go now and commit any crime you like, and if you are prosecuted, I shall plead for you gratis." And with this airy payment Shane was obliged to be satisfied. Smithwick tells a story of a beggar asking alms of Feargus. "Poor fellow!" cried Feargus, smitten with compassion. "Standy, can you lend me a shilling?" The shilling was lent and given to the beggar, whose gratitude was eloquently lavished on Feargus. "But," adds Smithwick, "Feargus never paid me the shilling."

August 30th. . . . Ran through some of Moore's Diary. He mentions, under date 9th April 1821, meeting Harry Bushe and his wife at Paris. Bushe was nephew maternally of my idol, Henry Grattan. I remember when a child of six years old being with the Bushes in Dublin for some days, and flying kites in

Mountjoy Square with little Gervase. . . . Letter from
Colonel Scott consulting me as to the mode of assuring
Louis Napoleon of his (Scott's) identity as nephew
of Lady Oxford, who plotted with Lady Holland to
effect old Bonaparte's escape from St Helena. . . .
Lady Oxford was at Paris when Bonaparte escaped
from Elba, and was privy to his design. Much of the
correspondence with his party in France passed through
her hands. The Bourbon Government became sus-
picious, but her ladyship was sufficiently adroit to
transfer the suspicion from herself to Lord Oxford,
who knew nothing about her manœuvres. He was
arrested, but soon set free and cleared from suspicion. . . .
Her dexterity was highly satisfactory to Bonaparte. . . .
Scott once visited Joseph Bonaparte in London, and
thanked him for his gracious reception, when Joseph,
who was aware of Lady Oxford's good offices, replied
that any member of Scott's family could meet no other.
. . . A duel story Moore tells in his diary reminds me
of the following :—Frederic Scott was rudely pushed
by some person in the pit of the Edinburgh theatre.
In the course of the scuffle his assailant waxed pugnacious, and demanded Frederic's card, at the same time
tendering his own. Frederic, who had no stomach
for a duel, quietly took from his pocket his tailor's card,
which he happened to have, and presented to the quarrel-
some gentleman some such legend as, ' Angus M'Kinlay,
tailor, 496 Lawnmarket.' The sublime disdain with
which the adversary passed from bullying to contempt
was very amusing. . . . When the Chevalier Stuart sent
me the German translation of *Saints and Sinners*, a title
subsequently plagiarised by Dr Doran, I at first felt
extremely vain of what I deemed a proof of its merit,

and I mentioned the translation to C. G. Duffy, who said, "That is fame." But my conceit was a good deal taken down on discovering that the translator had also brought out, at the same publishing house in Augsburg, a German version of another Irish story, which I charitably refrain from naming, and which struck me as such unmitigated rubbish that a translation of my book by a man who had so little discrimination as to translate the other, was certainly no compliment.[1] . . .

November 21*st.* This week two letters appeared in the *Cork Examiner,* one of them signed, 'A Catholic of Bere,' and both advocating the presentation of a testimonial from the Bere Catholics to me, in token of their gratitude for my having discomfited Puxley. There was a clever article supporting the proposal, which, however, I have written to reject. . . .

December 6*th.* Went to Cork. Travelled on the coach with the Reverend Mr Freke. . . . He knew, when a boy, the great Henry Grattan, and was often a guest at Tinnehinch. Grattan was delightfully playful with children. His dress at Tinnehinch was a court-cut brown coat. Freke said, "My relatives, the Tighes, all voted against the Union, but things are altered now," and so forth. I said I knew of no alteration that had occurred which could render it advantageous for Ireland that her national purse should be controlled by another nation. . . .

8*th.* . . . Found . . . letters from two western priests

---

[1] About this time Mr Daunt engaged in a brisk controversy with Mr H. L. Puxley, of Dunboy Castle, on certain points of Catholic teaching and practice impeached by that gentleman.—ED.

. . . from Father Endright, conveying hopes of Episcopal adhesions to the Disestablishment agitation, if the English Voluntaries consent to satisfactory terms of union.

21st. Got the address from the Berehaven Catholics, thanking me for having defended creed and country against Puxley's slanders. The letters signed by Puxley were, it seems, written by his brother-in-law, the Reverend Mr Waller. The address is signed by about a thousand persons.

29th. Read Mrs Crowe's *Nightside of Nature*. . . . My grandmother Wilson had a story of two English farmers travelling to some country town to transact business at a fair. They were friends, and having spent the day together, were desirous, possibly for mutual protection, to occupy the same bedroom at the inn where they dined. But the inn was quite full, and there was only one bed vacant, too small to accommodate more than one sleeper. One of the friends accordingly sought a bed in another inn, which did not, it seems, enjoy the best reputation. During the night the farmer who remained at the first inn was startled by dreaming that his friend appeared at his bedside, exclaiming, "Save me! save me! If you don't, I shall be murdered!" The dream awakened him, but when awake he speedily shook off the terror, saying, "It's only a dream." He soon fell asleep again, and dreamed that his friend reappeared, and more urgently renewed his appeal, saying, "If you don't come at once you will be too late." Again the dreamer awoke, and again satisfied himself that it would be foolish and idle to act on the visions of sleep. He composed himself once more to sleep, but immediately dreamed that his friend appeared a third time, ghastly and bleeding, and that he said, " You would not heed my previous calls. I have been murdered; but watch in the morning before dawn for a large cart loaded with straw passing out of the inn yard where I slept ; remove the straw, and you will find my corpse." This last warning he did not disregard. He provided help, watched the gate of the inn yard, saw, in the darkness that preceded the dawn, the cart passing out, as foreshadowed in his dream, stopped it, and found beneath the straw the murdered body of his friend. . . . When old Mrs Crawford of Tullamore was in her last illness, her daughter (my grandmother Wilson) attended her until pretty late in the night, and then returned to her own house, which was next door, and went to bed. She had not been very long in bed when there passed through the room a mighty sound as if of rushing wings. The sound seemed to enter from the wall next Mrs Crawford's house, and to pass out through the opposite wall. At the same instant a messenger knocked at the hall door to say that the old lady had just died. " And the rushing wings?" I said to Mrs Wilson, when she told me the incident, "how do you account for them?" " It was Azrael, the Angel of Death," said she, solemnly. She entertained no doubt of it.

CHAPTER XIX

Some Amusing Falsehoods—Major Spread's Leniency—Bulwer
and Scott—Spurgeon and the Queen—Disendowment.

1863. . . . *March 1st.* A lecture delivered at Bantry
by a Reverend Alexander Wilson has been sent me.
The reasonings are bosh, but their weakness is fully
compensated by the strength of the lies. One of these
is that Catholics can purchase for £4, 1s. 8d. permission
from their ecclesiastical magnates to murder father,
mother, brother or sister. . . . Says the Reverend A.
Wilson : 'For murder committed *by* a bishop, abbot,
chief of an order, or knight, each £50, 12s. 6d. For
murder *by* a friar or guardian of a monastery, £40, 9s.
For murder *of* a priest by a layman, £6, 2s.' Hence it
would seem that the Catholic clergy, by whom we are
to suppose this scale of prices was enacted, value the
lives of the laity at a much higher rate than they value
their own, since a bishop or abbot must pay £50, 12s. 6d.
for permission to murder anybody, lay or clerical,
whereas a layman can get leave to murder a priest for
the small sum of £6, 2s. The authority quoted for this
absurd string of lies is Anthony Egan, who, though the
parson does not mention it, lived in the age of Oates
and Bedloe, and was a renegade of the Achilli stamp.
. . . After he had trafficked as far as he could on Pro-

testant credulity, he is said to have returned, with what degree of penitence, heaven knows, to the Church he had deserted and maligned. . . .

April 20th. Apropos des bottes. Story of a benevolent duellist. Major Spread of Merrion Square, a crack shot, could hit to a hair's-breadth. He challenged, or was challenged by, a young man who had a passion for music, and played the violin enchantingly. They fought. " I treated him leniently," said the major ; " I could have killed him, but I didn't. I shot off three fingers from his bow hand and spoiled his music." There is a story, probably more *vraisemblable* than *vrai*, that Roger O'Connor had arranged to fight a duel with the first Earl of Bandon, who was renowned as a fire-eater. Time, 5 o'clock A.M. ; place, Desert graveyard. True to his appointment, Lord B. was on the spot, but his antagonist did not appear. Perhaps on second thoughts he considered that, being sprung ' from the royal race of Ireland,' it would be an unworthy condescension to fight a mere Union earl. . . .

July 19th. Youghal. . . . Walked to . . . the churchyard, where Hickman Watkins's grave is as bare of grass as ever ; Burke vowing that he twice sowed grass seeds on it and that they refused to grow.

24th. Sailed in the *Collieen Bawn* from Dublin to Glasgow. Saw in a Scotch newspaper that Spurgeon, the noted Dissenting preacher, joins a Scotch minister, named Candlish, in attacking the Queen for having inscribed a verse from ' Apocryphal ' Scripture on the cairn to Prince Albert. These preachers would not thus assail Her Majesty had she inscribed on the cairn a paragraph or two from their sermons.

25th. Arrived at Edinburgh. . . .

29th. Reached home at 9 p.m. . . .

September 23*d.* Read a book by a Mr Bennett of Bandon, called *A History of Bandon.* . . . It has some trifling particulars of the ancient O'Muirillys or Hurleys of Ballinacarriga and Ballyward, which Bennett spells Ballinvard. In a list of the persons indebted to one George Fenton of Bandon in 1641, he names 'William Mac Randal Hurley, Ballinvard, gentleman.' This designation apparently implies that William was the son of Randal ōge Hurley of Ballinacarriga, of whom the author records that he joined with, and fought hard for, the 'rebels,' and paid the penalty of ill success. His estates were forfeited as well as his castle, and Randal ōge remained a hunted outlaw till his death. He now rests in the little moss-grown graveyard of Fanlobbus, and sleeps his long sleep by the side of his faithful wife, Catherine O'Cullinane. . . .

October 25*th.* There have been meetings of the peasantry in Tipperary to renew their declaration of national Irish politics. I hear that a similar one is to take place between this and Skibbereen. . . . The taxation grievance helps largely to depopulate the country. People migrate when home presents no field for their industry. . . .

November 11*th.* Wrote a letter to the *Times* on the Anti-Irish State Church, signed, 'An Irish Catholic Landlord.' . . .

18*th.* The *Times* of the 16th came this morning. It contains my letter printed in a prominent part of the paper.[1] . . .

23*d.* Letter from the editor of the *Times*, enclosing

---

[1] This letter, and others that followed, produced a considerable impression at the time.—ED.

a note from Mrs Vavasour of Hazlewood Castle, Tad-
caster, inquiring the name of the 'Irish Catholic Landlord,' whose letter on the Anti-Irish State Church has
much pleased the querist.   I have authorised the editor
to gratify the lady's curiosity. . . .

25th. Wrote to the secretary of the Liberation Society
to beg that our English sympathisers may prepare
petitions to Parliament against that great national sin
—the 'Irish' State Church. The Archbishop of Cashel
writes to tell me that his brother prelates have determined on getting up diocesan and parochial petitions
throughout Ireland.   I do my poor best, urging or
soliciting the action of abler agitators than my failing
health permits me to emulate.   The *Nonconformist* re-
prints my letter to the *Times*, and calls it 'admirable.' . . .

December 8th. The secretary of the Liberation Society
writes to say that the Anti-State Church committee
have resolved against petitioning the present House of
Commons any more, deeming its prejudices insurmount-
able.   But they will help us all they can by articles in
the British press, and by giving the disendowment of
our execrable nightmare a prominent place in their
coming programme of electoral action. . . .

29th. Letter from the Archbishop of Cashel. His
Grace thinks it is capable of proof that the early Irish
Catholic Church was supported purely on the principle
of voluntaryism, and he has some notion of republishing
in a pamphlet an article on this subject, formerly contributed by him to a review.

CHAPTER XX

1864. . . . *January 6th.* Epiphany. The death of the Earl of Charlemont is announced. He was one of the few remaining members of the Irish Parliament. In 1843 O'Connell wrote to him, entreating him to join the Repeal agitation. He told O'Connell's envoy that he would return a written answer next day, but, so far as I know, omitted to write. O'Connell firmly believed that his lordship's principles were those of Irish nationality, but that his Whig friends would not allow him to act on them. . . .

February 7th. Letter from John Martin of Kilbroney, asking permission to insert my name in the list of a provincial committee of repealers. Although I see no grounds for expecting proximate triumph, yet I comply with readiness. . . .

18th. My daughter tells me a picturesque dream story. Sister J. F.'s father had two sons. One night he dreamed that he lay in bed with his two boys, one on each side; that the canopy of the bed was suddenly raised, and that a huge hand descended and carried off one of the boys. The child soon after died. In about a twelvemonth the father again dreamed the same dream, and awaking, he lay in an agony of fear lest the dream should be realised. His fear was too well founded. In a short time the remaining boy died. A year subsequently, the bereaved father dreamed that the same gigantic hand carried himself off. He made his will, prepared for death, and in a short time followed his sons from this world. Another story. One night the lads at a college in France were talking of graves, ghosts and sundry germane subjects. One student boasted of his freedom from superstitious fears. His companions dared him to walk alone to the end of the burial vaults under the church. He undertook to perform this deed of valour. At twelve o'clock he contrived to get out of the house ; the grated gates were unlocked, and the valiant student entered the dark abode of the dead. His companions in the dormitory awaited his return with some anxiety, but he came not. Alarmed at last at his non-appearance, they aroused the Prefect and President, and candidly owned what they had done. Lights were procured ; the vaults were entered, and at their farther extremity the unfortunate student was discovered on the floor quite dead, his soutane being caught by a nail in the adjacent wall. It could only be surmised that the nail having caught his gown in the dark, he, fancying he was detained by some unearthly hand, had died of fright. *Apropos* of ghosts. A spectre is said to haunt the road about half way between this place and Ballinacarriga Castle. One night when riding home late from Dunmanway, I found it nearly impossible to make my horse approach the spot of evil repute. He stared and winced and swerved first one way and then another, and would do anything but go on. I, of course, saw nothing unchancy ; but those who are learned in such matters say that animals are sharper than their masters in discerning the presence of spiritual beings. . . .

April 24th. Not very well for some time past. Rode to Brook Park and dined. . . . We looked over some old letters to my grandfather, interesting at least as holographs of men who made some noise in their day. Secretary Hutchinson ; the celebrated Earl of Bristol, who, as Bishop of Derry, raised a troop of volunteer dragoons in 1782 ; Lord Lifford ; Luke White, the bookseller, whose grandson has lately been raised to the peerage ; the notorious Paddy Duigenan, remarkable for infuriate hostility to Ireland and the Irish Catholics ; Howley, who was afterwards Archbishop of Canterbury, and who announces his presentation to a living in England, worth £200 a year, by the Marquis of Abercorn. Howley says, that although this seems insignificant when compared with 'your great Irish livings,' yet it is acceptable to him . . . from Lord Mountjoy, the descendant of the footman, sarcastically mentioned by Swift as " a fellow in Ireland, who, from a shoeboy, grew to be several times one of our chief governors, wholly illiterate, and with hardly common sense." (See *Swift's Letters to Gay,* 28th August 1731.)

May 8th, Sunday. Ballinacarriga. Before Mass I exhorted the congregation to sign the anti-tithe petition, and after Mass we had our tables superintended by the schoolmasters, who looked on at the work of signature. The petition was posted to Mr Dillwyn, M.P.

20th. The death of William Smith O'Brien is announced. He was in his sixty-first year. A braver, truer heart than O'Brien's never existed. . . . I remember the proud day when O'Brien introduced Henry

Grattan at Conciliation Hall, and moved his admission amid the cheers of a crowded and enthusiastic audience. One after another old confederates drop into the grave. . . . The busiest bit of Irish politics just now is Colonel Dunne's committee to inquire into Irish taxation. . . . Mr Napier's evidence was miserable. He advocated an equality of taxation between this country and Great Britain, dropping out of consideration the enormous inequality of the two debts, and the vast difference of relative taxable ability. . . .

June 29th. . . . Here is a story of a bull hunt told me by O'Connell many years ago. When the Great Dan was about sixteen years old, he joined a party, headed by a Mr Marcus O'Sullivan, to attack seven bulls that ranged the island of Deenish. This was a dangerous adventure, as the bulls generally resisted all attempts to land on the island. Marcus and his friends were all armed with guns loaded with bullets. When they reached the island they found the bulls all fighting each other, and one bull was killed in the taurine scrimmage. This reduced their numbers to six. Marcus fired at the largest of the survivors. The ball, grazing his shoulder, and tearing the flesh upwards, did not kill the brute, but rendered him furious. He rushed at Marcus, who could only save himself by flinging his person over a high rock that overhung the sea, and to which he clung by holding on to the long grass that grew in the crevices. The bull dashed headlong over the precipice, clearing Marcus in his descent, and was killed by his fall upon the rock some hundreds of feet beneath. There were then only five bulls. John Burke, a schoolmaster, presented his piece at one of them ; but the bull he aimed at appeared to anticipate his purpose, and rushed violently at the pedagogue, who, in his panic, did not fire, but sought safety by getting into some crevice where the bull could not follow him.　O'Connell said naively, "We youngsters, who had often been pestered with Mr Burke's teachings, were sorry our bothering schoolmaster was not killed !"　The bulls had soon another fight, in which three of them were pushed into the sea over the rocks and were drowned.　There remained but two, which were easily despatched. . . .

July 19*th*. Youghal.　Letter from —— announcing that John Henry Newman has sent me a presentation copy of his celebrated *Apologia pro Vita Suâ*.　I am grateful for the gift, and a little surprised that the great Oratorian should have thought of me.

23*d*. Henry Gumbleton of Fort-William arrived.　He is in the 60th Rifles.　He amused me with regimental stories and accounts of what he has seen in America. He has been in gambling-houses where each player had a pile of money and a loaded revolver before him.　The revolver was only to be discharged if the *vis-à-vis* either showed the least appearance of foul play, or looked as if he suspected it.　Some fellows had small revolvers in their wide trousers pockets, and would fire them through their pockets at the opposite player, on real or fancied provocation.

25*th*. Henry Gumbleton tells a story of Gervase Bushe, who is very deaf.　Some gentleman, who, I presume, had a facetious reputation, lost his father, and said to Gervase, next whom he was seated at dinner, " My father is dead."　" Capital fun ! capital fun ! ha, ha, ha !" exclaimed Gervase, not hearing the mournful words, but taking for granted that his funny friend had uttered some witticism at which it would be polite to laugh. Mrs Daunt says, that when Mrs W—— of this town died, her disconsolate husband put his hams and his candlesticks into mourning, decorating them with black paper.

August 3d. Returned home. . . . Found a card of invitation to the banquet to come off in the Rotundo on the 8th inst., on the occasion of laying the foundation stone of the O'Connell monument. . . . I am pledged to attend the contemplated Repeal meeting whenever it is held, and one political trip to Dublin will be quite enough for me just now.

9th. Letter from John Martin, asking permission to nominate me one of the Repeal Directory of five. . . .

September 8th. The *Times* not having printed my recent letter on the Viceroyalty and the State Church, Mr Carvell Williams sent a copy of it to the *Morning Star*, in last Thursday's issue of which it occupies a prominent place.

9th. The *Times* has printed my letter, though somewhat of the latest. . . .

10th. Letter from the Archbishop of Cashel warmly congratulating me on my letter. . . .

30th. The *Times* has published four letters of mine. The last was in reply to a Mr W. J. Lawson, who attacked some of my statements on Irish finance and its mismanagement. . . .

October 24th. The stir we have made about Irish fiscal wrongs has compelled the Government to issue a tract in self-defence. This is a report to the Viceroy by Dr Neilson Hancock on the public accounts between Great Britain and Ireland, and it is precisely such a combination of balderdash, falsehood and impudence as

might have been expected. J. B. Dillon is writing a
reply. . . .

   29th. There has been canvassing on behalf of R.
Longfield . . . in the town of Mallow. . . . I was once
returned for Mallow, having gone through a course of
agitation, and having been hooked in for disbursements,
which I could not afford, by promises of pecuniary aid
which were not realised. In London I was made very
ill by the late hours and the unwholesome atmosphere of
the House of Commons. Its political atmosphere was
still worse than its physical. I felt a painful sense of
humiliation at being delegated to represent an Irish
constituency in a foreign assembly. The House was
then engaged in passing the Irish Coercion Bill. . . . I
had no inclination to go anywhere. I declined an invitation to dine with the Speaker. . . . I was confined
to bed for some time with a feverish complaint, during
which I was attended with great kindness by Dr Baldwin,
M.P. for the City of Cork. There was a successful
petition against my return, containing a variety of allegations ; such as votes having been given me by persons
not entitled to the borough franchise, treating, bribery (!),
non-qualification, and other charges which I do not
now remember. I consulted O'Connell as to the course
I should take. He promised me his best assistance,
caught the breast of my coat, and said, in the most
fatherly and affectionate manner, " I shall treat you in
this as if you were my own son." . . . We had three or
four conversations on the subject, of which the result was
that O'Connell, who was personally acquainted with my
opponent, undertook to arrange with him that I should
withdraw, provided that certain changes (suggested by
O'Connell) should be made in the petition. . . . In the

confident expectation that this arrangement would be
effected, I arrived at Kilcascan early in April. I had
not been many weeks at home when intelligence reached
me that I had been unseated with costs. As I had confidently reckoned on the intervention of O'Connell to
prevent such an event, I was extremely surprised, and I
wrote to him to request an explanation. He excused
himself by saying that he had seen it stated in some
newspaper that I intended to defend, and that under that
erroneous impression he had omitted to make the promised arrangement with my opponent. . . . Had my
seat been in College Green instead of St Stephen's, I
would have struggled to keep it. Not the least disagreeable part of the affair was the bitter persecution
inflicted on my voters by their landlords. . . .

November 5th. Letter from J. B. Dillon announcing
that a new agitation for Tenant Right, Disendowment of
the State Church, and Free Education is contemplated
by the Bishops and a large number of laymen. He
hopes I will help. . . .

25th. Newspapers mention much excitement in Ger-
many occasioned by the execution of Muller, the German
assassin in London. . . . This reminds me in a roundabout
way of a story O'Connell or somebody told of the only
act of clemency I ever heard ascribed to Lord Norbury.
He had tried a murderer whose guilt was indisputable.
To everyone's astonishment he charged the jury strongly
for an acquittal. The Crown prosecutor ventured to
interrupt the charge by recalling to his lordship's recollection portions of the evidence that left no doubt of the
prisoner's guilt. " I know all that, my good fellow," responded his lordship in a sort of stage *aside*, " but I
hanged six men at the last Tipperary Assizes who were

innocent, so I'll let off this poor devil now to square matters." . . . O'Connell's duel with Peel was commonly talked of when impending, and O'Connell was apprehended and bound over to keep the peace. His unfriends suggested that this was done with his connivance. Pleading in court, before Lord Norbury, he urged an argument which the judge did not seem to appreciate. " I fear, my lord," said O'Connell, " that your lordship does not exactly apprehend me ? " " Oh, that would be impossible," replied the ermined punster; " there is no man so *easily apprehended* as Mr O'Connell." Illustrative of Lord Eldon's tenacity of office and its emoluments, O'Connell told the following incident :—" Eldon asked an old lawyer why he quitted the Bar. ' Because, my lord, I am old.' ' Why, I am older,' said Lord Eldon. ' My lord, I am deaf.' ' I am more deaf,' said his lordship. ' My lord, I am blind.' ' I am blinder.' ' My lord, I am rich enough.' Lord Eldon," said O'Connell, " did not add, ' So am I.' " . . . Another of Lord Norbury's puns. The State surgeon is entitled to wear military uniform. A gentleman to whom that functionary was unknown, asked Norbury, at a Castle levée, who was that distinguished - looking officer. " That officer," replied his lordship, " is the general of the *lancers.*"

December 28th. Dublin. Visited Dillon. . . . He divides the anti-State Church resolution into two parts. The Archbishop is to move the first, and I am to move the second.

29th. Our meeting went off very well. . . . My motion was seconded by Kenelm Digby, son of the author of the *Ages of Faith, Compitum,* etc. Kenelm, junior, is one of the handsomest young men I have

seen. He told me his classical instructor was Paley
of Cambridge, a convert to the Catholic Church,
and grandson of the celebrated Archdeacon of
Carlisle.

CHAPTER XXI

Mr Blake and the Teacher—Eccentricities of Cupid—An Ecclesiastical Highwayman — The Bishop's Leddy—A Nocturnal Visit — Bandon ruined by Free Trade — Government and the Fenians—Captain Groves, R.N.— A Lawyer outwitted—The *Cromwellian Settlement.*

1865.—*January 1st.* Heard Mass at the Catholic University. . . . After Mass I was shown through the University, the *ci-devant* mansion of 'Jerusalem' Whalley, or Buck Whalley, as he was indifferently called.

3d. . . . Attended a meeting of the committee. The *Times* correspondent says my speech was able and elaborate. . . . Went in the evening to John Martin's monthly meeting of the Repeal League. . . . Visited O'Connell's old friend, P. V. Fitzpatrick, on whom I do not find that years have made much impression. Story told by him of Anthony Richard Blake, when Commissioner of Public Education. Blake crossed the Shannon in an open boat unaccompanied by any of his official *confrères*, and met on the Galway side a sanctimonious-looking man in rusty black clothes, a teacher under the Board of Education, who took Blake for a Protestant. " Oh, sir," said this functionary, " I am spreading the gospel finely here. I go to Mass, and the priests all think I am a Papist, but I am cramming the children with the Protestant Bible and the Protestant Catechism *unknownst.*   Oh, I am spreading the Reformation wonderful, and the priests don't suspect a bit of it." " My good man," said Blake, "you certainly don't know that I am a Catholic." " Bless my soul," cried the teacher, " I never guessed that! Why, then, I suppose your honour is Mr Blake." " You never made a better guess ; I am Mr Blake." " Whisper, your honour," said the fellow, confidentially, " don't believe one word I said now. That is what I tell the Protestant Commissioners when they come my way. But faith, I'm training the children up in the true old religion. There isn't a man in the Board's employment that's doing more for Catholicity than I am." Fitzpatrick did not say whether Blake got the comical rascal dismissed. He also told a *mot* of V. Scully, smart enough. Whiteside, or perhaps some other Protestant champion, coming out of the House of Commons after a debate in which polemic bitterness had mingled, said, " I think all this controversy nonsense. I have been for forty years studying the case of the two Churches, and I cannot find any great difference between them." " My good sir," replied Scully, "you won't be five minutes in the other world before you will find out the difference."

11*th.* Letter from the secretary of the Liberation Society, saying that the committee have ordered the publication of my recent speech in a pamphlet for circulation in Great Britain. . . .

13*th.* The *Scotsman* throws cold water on our movement, but civilly says that my speech left nothing to be desired in the way either of ability or of candour. The *Caledonian Mercury* makes civil mention of our doings in a long and really able article ; one of the best I have seen. . . .

March 1st. Youghal. Father Foley, one of the curates here, came this morning to introduce me to Mr Barry, candidate for this county, who is now on his canvass. Barry is said to be a millionaire; is chairman of the Assam Tea Company; talks very orthodox patriotism; professes adhesion to the new association. . . .

9th. Eccentricities of Cupid. Mrs Daunt tells of the loves of a Miss P——, aged over fifty, and the Reverend Mr B——, rector of Templemichael, who is more than seventy. Miss P——, finding that the gentleman had succeeded to a property of £300 a year, made love to him, and contrived to elicit a promise of marriage. When matters had gone pretty far, he wished to recede, but the lady refused to relinquish her reverend prize. He offered her £200 to be released from his engagement, but Miss P—— would not take less than £400. This sum he was unable to give, and not wishing to encounter an action for breach of promise he married Miss P——. That lady had no one to give her away, except her nephew, a lad of sixteen. The young gentleman declared he would not give his aunt away unless she paid him ten shillings for the performance of that painful duty. She seemed to consent, but after the completion of the ceremony she put him off with a crown. Mrs Daunt said that, at a ball in Cork some years ago, Miss K——, daughter of the Protestant Bishop of Cork, fell, while dancing with an officer. Mrs K—— reproached the officer with not having upheld his partner. He replied that he would have done so if he had anything to hold, but that Miss K—— was squeezed into nothing by tight lacing. *Apropos* of Mrs K——, it is said that, not having brought out her purse, she asked

for some articles on credit at Carmichael's shop in
Patrick Street. " Impossible, madam," said the Scotch
clerk ; " the rule of the house is cash payments." " Oh,
but you might surely oblige *me*. Perhaps you don't
know that I am the Bishop's lady." " The Bishop's
leddy ! " echoed the inexorable Caledonian, " troth, an'
if ye were the Bishop's wife hersel, we wadna' break the
rule of the hoose for ye.'

March 27th. Dublin. . . . Met Captain Coventry
and his wife at my cousin's, Kitty M——. They are
Scotch, and I like the Scotch. Talking of the present
American War, he said there was no military skill displayed in it; all was brute force. When hosts were
killed, fresh hosts were poured in to fill up the gaps. . . .

April 26th. Letter from Colonel Scott, who says
that in the *Times* of the 16th of last December a biogra-
phical work is reviewed in which it is mentioned that
Dr Twysden, Protestant Bishop of Raphoe, finding his
diocesan revenue insufficient for his expenditure, supplied the deficiency by occasionally exercising the profession of a highwayman on his visits to England. In
1754 he stopped a gentleman on Hounslow Heath, and
desired him to stand and deliver. But the traveller answered with a pistol shot. The ball passed through the
Bishop's intestines, and his lordship's death was announced in the *Gentleman's Magazine* as having occurred
from inflammation of the bowels. . . . The story was
canvassed by some of Scott's neighbours. One Protestant gentleman was indignant that the *Times* should
print anything so derogatory to the fair fame of the
Anglo-Irish Church; whilst another, also a Protestant,
surprised Scott by saying that he did not think so
badly of Twysden, who robbed in a bold, straightfor-

ward manner at the risk of his life, while all the other Irish parsons robbed under shelter of the law. . . .

May 29th. Letter from the English Liberation Society announcing that they have placed me in nomination for election to their council. If I don't mistake, they paid me this compliment before, but I then declined the office, as I must also do now. . . .

26th. Last night, about an hour after midnight, I heard steps, and men talking in front of the house. The talkers seemed to make a circuit of the house, after which they knocked at the door. I asked, from my window, who was there. "Travellers." "Where from ?" "Ballyneen." "Where were they going ?" "To Skibbereen." "Then," said I, "travel yourselves out of that ; this is a strange and improper hour to stroll about the country." "Oh, is that the way ?" said the spokesman. He then conversed for a moment with his comrade, and after some delay they both departed. After leaving this they went to the gate lodge and called Singleton, the lodge-keeper, to admit them. One of them, he said, was dressed in a sort of military uniform, and announced himself as an American Fenian. He called for a drink of water, and, on paying fourpence for it, displayed a number of large gold coins. He told Singleton that he had come here to have a conference with me. S. replied that he would have a better chance of meeting me . . . in the daytime. The Fenian rejoined that when he should next come Mr Daunt should receive him were the hour two o'clock in the morning, or else he would burn the house. . . . To-day I apprised the assembled magistrates at Ballyneen of what had occurred. There have been nocturnal drillings of country lads and town shopboys by disbanded militia men. I told the magistrates that many poor fellows were induced to join the Fenian movement by a sense of great national oppression, which was not the less deeply seated because it was vague. . . .

July 12*th*, 13*th*. Both days canvassers, in the interests of Mr Barry, came here to ask my vote for the county. . . . Scully voted for the renewed imposition of the Income Tax on Ireland, alleging that his object in voting for that tax (which up to this time has drawn nearly nine millions sterling out of the country) was 'to recognise the unity of the two countries.' We must get rid of a gentleman who entertains such expensive notions of 'unity.' He is a 'Catholic,' forsooth. Hang your sneaking, anti-Irish Catholic !

22*d*. Went to Bandon. Plumped for Barry. . . . Scully nowhere.

August 5*th*. I have been slowly and carefully reading Colonel Dunne's Blue Book on Irish taxation. The fixed idea of the English members of the committee evidently is that Ireland has not the smallest right to her own public revenues; that England is entitled, under the convenient designation of 'the Empire,' to abstract them from Ireland at discretion, and is not bound to refund a farthing. The 5th clause of the 7th article of the 'Union,' which professes to guarantee to Ireland the use of her own money, never enters into their thoughts. Their sole system of Irish finance consists in grasping everything and refunding nothing, except the sums necessary for the support of the English interests in our country. . . .

8*th*. Went to Bandon. Mr W. C. Sullivan. . . . brought me through his tanning establishment. . . . He has also commenced a factory for the making of first-class 'uppers' by machinery. . . . Of the decay of Bandon he gave me the following account. In 1825, according to Lewis's *Topographical Dictionary*, it contained a population of 14,000, which, by the census of 1861, has dwindled to 6100. In the days of its prosperity, the town contained 7000 persons supported by the manufacture of linen, woollen, ticken, corduroys or cotton and leather. Bandon was the centre of a district that included Dunmanway, Timoleague, Kilbrittain, Ballyneen and Enniskean, all which places were more or less injured by its fall. Mr Sullivan ascribes the ruin of the manufacturers of Bandon to the removal of certain protective duties in 1825, after which date the country was exposed to the overwhelming competition of English (and other) manufacturers. . . .

25th. Mr Bence Jones sends me a printed statement of how he has managed his estate for a quarter of a century. It is a very shrewd and able paper, drawn up by one who has discovered the knack of making his land productive, not only of crops, but of money. . . .

September 1st. Wrote a letter to be read at the monthly meeting of the Repeal League. . . .

11th. My letter to the League was read. . . . and 'evoked expressions of dissent and disappointment from some of the members.' This was because I inculcated pacific agitation. . . . A priest from New York, a Father Evans, met me the other day in Cork, and said that the leaders of the Fenian society in America were enjoying handsome incomes from the funds subscribed by their credulous disciples.

12th. . . . When the priests condemned Fenianism in the confessional and refused the sacraments to persons connected with it, many of the Fenian youths of Cork gave up going to confession to priests who had been educated at Maynooth ; but some of them confessed to priests brought up in foreign seminaries.

17*th*. Tom Grier arrived. . . . Story told him by Dixie Clement of C. J. Fox. Fox having made a magnificent speech on some important question was met in the Lobby by a political opponent whom his eloquence had failed to convince. " Mr Fox," said the foe, " I admire your abilities, but—d—n your principles ! " Fox instantly retorted : " And I, sir, admire your sincerity, but—d—n your manners ! " The Government have arrested nearly thirty Fenians in Dublin and Cork ; the Cork prisoners having been betrayed by a fellow-conspirator named Warner, who, it is said, had reached the rank of colonel in the invisible army. This ' colonel,' having failed to get money for his support from the brotherhood, applied for relief at the Bandon workhouse, in which he spent three months. His circumstances being desperate, he resolved on replenishing his pocket by turning informer. . . . Colonel Scott once heard a discussion at Falkirk concerning the prudence of emigrating from Scotland to Ireland. " Life is not safe among the Paddys," said one speaker. " Ay," said another ; " but they only shoot their ain blackguards." . . .

October 4th. Story of Captain Groves, R.N., who insisted on disbelieving the existence of some dangerous sunk rocks to the north of Sicily, called the Esquerques. They were covered with about ten feet of water. An officer, subordinate to Groves, obtained a small vessel from Government, and from numerous fragments of wreck that floated in the neighbourhood of the rocks, he at last discovered their exact locality, and mapped them. Groves, perhaps jealous that the discovery was not made by himself, persevered in saying there were no such rocks, and pooh-poohed the map. Some time afterwards he was conveying the British Minister from Naples, and he ordered the pilot to steer directly over the course in which the rocks were mapped. The pilot remonstrated, but Groves was peremptory. . . . Groves then descended to the cabin, where the Ambassador said to him, " We should be near the Esquerques now." "They are all imaginary," answered Groves; "we are steering right over the spot where they are falsely said to exist." He had scarcely spoken when the ship struck with tremendous force. Her destruction was instant and complete. It was *sauve qui peut.* Boats were lowered hurriedly. Groves did his best to facilitate escape, but some lives were lost. On being urged to get into a boat, the unlucky, headstrong man declared that he would not survive his vessel, and wilfully perished with the wreck. . . . Story of the artist who was employed to paint Abraham preparing to sacrifice Isaac, and who represented the patriarch pointing a horse pistol at his son. . . .

20th. The Fenian conspiracy has its ludicrous incidents. A man named Jerry Coffey was imprisoned at Killarney, on the evidence of one Sullivan, who swore that he saw Coffey shouldering the handle of a brush in his father's brush shop. Four chimney sweepers marched through a town in this county (Passage, I think), shouldering their long brush handles, whereupon they were made State prisoners.

21st. . . . Grier tells a story of an old Miss Thewles, aged 75, who contested a property of £400,000 with a Widow Kelly. Judge Keatinge decided in Mrs Kelly's favour. Miss Thewles appealed from his decision to the

Court of Delegates, and obtained a reversal of the judgment. On the strength of this, her counsel, Mr Dease, married her. The widow had offered to compromise the affair by paying Miss Thewles £50,000 ; but Dease was so confident of her final success that he would not allow her to accept the offer. Meanwhile the widow appealed from the Court of Delegates to the Lord Chancellor, Blackburne, who confirmed Judge Keatinge's original decision ; so that poor Dease found himself indissolubly linked to his bride of 75, without the consolation of the expected tocher. I visited Father O'Keeffe, C.C., who told a story of a Whiteboy who, in 1822, got up and ostentatiously marched out of the congregation in the middle of a sermon of Father Doheny's against Whiteboyism. That night he joined a gang who attacked Mr Swete's house to get arms, and was shot dead. He also told an anecdote of a woman named Towgood, whom Parson Crosthwaite, late rector of Drimoleague, had induced to become a Protestant, which she continued to be for many years. After Crosthwaite's death, O'Keeffe, passing along a lonely bohereen among the Drinagh hills, saw Mrs Towgood on her knees in a state of great excitement, invoking curses on the soul of Crosthwaite for having induced her to embrace a religion in which she did not believe. . . .

November 7th. Dublin. Repeal meeting at the National League Rooms, D'Olier Street. I spoke for about an hour and a quarter, exposed the folly of Fenianism, but showed that the national discontent, which assumed a foolish shape more or less among the Fenians, was widely spread, deeply seated and well grounded. . . . Visited Sir B. Burke, who said some interesting things about his late visit to Rome. . . . He spoke of the ancient frescoes in the catacombs, and said that these old paintings, dating from the second century, represented the celebration of Mass precisely as we see it at the present day. Sir Bernard had an audience of Pio Nono, who received him and Lady Burke very graciously. When the audience was nearly at an end, the Pope said in French, "I hope you will bring up your children Catholics." "Why should I not?" said Sir Bernard; "I am a Catholic myself." The Pope had supposed he was a Protestant. In a day or two he had another audience of His Holiness, who inquired the state of religion in Ireland; in reply to which inquiry Sir Bernard bore witness to the Catholic fidelity of the Irish people.

9*th*. Visited Burke again. He lately met, at the dinner of some literary club, the Protestant Archbishop of Dublin (Trench), the Lord Chancellor, Dr Todd of Trinity College, and a mixed company of both Protestants and Catholics. Prendergast's late book, *The Cromwellian Settlement of Ireland*, was talked of. "It is a very able and a very interesting work," said the Lord Chancellor. "With what barbarity the Irish were treated! If I were driven into Connaught, and if the women of my family were treated as Prendergast describes the women of this country to have been, by ——!" (with a tremendous oath) "I would shoot every Englishman I met!" Archbishop Trench admitted the ability of the book, but added, "Of what religion, pray, is the author?" His Grace probably expected to hear the author was a Catholic, and was a little surprised when Burke said, "He is a Protestant." Went to the Four Courts to see Dillon. . . .

13*th*. Heard from the secretary of the Liberation

Society, who enclosed from the *Times* a long letter of a parson Hincks, County Down, proposing to settle the Church Establishment question by redistributing the revenues and dignities on a plan of what is called 'internal reform.' . . .

15*th*. Wrote to the *Times* under the signature of 'An Irish Catholic,' showing the absurdity and inefficiency of Dr Hincks' scheme.

24th. Lord Lifford has replied to my letter in the *Times*. Wrote a second anti-State Church letter to the *Times* in answer to Lord L.

28*th*. Looked through a book called *Life and Times of O'Connell*, compiled by a Mr C. M. O'Keeffe. He has stolen whole passages, in one case amounting to nearly twelve consecutive pages, from my *Ireland and her Agitators* and my *Personal Recollections of O'Connell*. I never met a sample of more shameless plagiarism.[1] . . .

30*th*. Letter from Dillon, asking my thoughts on the prudent management of the State Church question at the coming assemblage of M.P.'s in Dublin. Of course the voluntary principle is the only rational basis of this agitation.

December 15*th*. The *Times*, in a recent article on the conference of members in Dublin, seems disposed to back out of its recent hostility to the anti-Irish State Church; adopts Lord Lifford's phraseology in calling Disendowment confiscation, and recommends that the Catholic clergy of Ireland should be salaried by the State. . . .

25*th*. . . . A letter from the Liberation Society, giving counsel anent Sir John Gray's approaching

[1] N. 1892. O'Keeffe died in New York, 1891. His necessities accounted for his plagiarism.

motion against the anti-Irish State Church. Wrote at once to J. B. Dillon to apprise him and Gray of the views of our English allies. Hints have been dropped in the interest of the Government about subsidising the priests, either by stipends from the Treasury or by a slice of the endowments now possessed by the State Church. . . .

30*th*. Letter from the Archbishop of Cashel, who thoroughly concurs in my views, and says that no earthly consideration shall induce the Catholic Hierarchy to place their Church on any other than its present voluntary basis.

CHAPTER XXII

Mysteries of ' Fweeling '—Memoirs of Colonel Myles Byrne
—A Freebooting Landlord—A Cockcrowing Bridegroom
—An Uncommon Partnership—Mr Pennefeather's Carri-
age—A Belligerent Quaker.

1866.—*January 6th.* The Epiphany. The two curates,
Fathers O'Keeffe and Walsh, tell me that the popular
discontent is so great that a 'rising' perhaps may
happen ere the year is out. The Fenian, Stephens,
who escaped from prison, is said to be prowling about
the country in various disguises, swearing in fresh
conscripts. . . .

10*th.* Letter from Sir B. Burke asking my opinion
about an article he means to write on the justice of excluding the peerage of Ireland from the British House
of Lords. Wrote to tell Sir Bernard that the Irish
peers had a House of their own in Dublin, and that,
as they thought good to disfranchise themselves and
break up their establishment, I could not see that we
were called on to advocate their admission to any other
House. . . .

February 9th. Fenian arrests still going on. . . .
Shrovetide approaches, and as this is the close of the
marrying season among the people, there is a little
hymeneal activity, but not much. Those who don't
get married now will dismiss matrimony from their

minds till the approach of Lent, 1867. Conny Donovan, son and heir of one of my tenants, has been 'fweeling' about for a wife. 'Fweeling' signifies casting his eyes in various directions to see which of the collieens will suit him. . . . The offer proceeds sometimes from the lady. . . . I am told that my handsome 'Gow' at Currabegs received three intimations from as many collieens that they did not object to unite their fortunes with his. But the Gow did not avail himself of the kindness of any of his three admirers. . . . A few weeks ago I saw a smart-looking man coming down the road near my gate. I asked one of my boys who he was. "That's the matchmaker," was the answer. The occupation of that functionary is to attend fairs, wakes, markets, etc., and for a fee to suggest likely chances to young men and maidens; to find out the amount of fortunes, and to carry messages between the couples or their parents. . . .

17th. Received a well-written letter from a workingman in Manchester, named Richard O'Connor, who says, "I beg leave to thank you from the bottom of my heart for your noble letter which appeared in the Liverpool *Daily Post* of yesterday in defence of the morality of dear old Ireland." I was touched by this proof of Irish and Catholic feeling in exile. He states that the morals of the English in his own class are abominably bad.

March 3d. Sent for publication to the London *Morning Star*, a letter to John Bright, M.P., entitled, 'What causes Fenianism?'

6th. Read *Memoirs of Miles Byrne*, a Wexford 'rebel' of 1798, who emigrated to France, entered the Irish Brigade under Bonaparte, and became *chef de*

bataillon immediately after the Revolution of July
1830. He was 'forced,' he says, to take part in the
struggles of Ireland, by the outrages committed on
the people. . . . He says, at page 12, that the priests
did everything in their power to stop the progress of
the Association of United Irishmen; especially Father
John Redmond. . . . When the insurrection was at
an end, Lord Mountmorris, on whose loyalty some
shade of suspicion had rested, felt it necessary to
demonstrate his devotion to the ruling powers, and
as an effectual mode of doing this, he brought Redmond a prisoner to the British camp at Gorey, with
a rope round his neck, hung him up to a tree, and
fired a brace of bullets into his body. The only
part this ill-starred priest had taken in the Rebellion, was preventing the plunder of Lord Mountmorris's house at Camolin Park. . . . The book was
printed in Paris in 1863. . . . John Martin writes
to me of Byrne: " I knew Miles Byrne intimately.
Outside my blood relations, I never loved anybody
more affectionately. He was a beautiful character,
all gentleness and courage—all simplicity and insight
—all cheerfulness and gaiety and dignity; all happy
combinations of kindly and manly qualities and
virtues. . . . I never met a more lovable man.
Up to the last he was youthful in spirit and
temper."

29*th*. Read *Rob Roy* again. . . . What Scott says
of highwaymen reminds me of a story told me many
years ago by the driver of the Dublin and Limerick
coach. Passing along a part of the road somewhere
to the south of Naas, I observed an enclosed farm
partly planted, and which had something the look

of a greatly neglected domain. The owner was a farmer, whose ancestor, about a hundred years previously, had been placed on the ground as caretaker by an Englishman, who had then recently purchased the estate, and who was a total stranger in the neighbourhood. The English purchaser having installed the peasant in the situation of caretaker, disappeared, and was never afterwards heard of. The land remained in the hands of the occupant, whose right there was nobody to challenge, and to whose posterity it descended. My informant said it was supposed the English purchaser was a highwayman who had invested the gains of his profession in the purchase of the estate, and who went over to England to make one more *coup* at Bagshot Heath or Finchley Common before finally settling down as an Irish proprietor. This supposition received some colour of probability from the fact that a formidable freebooter was killed about that time near London in the exercise of his profession. An English innkeeper in Warwickshire once mistook Feargus O'Connor for a captain of robbers, and wanted to turn him out of the inn on a tempestuous night. Feargus got his mare into the kitchen of the inn, mounted her, made her play some tricks to which he had trained her, threatened the innkeeper with an action at law for expelling a traveller on vague and unfounded suspicion from a house of public entertainment, and contrived to keep his surly host in play until dawn, when the weather cleared up. I have told this story in a novelette I once wrote, called *Flora Douglas*. Had Feargus related his adventure to anyone who had read *Flora Douglas*, he would have been taken for a plagiarist.

A mistake of this kind befell a brother officer of Colonel Scott. The officer was greatly in debt, had nothing but his pay, and spent his life in all the misery incident to such a position. Suddenly a bit of unexpected good luck threw a wealthy widow in his way, and with commendable speed he wooed and won her. The whole affair passed so rapidly that, when the bridegroom awoke on the morning succeeding his nuptials, his first impression was a hazy disbelief of his own brilliant fortune. When he convinced himself, by gazing on his bride, that his marriage was not a dream, he jumped out of bed in a rapture of triumphant delight, and, rushing to the lobby, clapped his hands to his sides and crowed loudly like a cock. Scott told this story to a Mrs Ward who used to write historiettes for magazines. She asked his permission to dress up the foregoing anecdote for one of the monthlies; he gave it on condition of her suppressing the names of the hero and heroine. To this she agreed, and the little tale appeared, I think, in *Bentley's Miscellany*. Not long afterwards a friend of Scott was invited to dine with the officers, and, in the course of the evening, Scott asked him if he did not think Captain —— a very entertaining person. "Why, yes," was the answer, "but I fear he draws the long bow. Only think of his telling me a story about his being in difficulties, and getting out of them by marrying a rich widow, and how the morning after his marriage the delight of his improved position set him crowing like a cock; why, sir, he made free with a story I lately read in one of the magazines, and passed himself off as the hero of it." "Because he *was* the hero of it," said Scott, much amused at the mode in which his brother officer unjustly incurred the suspicion of appropriating from Mrs Ward's story an adventure which was in truth his own property.

April 16*th*. . . . Sir Colman O'Loghlen promises that he will write me his views before bringing in a motion for the enfranchisement of the Irish peerage under the notice of the House of Commons. . . .

20*th*. R. G. Daunt writes that a Mr Ogilvie of London has offered him, for the modest sum of £50, manuscripts deducing our descent, not from Dauntre, but from the Seigneur d'Athis, whose name underwent successive transformations of Dauntesy, Dauntre, Dantes, D'Aunt, Daunt. Some old jest book derives the name of Jeremiah King from Cucumber, through the successive modifications of Jerry King, Jer King Gherkin and cucumber. . . .

June 2*d.* Letter from General Dunne announcing that the Government have a Bill before Parliament for re-valuing Ireland, charging half the expense upon the counties, the object being to raise the valuation for the purpose of wringing increased Income Tax out of us. . . .

26*th*. . . . Dan Conner says the railway company (W. C. R.) is insolvent. Their carriages were seized by creditors the first week they commenced running, and keepers or bailiffs travelled for a few days on board the train in order to secure the receipts, but I hear the Company have extricated themselves from their difficulties.

July 3*d.* Letter from the Archbishop of Cashel advising me to write a circular note to the prelates of his province, requesting their active assistance in our agitation for the disendowment of the State Church. Wrote to beg his grace would also write to the prelates, bespeaking their acquiescence in my request. . . .

26th. Dublin. Visited Sir B. Burke, who mentioned an acquaintance of his, the Reverend Mr Eustace, who died a few years ago, aged 95. Eustace used to call himself Lord Baltinglass, in virtue of his descent from an old peer of that name, and Burke says his pretensions were well founded. He occasionally complained that religious bigotry was more inveterate of late years than he remembered it in his young days. He said to Burke, "When I was first appointed to a parish I found the tithes inadequate to enable me to keep a French cook, as my father had done, even though I had a private allowance in addition to my income as rector. I looked about for somebody to join forces with me, and soon hit off the parish priest. We took the same house, kept a French cook between us, and were capital friends. Now that is a sample of right feeling and religious liberality you won't find in the present day."

28th. Edinburgh. . . .

30th. Ushaw, Durham. . . .

5th August. The Protestant rector of this parish, Dr Butcher, has been given the State Church bishopric of Meath, vacant by the death of Dr Singer, who is said by the newspapers to have died worth £100,000. . . . Dr Butcher . . . has made himself exceedingly busy in propagating among the students of Trinity College the preposterous figment that St Patrick and the early Irish Church were independent of the Roman See. . . .

September 7th. Read the Reverend Maziere Brady's excellent pamphlet, demonstrating the falsehood of the State Church advocates who pretend that the Irish Catholic hierarchy, save two prelates, became Protestants at the 'Reformation.' Dr Brady proves that the whole hierarchy, with the single exception of Hugh Curwen, Archbishop of Dublin, lived and died Catholics.

October 5*th.* Leopold Shuldham . . . told me an anecdote of Feargus O'Connor. He was walking over Shehy Mountain with the late Mr William Shuldham and some ladies, when the path was crossed by a marshy vein about four or five feet wide, which brought the ladies to a standstill. Feargus, outdoing the exploit of Sir Walter Raleigh, flung himself on his back across the vein, and begged the ladies to do him the honour of walking over him to the opposite side.

16*th.* . . . Met Mr N——, who made some remarks on the exorbitant tithes of this and the adjacent parish of Kilmeen. He said that, when the Reverend E. Kenny was rector of Kilmeen, he was a great road-jobber, and, at the time of the 'composition,' he included his road-jobbing profits in the return he made to Government of the annual income he derived from his parish. By this ingenious scheme the tithe rentcharge of Kilmeen (saith N——) was inflated to its present large amount.

31*st.* Dublin. Visited Sir B. Burke. . . . Met The O'Donoghue, and urged him to attend the League meetings. . . .

December 5*th.* . . . Story in the *Limerick Reporter* of Mr Lysaght Pennefeather, a Protestant, son of a rector, and with many relations drawing incomes from the State Church, yet hating the system so cordially that he used to drive about the country in a gig on which, instead of armorial bearings, was painted a death's head and cross-bones, with a motto, 'To h——l with the tithes!'

7*th.* . . . T. M. Ray sends me a book by the late John O'Connell. . . . He gives a specimen of Ebenezer Jacob's style of ferocious oratory on the hustings, which reminds me of Morgan O'Connell's account of the acrimonious dialogue between that gentleman and a fishmonger, into whose shop Ebenezer went in search of fish for supper, one night on his way home from the House of Commons. Inspecting one by one the various fish displayed upon the marble counter, Ebenezer at last took up a lobster, but fastidiously replaced it, saying, "Faugh! it stinks!" "I'll trouble you, sir, not to touch any fish that you don't intend to purchase," said the shopman, very testily. "Confound you, sir!" roared Ebenezer, "do you know who I am? I am a member of Parliament, sir, and if you presumed to be insolent, I'd pitch your stinking fish into the street, and kick yourself after it!" So saying, Ebenezer swaggered out in all the glory of having bullied the fishmonger. Ebenezer was understood to be a Quaker; but it must be owned that his style of eloquence does not characterise the Society of Friends. John O'Connell says he acquired it in the navy. . . .

CHAPTER XXIII

Anti-State Church Meeting—A Militia Officer's Mother—
An Anti-Malthusian Beggar Woman—A Dishonest Uncle
—Roger O'Connor's Band of Robbers—Dr Todd's *Life
of St Patrick*—Mr Carvell Williams's Irish Mission—The
Bishops affirm the Voluntary Principle—The Glorious,
Pious and Immortal.

1867.—*January 4th.* Letter from the Archbishop of
Cashel, endorsing the doctrines of Voluntaryism, as
expressed in my letter in answer to Aubrey de Vere,
and informing me that the Cardinal (Cullen) is of the
same opinion.

5th. Dublin. . . . A heavy fall of snow last night.

7th. Conferred with Sir John Gray and Alderman
M'Swiney concerning the shape of my resolution to-
morrow.

8th. Attended the meeting of the Association.
Letters of support from many prelates. The Bishop
of Ross demands the secularisation of the State Church
revenues. My resolution, pledging the Association to
Voluntaryism, is unanimously carried.

22d. Home. . . . Someone sends me a copy of the
Tablet of the 19th, with a leading article against my
speech in Dublin. The writer tries to exhibit me in
antagonism to the Pope, because I am a Voluntary, and
he tries to show that I calumniate the Irish Catholics

because I assert that they would lose confidence in their priests if the latter were subsidised by the hostile Government of England. . . .

26th. Letter from the Archbishop of Cashel, saying that my presence in Dublin, and my speech, have done immense service. He adds, in a postscript, " Don't mind that *Tablet !* "

February 14*th.* Since the commencement of the month I have written two letters to the *Freeman's Journal* in rejoinder to Mr Aubrey de Vere, who published in several journals a commentary on my views respecting the Church Endowment question. . . .

28th. Found in my desk a few memoranda of a queer Mrs Loftus, whom I remember in Tullamore in my young days. She was daughter of a Sir Thomas Ashe. When her eldest son died, her grief found expression in the following manner : " I am the most unfortunate of women ! I have, on the same day, lost my eldest son and my pet dog ! " She had a second son, Edward, whom I also remember. He was an officer in a militia regiment, and his mamma asked his brother officers, as her son Edward was so delicate, to perform his military duties for him in rotation. Her maternal solicitude impelled her to send her kitchen-maid to follow Edward, holding an umbrella over his head as he marched with his men on a wet day. " Pray go home," said Edward, to the kitchen-maid. " Oh ! sir, let me folly you ! The misthress will kill me if I don't hold it over your honour's head ! " . . . A very gratifying letter from the Bishop of Cloyne, fully sympathising in my anti-State Endowment views.

March 1*st.* Letter from the Archbishop of Cashel expressing his unaltered concurrence in the policy I advocate.

7th. The Fenians have ' risen,' as the saying is, simultaneously at several places in Leinster and Munster. They are chiefly young men whose zeal lacks the balance of discretion. . . .

16th. Letter from Mr Carvell Williams. . . . He seems to think that this Fenian affair may accelerate the disendowment of the State Church by compelling statesmen to take measures calculated to remove or diminish the prevalent disaffection.

20th. Letter from Scott, who . . . tells a story of a very loyal gentleman in the neighbourhood of Ballintra, who in order to render his loyalty very conspicuous, employed men to watch his house at night. " One of the men so employed," says Scott, " was a youth who had sometimes carted turf for me; but instead of looking out for Fenians, he eloped with his employer's daughter. They reached Glasgow and got married before the lady's papa could catch them. "

April 7th, Sunday. A beggar woman with a baby asks alms at the window. " Madam, why do you not go to the poorhouse ? " " Musha, bad luck to it for a poorhouse ! I was in it before and eleven of my childher died in it ! " " And had you eleven children ? " I asked with some surprise. " I had fifteen, your honour," responded the prolific mendicant, who seemed not much above thirty years old. When the Poor Law was first introduced, a Dublin beggar woman, whom, in answer to a prayer for alms, a gentleman referred to the poorhouse said, " This Poor Law is a grand thing for the sowls of the jintlemen." " Why ? " " Bekaise now when we axes for alms, they only say, ' Go to the poorhouse,' but before there was a poorhouse they used to say, ' Go to the d—l ! ' "

28th. . . . The National Association have adopted the form of anti-tithe petition I sent up, praying for the secularisation of the revenues.

May 1*st.* Curious fanaticism in England. The widow of a rich grocer, thinking with Dr Cumming that the end of the world is at hand, takes it into her head that the Last Judgment will be held in her drawing-room, and spends £40,000 in fitting up that apartment for the grand occasion. . . .

26th. Not well, and was late for Mass. One of the Earls of Traquair was often late for Mass, and would saunter lazily into the chapel when it was half over, saying, in a listless, careless way, "I believe I'm late." One day the priest rejoined: "Take care, my lord, that you're not too late for Heaven." . . .

June 10*th.* . . . Story of a parson, Stratford, who was made trustee for his nieces, I suppose in the last century. He contrived to get hold of their property for his own children. His nieces went to law with him, and after much expense succeeded in putting him into jail. As the law then stood, they could not recover the property while the reverend gentleman remained incarcerated. He had the alternative of imprisonment or restitution, and he chose imprisonment. So he remained in jail till the day of his death, enjoying himself with a capital *cuisine* and jovial society, and succeeded in diverting the property to his own posterity.

26th. Letter from the secretary of the National Association, asking me to send up a resolution on the State Church to be moved at their meeting next Thursday, and a letter to be read at the meeting.

Duffy, the publisher, asks me to write a life of O'Connell. . . .

July 12*th.* This is an Orange anniversary. *Apropos* of Orangeism, I was told recently that Orangeism was the indirect occasion of the Honourable Captain Maude's conversion to the Catholic Church; he is now an Oratorian priest. He was on a visit with an Ulster parson, on whose church steeple was hoisted an Orange flag, and when Maude saw the flag, and heard the ferocious howling of the brethren on one of their field-days . . . he asked his reverend host whether it was not very wrong to tolerate such truculent insults to the population, who were admittedly well behaved and inoffensive. " I cannot help it," replied the clergyman; " I disapprove of these displays as much as anyone, but if I tried to interfere with them I really could not stand the place against the Orangemen." The answer struck Maude deeply. Here was a rector, coerced by the ruffian pressure of his bigoted and senseless flock to tolerate a system of outrageous party insult. Thus far there was no question of theology involved; but the incident led to a train of reflection and inquiry that ended in Maude's adoption of the faith to which the Orange zealots were so violently hostile. Story of old Jeffreyes of Blarney Castle 'on his keeping.' Shut up in his castle, he defied the powers of civil law, and being as secure from personal arrest as bolts and bars could make him, he collected in derision the numerous legal writs and notices served on his agents, and papered a room with them. . . .

August 7*th.* Mr W. J. Fitzpatrick kindly sends me an acceptable gift, his *Sequel to the Sham Squire.*

His appendix, which he calls a portfolio, contains a statement given on the authority of an old servant, that Roger O'Connor had a gang of robbers in his employment at Dangan, and that when leading them to attack the Athlone coach he threatened to shoot any who should lag behind. Roger was equally unscrupulous and entertaining; he could employ brigands to rob the mail and charm a refined coterie with his wit. . . .

24th. Read the *Life of St Patrick*, by Doctor Todd; an interesting book, calm and scholarly. Todd is a clever fellow, but the following lapse is amusing. St Patrick, in the agony of a nightmare, felt as if a great stone had fallen on him. He was unable to move a limb, and he says, "How it came into my mind to call out 'Helias!' I know not; but at that moment I saw the sun rising in the heavens, and while I called out, 'Helias! Helias!' with all my might, lo! the brightness of the sun fell upon me and straightway removed all the weight. And I am persuaded that I was relieved by Christ, my Lord." Dr Todd, *apropos* to the above invocation of Helias, says, "It is strange that this curious anecdote should have been taken as a proof that St Patrick practised the communion of saints. If this was an invocation of a saint, and if it was the custom of the time to invoke saints, and more particularly to invoke Helias as a saint, why did St Patrick say, 'I know not how it came into my head to call upon Helias.' Do not these words clearly prove that to invoke saints, or, at least, to invoke Helias, was a somewhat unusual thing in St Patrick's day?" Dismissing with this reasoning the idea that St Patrick was guilty of invoking a saint,

---

[1] *Query:* Helios?—ED.

Dr Todd suggests that the true reading of the passage is not Elias or Helias, but probably, " Eli, my God," which word the copyists, not being able to understand, made *Helias.* " It is therefore not improbable," says Todd, "that Patrick may have known the word *El* as a name of God or of Christ, and in his distress may have cried out, ' Eli, Eli ! ' " . . . Very good. . . . but one might as well say, " If this was an invocation of God, and if it was the custom of the time to invoke God, why did St Patrick say, ' I know not how it came into my mind to call upon God ' ? " Do not these words very clearly prove that to invoke or call upon God was a very unusual thing in St Patrick's time ? ' . . . *Quod nimis probat, nihil probat.* . . .

September 6th. Arrived, Mr Carvell Williams, secretary of the English Liberation Society, who has come to Ireland on an anti-State Church mission. . . .

7th. After breakfast Mr Williams set off to the Bishop of Ross at Skibbereen. He will visit many bishops, and will go to the north to test the feeling of the Presbyterians. He seems to be a highly intelligent and practical man of business, whose heart is in the cause of Disendowment.

26th. Letter from Scott, who is at Caen. He reports that his cousin-german, Lady Anne Harley, was converted to the Catholic Church some time ago, and lives in Italy. The Pope has made her a countess in her own right. " No great promotion," says Scott, ' for the daughter of a British peer." Her Italian title is Georgio. . . .

October 2d. Received the *London Review* of the 28th ult., containing my last article on the State Church. . . .

8th. Letter from the Archbishop of Cashel announcing the good news that the bishops, at their last meeting in Dublin, unanimously concurred in rejecting the principle of State support for the Irish Catholic Church, and recommending that the revenues should be applied to the uses of a poor rate. There is nothing now to interrupt an alliance with the English voluntaries. Verily, I have not laboured in vain. . . .

November 15*th. Dublin.* Henry Macfarlane went to hear the speeches delivered last night at the Historical Debating Society, where the name of William III. was much cheered. I remarked that the idolatry rendered by the Irish Orangemen to William had only two Irish facts to support it ; one, that he destroyed the Irish woollen trade ; the other, that he broke the Treaty of Limerick. . . . It may be remarked that William's real sentiments were not bigoted. When free from evil influence, he was so tolerant, that the Irish Orangmen, did they know his genuine disposition, would abate their enthusiasm very considerably. . . .

December 6*th.* Received an invitation to attend a funeral procession in honour of the Manchester martyrs. . . . I cannot go to Dublin, but I addressed to the secretary a letter expressing my high appreciation of the three poor fellows hanged at Manchester. . . .

16*th.* Letter from John Martin, announcing that the Government intend to prosecute him for sedition. . . . Future funeral processions in memory of Allen and his fellow martyrs are prohibited by proclamation. . . . A great explosion in London on Saturday is announced. A great part of the wall of Clerkenwell prison, where Burke the Fenian is confined, was blown down. . . .

29*th, Sunday.* Congregation disturbed by a mad woman. She fancies that the world is in a conspiracy to deprive her of her husband. (She fancies the husband too, for she never had such an adjunct.)

CHAPTER XXIV

Portrait of a Noble Lord—Mr Gladstone's Adhesion to Disen-
dowment—Mr Gladstone explains—Travelling in Swift's
Time and Since—Mr Daunt invited to Stand for Wexford—
Lord Lisle's Visit to his Property—Sir Francis Burdett and
Roger O'Connor—Roger O'Connor and Colonel Burrowes
—Adventures of Roger O'Connor's Family—The Incompar-
able Finina—Humours of Electioneering—Drinking Him-
self into Popularity—' Who killed His Washerwoman ? '

1868. . . . *January* 14*th*. Letter from Mullany's cor-
rector of the press, announcing that two cancels I had
ordered [1] are in the printer's hands. One of the can-
celled passages contained a description of an aristocratic champion of the State Church, which, on reflection, I thought might be recognised. It was the
portrait of a peer whose red, round, unmeaning face
was a faithful index of the mental stolidity of the
sensual *bon vivant*, whose corpulent person was encased in stays and padded garments to supply, so far
as possible, the symmetry denied by nature ; a bloated,
superannuated fop of Paphian reputation ; the scourge
of his Catholic tenants, and sometimes caught as
a prize to preside at what were termed religious meetings. How frequently do we find sectarian partisan-
ship associated with wretched morality ! This is un-
happily true both of Catholics and Protestants. . . .

[1] In his book *Ireland and Her Agitators*.

24th. Letter from Mr Goldwin Smith, acknowledging a pamphlet I sent him. He says, "You know my desire is for a just union, with due respect for the principle of national self-goverment, so far as is compatible with union. But I confess there seems at present little chance of the Union being made just, and I fear that to Repeal—which I strongly deprecate—we shall come after all." . . .

February 5th. Letter from one Denis Rellihan stating that he had a bill of £75 against my committee at the Mallow election in 1832, and requesting assistance from me in this present year—1868—as the committee did not satisfy his claim at that period. I wonder if I am the only person on whom election claims were made at the end of thirty-six years. . . .

25th. Letter from Mr Baxter Langley, candidate for Greenwich, assuring me that he is a repealer of the Legislative Union, and a political reformer, and asking whether I could do anything to aid him in his candidature.

26th. Wrote to Mr B. Langley, expressing a wish for his success. . . .

18th March. The *Nonconformist* has a favourable review of *Ireland and Her Agitators* from an English standpoint, and says that I have probably done more than any other living man to keep alive the Voluntary principle in Ireland. I have indeed done all I could. I have suffered severely both in mind and body by my politics, but if my efforts—the efforts of a very insignificant agent — can be of any appreciable value in promoting ecclesiastical Voluntaryism in this country, I shall not regret my losses.

23d. Circular from Messrs Voelcker of Vienna, informing me that my name has been registered in some lottery scheme. . . . The late Lord Cloncurry told me he once bought a ticket in a German lottery, which entitled him to a prize of £7000. The managers neglected to answer his applications for payment, and he was obliged to sue them in a German court. After some litigation they paid him, as well as I remember, £4000, but he never recovered the whole amount.

25th. Mr Gladstone, out of office, has seen fit to throw down the gage of battle to the defenders of the State Church, and to proclaim his devotion to the cause of Disendowment. The question has arrived at a stage of great importance when he thinks it worth his while to turn it into a test of party, and to propose resolutions of Disendowment and religious equality. For this we may thank our good allies, the English Voluntaries. They have effectually helped us to work up the question to its present high position, and I, with all due modesty, may thank my patriotic self for having been mainly instrumental in promoting and cementing the alliance between them and the Irish Catholics. The work on this side of the Channel was commenced at Clonakilty on the 15th of August 1856, and continued ever since with more or less activity.

April 6th. On the night of Friday, or rather on Saturday morning, Gladstone's resolutions were carried by a majority of sixty. All will go well if the Irish Catholics continue, as I think they will, faithful to the English Voluntary alliance. I have hitherto kept the committee of the National Association quite straight in this matter, and I hope that the combined influence of the English and Irish friends of Disendowment will force Gladstone to adhere to the policy he has adopted. . . .

18*th.* Gladstone's Disendowment scheme seems no better than a sham. He talks of capitalising the ecclesiastical State revenues of Ireland, and giving two-thirds of the proceeds to the Protestant Church in perpetuity. The remaining third he will probably appropriate so as to increase Government patronage by its means. His purpose, as at present stated, seems to be to fortify the grievance by investing one-eighth of the people with two-thirds of the Church property, in a mode well devised to protect the endowment from future attacks, and then by some dexterous legerdemain to make the residue a fund for clever jobbery. . . .

May 11*th.* Dublin. Arrived in town, having caught a severe cold *en route.*

12*th.* The day of the conference (of the National Association). The cold . . . destroyed my voice so that I could not make a speech. Being rendered dumb I was placed in the chair. . . . After the meeting I wrote to Mr Carvell Williams expressing my doubts about Mr Gladstone's purposes. . . .

13*th.* Visited Fisher at the Heralds' office. . . . Fisher knows an old Mr Orpen, who told him that one day, in 1797, when walking with a friend in Cork, Bob Conner of Fortrobert accosted him with a jubilant countenance. " Orpen, my dear fellow," said Bob, in a tone of triumph, " I have got evidence that will hang them as round as a rope ; " and so saying, Bob passed on. " Who is Mr Conner so anxious to hang ? " asked Orpen's companion. " His brothers Arthur and Roger," replied Orpen, to the great amazement of the inquirer.

18*th.* Letter from Mr Carvell Williams, who has

communicated with Mr Gladstone. Mr Gladstone denies that he ever meant to capitalise the revenues, or to give the Episcopal clergy anything beyond compensation for life interests. . . .

26th. Read a good deal of Macaulay's captivating *History of England.* In his entertaining account of England in 1685 he compares the past and present rate of travelling in that country. Here in Ireland we have our contrasts also. Of course, relays of swift horses could achieve a rapid journey when people rode post ; but what were called ' expresses ' in comparatively recent times, seem marvellously slow. As for private carriage travelling, my grandfather Wilson used to occupy three days in travelling from Moyle to Dublin. The distance, I think, is about ninety Irish miles. The Gumbletons usually took two days to travel from Castlerichard to Cork. . . . In 1735 the Protestant Archbishop of Cashel invited Dean Swift to Cashel, telling him as an inducement that he had a turnpike road to Kilkenny, with good inns at the end of every ten or twelve miles. But from Kilkenny to Cashel the distance was twenty long miles, bad road and no inn at all. In the midst of the desert, however, his grace tells the dean that he will find a hospitable parson in a cottage at the foot of a very high hill. " Here," said the prelate, " I design to meet you with a coach ; if you be tired you shall stay all night, if not, we will set out about four and be at Cashel by nine, and by going through fields and byways, which the parson will show us, we shall escape all the rocky and stony roads that lie between this place and that, which are certainly very bad." From this it appears that his grace's coach would take five hours to go ten miles. . . . ' Expresses ' travelled at the rate of four miles an hour.   An express from Dublin to London cost £6, 15s. 5d. ; to Chester £2, 2s. 1od. . . . to Edinburgh, £5, 6s. 4d.   Towards the close of the last century and the beginning of the present the mail coaches were forty-eight hours on the road between Cork and Dublin. In 1826 they ran the distance in twenty-four hours ; in subsequent years the time was abridged to twenty-two, to twenty-one, and in summer to twenty, and even eighteen, hours.   How steam has eclipsed all that ! . . .

June 8th. The *London Review* contains my (anti-State Church) article and letter, but the editor has suppressed my signature at foot of the letter, and substituted ' J. H.'

13th. Letter from the editor, apologising for the substitution of ' J. H.' for my signature, and explaining that his reason for the change was that, when on a former occasion he published two letters of mine on the State Church, he was sharply attacked by some Protestant friends for allowing full swing in his columns to a Catholic politician upon such a topic.   So he deems it prudent to hide the Catholic politician behind the mask of unmeaning initials.

22d. . . . A letter from a person whom Dr Furlong, the Catholic Bishop of Ferns, had requested to ask me whether I would consent to stand for the County Wexford at the next election. . . .   Very kind of his lordship, but it would not do ; I am too old, too poor, too infirm.

29th. The House of Lords have rejected Gladstone's anti-State Church Bill by a majority of ninety-five. This was of course to be expected.   The surrender of the Lords is only a question of time. . . .   The question has made immense progress since 1856. . . .

30th. A widower of Miss M'Farlane's acquaintance

has married a widow. The bridegroom contributed six children to the family circle and the bride contributed eight. . . . Here, too, Hymen has been busy. A lame tailor who uses a crutch made love to a country girl who was also admired by another tailor. The rivals are said by the gossips to have fought each other about the girl ; her lame beau is stated to have beaten off the other with his crutch, and to have received the hand of his mistress as the guerdon of his chivalry.

July 15*th.* The papers announce the death of Lord Lisle in his eighty-sixth year. His mother was a cousin-german of my grandmother Daunt. The old gentleman was a permanent absentee. There was a queer story in the *Cork Reporter*, about twenty-five years ago, of his coming to Ireland to see his estate, ordering post horses in Cork, going part of the way to Mount North, getting tired on the journey, and ordering the postboys to return to Cork, without having visited his property.

August 1*st.* I was seized yesterday with a sudden and violent attack of illness, which laid me so prostrate that I thought it only prudent to send for the priest. He administered Extreme Unction, and I am now much better. A general officer, during the Crimean campaign, asked Father Caswall how it happened that a much larger percentage of sick and wounded Catholic than Protestant soldiers recovered. Father Caswall said he had no other mode of accounting for the fact than that the Protestants were destitute of the Sacrament of Extreme Unction which the Catholics received, and of which one result is, that the patient recovers if God sees that his restoration to health will conduce to his spiritual benefit. . . .

September 9*th.* Letter from W. J. Fitzpatrick, the

author of the *Sham Squire*, with proof slips of a preface to the fourth edition of *Ireland before the Union*
in which he chronicles some of Roger O'Connor's extraordinary doings. Fitzpatrick states that the memorable
robbery of the mail coach was undertaken by Roger at
the instance of Sir Francis Burdett, in order to intercept
a parcel of letters which were to be used in an action at
law against Sir Francis, who had ascertained that the
letters in question were to be conveyed by the identical
mail which he instructed Roger to rob. Roger got hold
of the letters and thereby saved Sir Francis from the
threatened lawsuit. Roger was tried for the robbery at
the Trim Assizes, and Sir Francis—the instigator of the
robbery—figured prominently among the witnesses
whose testimony to his unimpeachable character contributed to his acquittal. Roger's exalted pretensions
were extremely amusing. On his plate was engraved
the royal crown of Ireland. A tradesman addressed a
letter to him, ' Roger O'Connor, Esq.' Roger reprov-
ingly said to him, " I thought you knew my name."
" Well, sir, I think I do," was the reply. " No, sir, you
don't," rejoined Roger; "you should have addressed
your note simply ' O'Connor.' There is but one true
O'Connor in Ireland, and I am the man ! " Fitzpatrick
tells the story of the robbery in Dangan park, as if the
immediate victim was Thomas Doyle, a postmaster, who
is stated to have been the messenger employed by
Colonel Burrowes. . . . The version I have hitherto
believed in is different. According to it, Burrowes was
the agent of Lord Wellesley, from whom Roger had
bought Dangan for £30,000, the purchase money to
remain in his hands for a time at five per cent. At the
end of six months Burrowes called on Roger at Dangan

for £750, being the first half-year's interest. Roger, who possibly had not the money on hand, replied he had been advised there was a flaw in the title to the property, and that until this could be set right he begged to postpone payment—all a trick to gain time. Burrowes, instead of parleying, went to Dublin, and at the earliest possible period obtained an order for prompt payment from the Court of Chancery. Armed with the Chancellor's order, he came again to Dangan, and was courteously received by Roger, who told him that his doubts about the title were removed, and that he would at once pay the £750, which sum he then counted out in pound notes. " I shall thank you to endorse the notes," said Burrowes. " Nay," said Roger, "you have put matters between us on a legal footing ; if you show me the Lord Chancellor's order to endorse these notes, I will of course obey it ; but otherwise you must excuse my taking the trouble." Colonel Burrowes then departed with his big bundle of notes, which, not being endorsed, could not be identified if stolen. At a part of the park where the avenue passed through a thicket, out bounced a gang with blackened faces, dragged the Colonel from his horse, enveloped his head in a sack, pinioned his arms, and rifled his pockets of the money he had just been paid by Roger, into whose possession the 750 bank notes were speedily restored by his confederates. Roger, in or about 1812, occupied a hut during the erection of a cottage near Connorville, in which he intended to fix his abode. He employed himself in the composition of a work which he intended as a refutation of the Mosaic account of the Deluge. Of this achievement he boasted with the characteristic exclamation, " Ha ! I have Moses on the flat of his back now!" . . . I once asked a near relation of Roger whether he had not two thousand a year. "Not he!" was the answer; "but he thought he *ought* to have it, and so he spent it." When Dangan Castle was burned (mysteriously), Roger's sons and daughters were forced to fly; '*sauve qui peut*' was the order of the day. Fortrobert occurred to them as a haven of refuge. It is about 180 Irish miles from Dangan, and the three young gentlemen, Arthur, Feargus and Roger junior had only one guinea among them. With this sum, and a grey pony, they started on their journey. I remember being much amused in my boyish days with Roger's comical account of the tricks by which they contrived to travel without spending their solitary guinea. They rode the pony alternately on the plan of 'ride and tie.' They enjoyed the hospitality of the farmers along their route. At one snug farmhouse Arthur evoked the generosity of a hippish *vanithee* by pretending to be a doctor and prescribing for her ailments. At another place they secured a good breakfast by pretending to treat for the tenancy of a farm which was shown by the landlord's agent. By this and similar devices they managed to reach the end of their long journey with their guinea unbroken. Walking up the avenue at Fortrobert, the three youths indulged in speculations on the sensibilities of Bob Conner's three daughters. They established themselves at Fortrobert and found favour in the eyes of the co-heiresses; Arthur marrying his cousin Mary, Roger marrying Elizabeth, and Anne, the eldest, bequeathing to Feargus (whom she did not marry) a life interest in her third of the Fortrobert inheritance. Meanwhile, Roger senior was seized with a desire to educate a peasant girl named Sullivan the daughter of a fish-seller, whom he met among the Bantry Mountains. Of course, as he undertook to enlighten Miss Sullivan, he discarded her vulgar baptismal appellation, and called her 'Finina.' In a copy of his *Chronicles of Eri*, which he gave her, he styled her 'my more than daughter, Finina O'Sullivan.' They went to reside at a cottage near Ballincollig. His daughter Harriet visited him there, and asked him for pecuniary assistance. He replied that he had nothing of his own to give, that all he had, his whole means of subsistence, were derived from the bounty of the incomparable Finina. Their *liaison* was said to have been purely platonic. After his death, in 1835, Harriet again visited the cottage and had a scuffle with Finina for some of the movables. . . . Finina had the best of the skirmish, although I think Harriet had some little success.[1] Roger was renowned for the charm of his manners as well as for the desperate exploits that made his name notorious. At a public ball in Kinsale, a card-playing lady had a partner at whist whom she had never previously seen, and who was not introduced to her by name. During the game he delighted her with his wit, and his extraordinary powers of captivation. He withdrew rather early, and when he was gone, she inquired the name of the fascinating old gentleman. " That, madam, is the celebrated Roger O'Connor." The lady burst into tears (*dit-on*) and exclaimed, " How that charming man has been slandered! What dreadful things they say of him! Well, it will be a lesson to me to be slow in believing reports to anybody's disadvantage."

[1] The Diarist affirmed that, *inter alia*, she managed to secure a blunderbuss, a turkey-cock and a blanket.—Ed.

October 1st. Mr D'Esterre Parker of Cork sends me his pamphlet on the operation of the Poor Law, in which he shows that poor rates increase as our population decreases. When our population was over eight millions, Mr Nicholls, the English Commissioner appointed by Lord John Russell to report upon the subject, estimated the annual cost at £295,000. But now when the population has diminished to 5,774,543 souls, the expense of the Poor Law amounts to £824,442, 4s. 1d., thus furnishing one more to the innumerable proofs of English incapacity to legislate for Ireland.

6th. Public meeting in Dunmanway to sustain M'Carthy Downing's candidature for the county. I consented to be chairman. The platform broke down during my speech, but was soon set right. Talk after the meeting. Ten or eleven candidates for Athlone, including some English adventurers, one of whom, a rich Jew, or else a convert from Judaism, scattered money broadcast, part of which was devoted to an enormous purchase of whisky and porter. One of the candidates was shipped back to England in a violent fit of *delirium tremens*. The gentleman who told this anecdote also said that Sergeant Barry, who is canvassing Dungarvan, declares that he can stand any portion of electioneering worry better than the drinking; but he is expected to imbibe large quantities of whisky punch day and night with successive batches of electors; and failure in this terrible duty would seriously imperil his popularity. . . .

November 26th. Letter from Mr Joseph Whittaker of Dukinfield, Cheshire, who describes himself as a working-man, one of the large number of working-men newly admitted to the franchise by the late Reform Act. On his own behalf, and on that of his *confrères*, he asks me to furnish him with information on Irish questions, in order to use it in our favour at the coming elections. This poor fellow writes in a very friendly spirit, which, as far as it exists in his class, I ascribe to the teachings of the Liberation Society.

November 11*th*. Attended the Poor Law Board in Dunmanway to get the Guardians to adopt a petition to Parliament for the conversion of the State Church into poor rate. . . . This is an excellent project, *ac mihi plaudo* for setting it going. It may, if successful, save Ireland from being robbed of her Church revenues for the benefit of the English exchequer. . . .

19*th*. Letter from the English working-man, Whittaker, expressing great sympathy with Ireland, and asking me to give lectures on Irish affairs at Dukinfield, where he offers me the hospitality of ' such fare as a working-man can give.' This really is touching. . . .

26*th*. Polling for the county at Bandon. M'Carthy Downing returned by 8100 votes; Smith Barry by nearly 7000. . . . Some of the people were distrustful of Downing, "for," said they, "he is an attorney." . . .

December 5*th*. . . . Story of a hot election contest, I know not where, perhaps fifty or a hundred years ago. Old M.P., not very popular, solicits re-election, backed by some score or two of steady friends. Opponent, a flashy talker, tickles the multitude to the top of their bent; shouts of laughter, vociferous cheering, tremendous excitement and enthusiasm; feelings of the audience clearly in favour of the flashy talker. Old M.P. is not eloquent; can think of no way to overthrow his opponent's popularity except by creating a conviction that he had committed a terrible crime. " I have one question," he says, " to ask my eloquent rival, and only one, and I

beg of you to mark well his answer. Tell me, sir," said
he, addressing that gentleman in a tone of stern and indignant virtue, " *who was it that murdered his washerwoman ?*" " Ay, tell us that," chimed the band of cla-
queurs with scowling glances and appropriate gestures of
indignant horror. The fickle and easily-duped crowd in
an instant adopted the belief thus insinuated ; the funny
hits, the glowing profession of patriotism, the eloquent
appeals were forgotten, and a loud roar of popular wrath
drove the supposed assassin of his laundress from the
hustings, and left the field in possession of the old
M.P. . . .

   19*th*. The Board of Guardians of Kanturk, Mitchelstown, Kilkenny and Cork have adopted my petition for
converting the tithe into poor rate.

   26*th*. Letter from Mr Carvell Williams on the gratifying results of the late general election. Mr Gladstone
has got a majority on the Church question, but it
remains to be seen how far his majority will pull
together. . . .

CHAPTER XXV

1869.—*January* 12*th.* Dublin. We had a private conference at the Association Rooms before the public
meeting commenced. I was anxious to move a resolution advocating the payment of poor rates from the
ecclesiastical revenues, but I found most of our associates
strongly opposed to a measure which they thought
would confer a benefit on a body of men whom they
hate as much as the landlords. . . . A prevalent notion
of the committee was 'to leave it all to Bright and
Gladstone.' . . . Besides, the tenants have to pay their
proportion of poor rate as well as the landlords.

14*th.* Visited Sir B. Burke. . . . He says that
Longman advised him to retrench his Irish stories, as
they were not serviceable to the English popularity and
sale of the work (*Vicissitudes of Families*). The same
black prejudice for ever!-. . . Francis (Colonel Macfarlane) said, speaking of his Indian career, " I extended
my hospitality indiscriminately to priests and parsons.

I really cannot think the Jesuits are as bad as they say. I received some of them in India, and they seemed to be hard-working and self-denying." . . .

March 8th. Gladstone introduced his bill for disestablishing and disendowing the anti-Irish State Church Establishment last Monday. His speech is very able. The scheme, as set forth, is undoubtedly, to some extent, a disendowing scheme ; but objectionable in not going as far in that direction as Gladstone might have done with propriety, and with full consideration for the vested interests of existing incumbents. His capitalisation scheme is, in fact, a plan for re-endowment, by which several millions of money obtained by the sale of Church property will be permanently abstracted from the Irish public and appropriated to the ecclesiastical uses of the present State Churchmen and their successors. (A correct forecast.) This is anything but religious equality, and cannot be accepted as a final settlement by the Irish nation. . . .

18th. Someone sends me the *Bradford Observer* announcing the return of Mr Miall to Parliament for that borough. Wrote to Miall to express my delight at his return, and to congratulate him on the enormous advance our noble cause has made since the day—15th August 1856—when I first attempted to get up at Clonakilty an Irish response to his anti-State Church movement. . . . Surely the best thing I ever did for Ireland was to effect that alliance with the English Liberation people, which at last bids fair to result in the overthrow of State Churchism among us. I don't very much like Gladstone's plan. It is ridiculous to bestow the name of ' religious equality ' on a scheme that gives permanently almost £6,000,000 sterling to the members of the State

Church,[1] while the Catholics neither ask for nor get anything.

24*th*. Dublin. Visited Sir B. Burke, who produced somebody's peerage, in which an English peasant girl, daughter of a labourer, is made to figure as the daughter of T—— S——, Esq. of —— Hall. A gentleman of fortune first engaged her as kitchen-maid, advanced her to be housemaid, and finally married her. Her son was created a peer.

25*th, Annunciation*. Visited Burke again. . . . He talked of publishers and publications. " I'll tell you," said he, " how I was treated by Mr —— " (naming a first-rate London publisher). " I sold him a work for £300 down ; the bargain provided for his giving me a further sum of £100 if a thousand copies should be sold within twelve months. When the twelve months had nearly run out, the sale stopped at nine hundred and fifty copies. The moment the year expired the sale recommenced, and fifty copies were sold in a week. So I was done out of my £100." " There is your honest John Bull for you ! " cried Fisher, as if the story was a confirmation of his evil opinion of the English. . . .

April 19*th*. Dined at Brook Park. Story of a stupid magistrate before whom a man was charged with striking another with a pair of tongs. " A *pair* of them ! " exclaimed the justice, " why, it would have been bad enough to strike him with *one* tongs, but the prisoner must have been the d—l entirely to strike him with a pair of them ! "

28*th*. My sixty-second birthday. Long letter from Scott, written on board the French steamer *Cydnus*.

---

[1] The Act, as finally passed, gave them £10,000,000 under the name of compensation.

He has been associated by the French Government with the Count de Vogüé in a commission instituted at the Duc de Magenta's suggestion, to inquire into the feasibility of establishing an Irish colony in Algeria. They were entertained on their official ramble by an Arab chief. A sheep was roasted entire and spitted on a pole, in which fashion it was borne to table. The roast was so good that the Count frequently recurred, during the day (and night), to the delicious recollection, exclaiming rapturously from time to time, '*O, quel mouton !*'
. . . Scott thinks that, should the Irish colony be decided on, occupation might be found for my son in connection with the scheme. . . .

May 3*d.* On Friday night, in a debate about Ireland in the House of Commons, Mr Bright said, " For once—for the only time in the history of the Union between Great Britain and Ireland—there is a Parliament which is willing to do justice to Ireland ! " What an avowal !
. . .

8*th.* . . . Gladstone's Bill has as good as passed the Commons. It falls so short of what a Disendowment Bill should be that I shall not be sorry if the Lords reject it. . . .

16*th.* Read the new and enlarged edition of Bennett's *History of Bandon.* There is an appendix devoted to the Bernards of Palace Anne, one of whom is stated by Bennett to have practised such overpowering hospitality that his guests never *walked* from the dinner-table, but were always *carried* by their servants, being too drunk for unassisted locomotion. The male heir of the family, Francis Bernard, was disinherited by old Tom Bernard in favour of the son of a sister, and the circumstance that led to his disinherison was this : When a boy, he was taken by his mother to visit the Palace Anne family. Walking through the garden, his mother said to him, " Is not this a beautiful place, Frank ? This will be yours hereafter." The words were overheard by Tom Bernard's childless wife, and nettled her so much that she resolved to disappoint the speaker's expectation. She induced her husband to make a will disinheriting Frank, and transferring the succession to his nephew, Arthur Beamish, who took the name of Bernard on condition of the inheritance. . . .

June 10*th*. Letter from John Martin, who tells me he was visited by a F.T.C.D. on the subject of Gladstone's Bill. . . . " We Protestants," said the ' Fellow,' " were employed in Ireland to do England's work in keeping down the Catholic population, the bulk of the Irish people. We bargained for certain advantages in return for that service. We have manfully trampled down the fellows these two hundred years in fulfilment of our bargain, and now the English think they can do better without us. . . . Well, we are not afraid of our Catholic countrymen. If they wish to hurt us we are able to hold our own. Barring religion, we sympathise far more with them than with the English. Our material interests are the same with theirs as Irishmen. I hate the English. They are most arrogant, most insolent, most greedy, most hypocritical, most stupid. Let us have an independent Ireland, and have done with England ! " This is a grand burst of patriotism. . . .

28*th*. Letter from the Lord Chancellor with an explanation of the mode in which Gladstone's Bill would work; he tells me the only money it would divert from Ireland is the *Regium Donum* and the Maynooth grant. Can O'Hagan be right ? . . .

July 12*th.* Wrote to the President of the National Association, denouncing the impudent scheme (Lord Westbury's) of bribing the Catholic priesthood with a beggarly slice of the Church property. . . .

24*th.* The Lords have passed Mr Gladstone's Church Bill with some mutilations, to which the Commons finally assented on a conference. The bill is a wretched abortion, in fact it is pretty much such a sham as might have been expected from an English Parliament. It pretends to disendow the State Church, which it re-endows with about five-eighths of the Church property in a capitalised shape.[1] . . . If Gladstone were an honest friend of Ireland, he could have averted all danger by withholding the power to capitalise. To be sure, it is a queer 'disendowment' that sends off the parsons with five-eighths of the money in their pockets.

26*th.* This morning's paper announces that the Bill has received the Royal assent. . . . Now that the Bill has passed let me briefly review my own share in the agitation. In 1856, I and a few others commenced it in Ireland by a meeting at Clonakilty in response to Mr Miall and the Liberation Society. Thenceforth I kept up a correspondence with the Liberation Society on the one hand, and with some leading Catholic prelates on the other, in the hope of getting both parties to work in the same harness. It was no easy task to get the Irish ecclesiastics to place confidence in the Liberation people whose anti-Catholic bigotry in theological matters was notorious. . . . In December 1864, poor Dillon, P. P. M'Swiney (then Lord Mayor of Dublin), and the Catholic prelates founded the National Association, and the ques-

[1] *N.B.*—In a previous entry in the Diary is noted Mr Gladstone's disclaimer of all ideas of capitalisation.—ED.

tion, whether to adopt Voluntaryism or a division of the endowment between the Churches, then hung on the balance among some of the founders. Dillon was strenuously pressed to avoid the Voluntaries and to pin our faith to such people as Russell, Grey, and the slippery Whig party in general. I told him that such a course would destroy our chances of being emancipated from the State Church. He pressed me to go up to town and move a resolution at the inaugural meeting. Most of the bishops, including Archbishop Cullen, attended, and I preached the most out and out Voluntaryism. Matters thenceforth went on more smoothly till Mr de Vere and some less able men got up a little agitation for division of the spoils between the Catholic and Protestant Churches. This project I successfully opposed in and out of the National Association. . . . My admirable friend, Dr Leahy, Archbishop of Cashel . . . wrote, " What we want is Disendowment, not Endowment." Meanwhile, the English Voluntaries agitated far and wide. They brought our question into every corner of England and Wales. Without their alliance the Irish Catholics could not rive the chain. On the other hand, the English Voluntaries could have done nothing without us, for had we been silent, their efforts would have been met with the plausible assurance that they were meddling with a question which did not concern them. In fact, our joint action was indispensable to success, and it was I who originally created or promoted our alliance. . . . Recently attempts were made to renew the miserable policy of partition by bribing the Catholic priesthood with two millions' worth of manses, glebes, etc. . . . I fought against it here and the Liberation people did the same in England. It happily failed, and the Bill passed without it. On the whole, I daresay, we have a sort of qualified triumph, nothing to boast of, considering that the result of nearly thirteen years' agitation is a measure that enables the parsons to walk off with ten or eleven millions of our money in their pockets, *that still extorts from us the rascally tithe rent charge*, and that swindles Ireland of the amount of Irish taxes heretofore kept in the country by Maynooth and the *Regium Donum*.

August 2d. The reception of the Bill by the Protestants in this quarter is comical. On Sunday last the Reverend Mr Myles announced from his pulpit at Dunmanway, that England had separated herself from God. "We Irish Protestants," said he, "have always been faithful to her, and now she requites our fidelity with desertion. Cæsar has cast us off. I will not preach disloyalty, but I will say this,—let Cæsar take care, of himself for the future without our assistance." . . .

7th. Alderman M'Swiney writes to me complaining of a letter in the *Freeman's Journal* from a certain Father Ryan, P.P. of New Inn, Cahir, in which the sole and undivided glory of the Church Bill is given to Sir John Gray, J. F. Maguire and John Mitchell. M'Swiney is indignant that Ryan ignores all the other soldiers who fought in the campaign, and asks me to set Ryan right by a statement in the newspapers. I shall comply, though, in fact, the Bill is nothing to excite anybody's pride at having promoted it.[1] . . .

17th. Arrived here Scott and Mr Leonard, commissioned by the French Government to establish an Irish

[1] The *Freeman's Journal*, for obvious reasons, would not print Mr Daunt's letter.—Ed.

colony in Algeria. They are come to collect the colonists, who are not to exceed thirty-seven families; each head of a family being required to bring with him at least £100. The land in Algeria is offered on (apparently) most tempting terms. Scott and the Count de Vogüé recently inspected the territory on which it is proposed to plant the emigrants, and their joint report determined the Government to proceed with the scheme, which was originally devised by Marshal MacMahon. My son is nominated to the command of the colonists *en route* to their destination. . . . Scott says that investments in the purchase of Algerian land will realise a fortune for the lucky purchaser. . . . He tells a story of a French sportsman who went out with his gun and failed to hit anything. Ashamed to face his wife at night with an empty game-bag, he purchased some partridges in the market, and presented them to madame as having been killed by himself. She saw at a glance that they were in a state approaching decomposition, and slyly said to monsieur, " It was indeed high time to kill them ! " Leonard says the grandsons of General Arthur O'Connor (the ' United Irishman ') live in good style at Paris. Their mother is a Grouché, and she requested Leonard to get the O'Connor pedigree, which I have promised to give him.

18*th*. Exit Leonard *en route* to Skibbereen to interest the Bishop of Ross in finding out suitable emigrants. He takes with him two magnificent Sèvres vases from the Empress Eugénie to the Bishop as a prize for a bazaar, also some very curious ware from the town of Limoges. Scott says the Count D'Orsay died in a state of penitence, deploring his past irreligion. He pointed to a sword that hung in his room, and said, " The only pious act I ever performed was running that sword through a fellow who spoke disrespectfully of the Blessed Virgin." Scott mentions that during the mania of the 'Papal aggression' in England, in 1850, a vindictive old Irishwoman in London was attended *in articulo mortis* by a priest, who assured her that if she did not forgive her enemies their offences she could not obtain the forgiveness of her own. "What are you," said he, "compared to the Blessed Virgin? and yet see to what outrages she is exposed; they have recently burned her in effigy." "That is all very well," replied the woman, "but she has a Son who is able to avenge her, while I am a poor craythur, with nobody to raise a fist for me." Scott had Dr Harris, the Protestant Bishop of Gibraltar, among his travelling companions when on the Mediterranean recently; he says the Bishop told him the profligacy of the 'upper ten thousand' in England, male and female, is tremendous. Scott tells a story of a party of ladies and gentlemen who were at a picnic somewhere in the Roman territory. While they were eating their repast, a handsome brigand of courteous manners, fully armed, suddenly appeared, and, gracefully bowing to a gentleman, suggested that he had probably some superfluous money about him, at the same time holding out his hand for a donation. "I trust," said the brigand, "that the willing generosity of the present company will obviate the necessity of my summoning the assistance of my friends, who are not far off." The gentleman took the hint, and delivered his purse. The robber next addressed a lady, "Signora, that is a beautiful brooch; I shall feel extremely grateful if you will have the goodness to give it to me for my wife." The brooch was yielded, and the elegant robber proceeded to levy contributions on the rest of the company. When he had robbed them all round, he thanked them for the polite readiness with which they had surrendered their property, and said that he felt bound to requite them by contributing to their amusement. So saying, he sat down, helped himself to some of the viands, and then sang very agreeably, after which he bowed, once more thanked the company, and departed. Scott says that Professor Playfair told him of a gentleman who had whistled on Sunday in a Glasgow hotel. The waiter immediately checked him for his immorality. "Why, surely there's no harm in whistling, is there?" said the whistler. "Ay, but there is, sir," responded the waiter, solemnly; "ye may get fou an' ye like, or ye may . . . but ye manna whistle at no rate on the honourable Sabbath." . . . Scott mentions an English lady with a fortune of £14,000 at her own disposal, who proposed marriage to an Arab chief, with whom she was desperately enamoured. The chief was quite ready to marry the lady, but refused to discard three wives who formed his previous conjugal stock. As the lady required as a *sine qua non* the sole possession of her fascinating savage, the treaty was broken off. Scott said, "Do you know who Lady H——d had been?" "No." "She had been the wife of Sir G. W——, and Lord H——d took a fancy to her. He bought her from her husband for £15,000, a divorce bill was quietly passed through Parliament, and Lord H——d married the *divorcée*," who, it may be added, figured for a long time in ultra-fashionable life. Dr Cumming, the great Presbyterian notoriety of London, writes a letter to the Pope requesting permission to attend the forthcoming General Council, and to speak there. This is delicious.

Long ago, Cumming predicted the extinction of the Papacy in 1866 or '67, and the end of the world shortly after it. . . .

September 15*th.* Found an old letter of my own with a *mot* of Sam Lover's. Meeting him one day in London, I told him that I had seen in Chelsea church-yard a potato crop growing among the graves. " That is death in the pot," said Lover.

26*th.* Presided at a meeting of the parishioners of Enniskeane (to which parish I don't belong) to raise funds for the erection of a new church. A farmer named Driscoll having given in his name for £20, I expressed surprise at the large amount of his subscription. " Oh," said one of my tenants (not publicly, however), " he never will pay it." " Then why give his name for it ? " " Wisha, them Driscolls are greatly given to bragging, and that fellow has a son to get married, so he thinks—! " I could not help laughing at the notion that Mr Driscoll thought he could better his son's chances among the rustic heiresses by diffusing the belief of his own wealth through the pretext of a large contribution to the church. . . .

October 30*th.* The papers are filled with comments on, and biographies of, the late Earl of Derby, who has just died at the ripe age of seventy. Regarded merely as an orator, Lord Derby was, in my opinion, the best I ever heard. There was in his public speaking a force, a fire, an elegance, a spontaneity which I never found combined to the same extent in any of his competitors ; what he said had pre-eminently the air of being purely the emanation of the moment. He and O'Connell were pitted against each other night after night during the Coercion debates of 1833. He was then Mr Stanley.

On nights when the Speaker occupied the chair, and when the rules of the House restricted each member to one speech, Stanley seemed to me to have the best of it. O'Connell laboured under the damaging consciousness that the large majority of his audience were against him, while Stanley had the encouraging knowledge that every word he uttered would find a ready echo in the breasts of that majority. I remember one night in particular, when Stanley hit O'Connell very hard for having said at a recent public meeting that the House of Commons consisted of six hundred scoundrels. "How anyone," said Stanley, "with the slightest pretensions to the character of a gentleman, could utter such language, I cannot understand." "Admit the words," said Feargus O'Connor, "and justify them." But O'Connell denied having said them. . . . On the other hand, on nights when the Speaker left the chair, and when the House was in committee, each member could speak as often as the assembly would listen to him, and in the interchange of short speeches O'Connell had a very decided advantage over Stanley. . . .

31st. Arrived last night, Colonel Scott. . . . He spoke of duelling, and said that when the Parton estate was forfeited in some civil commotion by one of his Glendonwyn ancestors, and was put up to auction by the Government, all the gentlemen of the County Kirkcudbright threatened that if any person should bid for it against the heiress he must cross swords with them all in succession. This gallant menace scared away all competitors, and the heiress re-purchased her patrimony for a small sum. . . . Talking of tenures, leases, etc., Scott said that many of the tenants of the Highland chieftains held their lands on condition of following the chief into battle.   In 1745 some tenants refused to follow their Jacobite leaders to the field, whilst others, as everybody knows, were willingly enrolled in clan regiments.   After the civil war had terminated, the tenants who had refused to take up arms for Charles Edward were ejected from their lands by the ruling powers, inasmuch as by their refusal to follow their chiefs to battle they had broken the conditions of their tenures.   They pleaded, that by taking up arms they would have incurred the pains of treason, which included the forfeiture both of lands and life.   But their plea was disregarded, and they were left to console themselves as they best might by the reflection that they were not hanged. . . .

November 1st. . . . Scott talked of a Scotch clergyman, the Reverend Mr Y——, whom his aunt, the late Miss Glendonwyn, had presented to the parish of Parton.   On preaching his first sermon he was seen to be tipsy in the pulpit.   He had many good qualities, but for his unfortunate addiction to drink was deposed by the General Assembly of the Kirk.   Shortly after his deposition one Neilson, a cabinetmaker, and a partisan of the reverend gentleman, appealed to Scott in his behalf.   " Why, what can I do for him ? " said Scott.   " Just this," returned Neilson ; " you can speak a word to Bishop Gillis to provide for him in the Catholic Church, and dootless the Bishop will oblige ye.   Mr Y—— is ready to turn Papist."   Scott protested that the Bishop would certainly refuse to comply with such a request.   Neilson was at first incredulous, but on Scott's assuring him that what he asked could not possibly be granted, he answered,—" Then that's a d—d shame, I must say. If ane o' *your* priests got turned out o' your Church and became a Protestant, our folk wad tak' him by the hand, and I'se warrant he wadna be lang unprovided for." Scott mentioned a young gentleman who was strongly advised by a friend to marry an attractive young lady. " She is a splendid creature," said the adviser ; " such manners, such beauty, and I can tell you she has a good long purse; but there's nothing in *that ;* her greatest merits are her heavenly disposition, her angelic temper, her household management, and her many accomplishments." The swain was induced to marry the girl, and found that she had not a farthing. " You told me," said he, re-proachfully, to her eulogist, " that she had a good long purse."   " Yes," returned the other, " but I also told you there was nothing in it."

2*d*. Exit Scott, who must go to Ballintra before returning to France. He mentioned that a Dublin police officer told him that at the time of Major Sirr's death the most horrible, preternatural noises were heard in the apartments the major had occupied in the Castle —the exultant shrieks of fiends who were come to carry off his soul 'to its ain place.' . . . Scott gave an in-stance of the practical results of lax casuistry in inju-dicious hands. A woman in Queenstown, who sold milk largely adulterated with water, informed a mis-chievous casuist that she habitually did so. That person told her that the iniquity of the deception be-came much lessened when sanctioned by the general practice of the neighbouring milk-sellers. Fortified with this clever distinction the woman apprised the other milk-vendors that nothing but general practice was needed to render the aqueous mixture consistent with honesty. Thereupon they all agreed to make the practice general, and Cove was forthwith deluged with milk-and-water sold as pure milk.

18*th.* Read over some eleven letters in an old magazine describing the west of Clare. The mention of Kilrush reminded me of Mrs ——, who, having been separated from her husband, took up her abode in one of the hotels of that gay village. After dinner, of which the first night of her arrival she partook alone, the waiter coolly shut the door, and took his seat at her side. She rose from her chair, and with much dignity reproved his impertinence and ordered him out of the room. He burst out laughing, and begged pardon for the liberty he had taken. " In fact, madam," said he, " I am not what you suppose. I am Mr ——, and merely adopted the guise of a waiter to have a nearer view of your distinguished attractions than I could have otherwise found means to enjoy." The compliment soothed Mrs ——, and she graciously permitted the gentleman to admire her for the rest of the evening, so at least goes the story. .... My grandmother's family were constantly visited and often bored by the officers of the Tullamore garrison (among whom figured a Lieutenant von Bismarck). One day the old lady expected a clergyman . . . on business, and as the intrusion of idle, lounging, gossiping redcoats would have been especially inopportune, she desired her servant to exclude every visitor but Mr Maxwell. The parlour-maid was a recent acquisition and knew neither the parson nor the officers personally, so that Mrs Wilson was obliged to say, "Admit the visitor in the black coat, but keep out any callers in red coats." It so chanced that one of the greatest bores of the regiment, encased in a black coat, called at the house a few minutes in advance of the time appointed for the parson's visit. The servant, acting literally on instructions, marshalled Captain —— into the drawing-room, to the vexation of the inmates ; possibly also to their amusement. I know not whether he belonged to the regiment whose colonel received the following invitation :—" The Earl and Countess of Charleville present their compliments to Colonel F——, and request the honour of his company at dinner on Thursday, the 16th inst., and the company of as many of his officers as know how to conduct themselves properly." . . .

CHAPTER XXVI

Attacking Otters *en grande tenue*—Newman on Miracles—
Political Fusion of Catholics and Protestants—Fly-Fishing
Extraordinary—Mr Daunt pleads Home Rule before the
Corporation—Westmeath Election and Lord Hartington—
Mr Daunt's Daily Life at Kilcascan—He would be a
Gentleman—*Nouveaux Riches* Hospitality.

1870. — *January* 23*d*. Been pruning trees constantly
with D. Singleton, who is *my* Tom Purdie. He tells
me the people are very angry and indignant at the misconduct of the Longford clergy in rejecting John Martin.
D. says he never heard such *damning* at the priests
as the people uttered in their angry comments on the
Longford election. . . .

February 1*st*. Letter from Lady Queensberry . . .
asking why my project of an address to the Queen from
the Irish dispersed over the globe demanding Repeal is
not carried out. . . .

April 5*th*. Letter from Colonel Scott, saying that the
Irish emigrants to Algeria are getting on well when
honest and sober, but that a large number of them
(seduced by the cheapness of the brandy) became
drunkards, and struck for exorbitant wages. These
rascals were of course sent adrift, and may thank themselves for their misfortunes. . . .

28*th*. Cork. Walked into Mulcahy's bookshop, and
found he had got a batch of the new edition of my

Catechism of the History of Ireland. He told me that he never sold so large a number of copies of any shilling book as he has sold of this little compendium of our history. Louis Napoleon has **given** a bourse in the Lycée Impérial at Caen to Scott's second son Harold.

June 20th. Heard among others from C. G. Duffy, who promises that whenever Ireland shall move in earnest for Repeal, the movement shall be well backed up from Australia. . . .

29th. Letter from John Henry Newman on infallibility, in reply to some queries of mine.

July 1st. A party of townspeople from Cork, Kinsale, and Innoshannon, came to-day with tremendous preparations for the destruction of the otters; long otter spears, big jack-boots stuffed with gravel to receive the bites of the exasperated animals, a horn which was gallantly blown by some of their attendants—in short, a terrific apparatus according to their notions of the sport, but the otters did not make their appearance.

15th. . . . Letter from T. D. Sullivan, saying that he ascribes the small number of priests who have heretofore joined the Home Rule movement to a fear on the part of the clergy, that if they came more numerously into it, they would frighten the Orangemen and Protestants from joining it ; whereas I suspect that the priests are kept back, as a certain parish priest tells me that he is, by the number of Tory names on the committee. Miserable jealousies and fears ! . . .

August 12th. . . . The Prussians have had two victories over the French at Wissembourg and Woerthe. . . . The country people here evince the strongest French sympathies. They come to ask me the latest French news with infinite eagerness. One fellow said,

" If the French are beat, Ireland's beat."   Another said,
" Sure the French are ourselves." . . .   A butcher said, " I
am a poor man, but I'd willingly give that cow " (he had
just killed one) " if by doing so I could get the Prussians
beat." . . . Letter from Scott, who has been enrolled in
a corps of volunteers called out for the defence of Caen
and its neighbourhood.   He says that Prussian agents
and Prussian gold are at work to stir up a revolutionary
movement, and it is against this that the volunteers
have most chance of being called to act. . . . Letter
from John Henry Newman.   Here is one Englishman
at any rate for whom I entertain the most profound
veneration and very strong regard. . . .

October 3*d*. Letters from Isaac Butt and John
Martin urging me to go to Dublin to help the Federalist
Association.

19*th*. Wrote to Dr Newman to thank him for his
Essays on Miracles; of which book he has very kindly
sent me a copy of the new edition.   An able and
interesting work, marked by candour, learning, and
great precision of thought.

26*th*. Letter from Newman.   Speaking of exaggerated stories of miraculous occurrences, he says,
" The exaggerations which you notice are very injurious
to the Catholic cause, but at the same time, from the
nature of the case, they cannot be helped.   Forgeries,
corruptions, and delusions are the shadows of the truth,
and in that way are indications of its presence.   What
is Protestantism itself but such a shadow, implying (as
we may trust), in those who profess it, some portion of
that truth which it thus witnesses."

28*th*. Letter from Scott containing a communication
to the exiled Empress of the French. . . .

November 4th. Letter from Commandant Duperré acknowledging Scott's communication. . . .

15*th.* This day a great meeting was held in Cork to express sympathy with the Pope, who is undoubtedly wronged by Victor Emmanuel. . . . Letter from Captain Dunne, who says the Federal principle is praised by the *Edinburgh Courant*, and that a similar movement in Scotland to recover domestic legislation is advocated by the editor. . . .

December 3d. Wrote a long, urgent letter to the Archbishop of Cashel, pressing on his grace the reasons why the Irish prelacy and priesthood should take an active part in the movement for Home Rule.

8*th.* Letter from the Archbishop; agrees with me on all points except that he cannot conquer his distrust of the ex-Tory patriots who are prominent in the Home Rule movement. . . .

1871.—*January 7th.* John Martin has been elected for County Meath by a majority of 486. . . .

18*th.* Letter from the editor of the *Limerick Chronicle* (the Conservative journal of that city) inquiring if I would contest the County Limerick against Mr Monsell, and saying that several Limerick solicitors would readily undertake the professional agency without fees if a true and reliable Nationalist could be induced to stand. Of course I refused. . . .

19*th.* Got a copy of the *Limerick Chronicle* with a letter from 'A Protestant Elector,' advocating my candidature as an old and tried Nationalist.

February 1st. Dublin. Visited Sir B. Burke, whose Castle intercourse creates in his mind a prejudice against Repeal, even in the modified shape of Federalism. . . .

4*th.* Interview with Reverend J. Galbraith at the

Nation office ; we were arranging who should speak to the toasts at the approaching dinner to John Martin.

6th. Banquet to Martin at the 'Antient Concert Rooms'; Mr Shaw, M.P. for Orange Bandon, in the chair. . . . All passed off most brilliantly. A wonderful fusion of Catholics and Protestants, Conservatives and Radicals, all banded together in the national cause. . . . Among the guests was Dr Maunsell, proprietor of the Tory *Evening Mail.* . . .

22d. Very acceptable letter from the Bishop of Ross, holding out a prospect of his joining the H. R. Association at the head of his clergy.

March 1st. Draft of 'Address to the Irish People,' partly drawn up by me, partly by Isaac Butt, forwarded to me for revision. . . . It was unanimously adopted by the Association. . . . Story of a young Tipperary squire who was salmon-fishing at the foot of the lawn stretching before a house which was inhabited by a young lady to whom he was paying his addresses. The gentleman's line, which he had thrown back for a cast, caught in something ; on turning to discover the cause of the obstruction, he saw that the hook was fastened in the tail of a bull which had been grazing near the river. The bull was hooked in a sensitive part, and galloped off bellowing, attended by the cows, at full speed, and by the fisherman, whose impulse was to save his line and recover his fly at all hazards. The bull took his course towards the mansion, bellowing and galloping—the gentleman scampering after him, rod in hand, and in this fantastic fashion did the herd and their human escort arrive at the hall door, at which the gentleman's fair friend was standing. It was no time for ceremony, but the lady stared in surprise at her admirer as he shot past. The narrator of the story, old Smithwick, omitted to say whether the adventure produced any change, favourable or otherwise, in the state of her affections, or whether her lover was able to rescue his fly. . . .

27th. Letter from C. G. Duffy. . . . asks me for my account of the dispute between the Old and Young Irelanders in the Repeal Association, as he thinks of writing something on the subject. I wrote to him that I thought the secession of the Young Irelanders from the Association in 1846 a great mistake, though not without an apology.

April 3d. Letter from the Archbishop of Cashel assigning as a reason why some prelates are slow in joining the Home Rule movement, their want of confidence in the motives of some of the Protestant leaders, who, his grace says, look on the movement as *identical with a movement against Rome Rule.* Wrote to the Archbishop that we were only concerned with the acts, not the motives, of our bigoted allies, and that the very same objection would, if acted upon, have withheld us from taking part in the struggle for Catholic Emancipation and Disestablishment. The former was supported by Mr Percival and others in 1829, on the ground that the Papists, when freed from legal disqualifications, would no longer consider it a point of honour to adhere to Popery, and that numerous conversions to Protestantism would be the probable result of the Relief Bill. . . . The Catholics were not such fools as to refuse to co-operate with the Percivals and their imitators for no better reason than that their motives in supporting our demands were crotchety and anti-Catholic. . . .

28th. . . . Letter, or rather envelope, from someone unknown, enclosing an epistle extracted from the *Times* of April 14th, with statistics of the crimes in Catholic countries. The writer says that in Vienna there are 118 illegitimate births in every 100, and in Rome 243 in every 100. He does not explain how the Viennese and Roman profligates contrive to have more bastards than births. . . .

May 3*d.* Letter from the Limerick and Clare Farmers' Club, urgently requesting my presence at the Home Government meeting in Limerick on the 18th, which Mr Butt is to attend. Must decline the invitation for sufficient reasons. . . .

30*th.* Letter from Townsend on the horrors in Paris, which city, he says with truth, is now like hell in misery as it had previously been like hell in wickedness. . . .

June 14*th.* Letter from Mr Carvell Williams, announcing that the Liberation Society have for the third time chosen me as a member of their council. Again I must decline the office, for I neither could nor would go to London.

July 4*th.* Letter from Martin informing me that the Home Government Council are about to request me to state our case before the Dublin Corporation, in conjunction with himself and Galbraith. . . .

18*th. Dublin.* We met to-day in the great hall of the Royal Exchange, which was admirably fitted up to accommodate the audience. The hall was crammed. The Lord Mayor was in the chair. He and the corporators wore their scarlet robes in honour of the occasion, and the brilliant colours, the anxious and animated audience which included many well-dressed ladies, the white marble statues of Grattan, Lucas and O'Connell, and the noble-pillared hall formed on the whole a scene at once interesting and picturesque.

. . . I began, Martin followed, and Galbraith finished in a noble, generous, truly Irish speech. We were cheered throughout with irrepressible enthusiasm. It was altogether a very gratifying sight. . . .

19*th.* Martin, Galbraith and I met in the back parlour of the *Nation* office to talk over our exploits, and *de omnibus rebus.* Galbraith told a story of the late Tom Reynolds abusing the parsons in a speech. " The fellows take the tenths from you—ay, and they would take the twentieths if they could ! " . . . Captain King Harman called to inquire my address, and finding I was in the *Nation* office, came up and introduced himself. He said, " I never was so stirred by a speech as by your speech of yesterday. I have sent three dozen copies of the report of the meeting to England. We talked of the late Westmeath election in which P. J. Smyth, the Nationalist, has had a walk over, the Government candidate, Sir John Ennis, having retreated from the contest. At an early stage of the canvass, Lord Hartington telegraphed to Sir J. Ennis, ' Is Smyth needy ? ' Ennis replied, ' Yes.' Hartington telegraphed, ' Then buy him off—let him name his price.' But Smyth was not to be bought." Captain King Harman added, " If Smyth had been induced to retire, there was a worse man behind him—namely, myself." He told us that the late Bishop, Dr M'Cabe, had his heart broken by the scandal entailed on the diocese by the conduct of some of his clergy in the Longford election. I asked, " Is the new Bishop of Ardagh (Dr Conroy) all right ? " " He is," answered King Harman. " Sir John Ennis civilly requested that his lordship would permit him to contribute to the furnishing of the new episcopal residence. The Bishop assented, and Sir John thereupon sent his lordship a cheque for £800, but when the Bishop found that this liberal advance was meant as a douceur for parliamentary support, he returned the cheque." That Captain King Harman should act and speak as he does, would have horrified his grandfather, the late Lord Lorton. . . . I looked into Lord Clare's great speech for the Union, and felt astounded at his lordship's magnificent capacity for lying. This led us to talk of lies and liars. Martin said that Mr Mitchell divided liars into two classes, good liars and bad liars, bad liars being those who hesitate and utter their inventions with some timid reserve; good liars being masters of the art, who stop at nothing, Martin said that Mitchell presents Bismarck as a specimen of what he calls a really good liar. . . .

August 9th. Received an invitation to a monster meeting to be held in Dundalk, for Home Rule, on the 15th inst. . . . Invited also to the banquet to be given in Dublin on the 17th inst. to the Comte de Flavigny, the Duc de Feltre and other French notables, among whom a son of MacMahon will perhaps appear. Sorry to decline, but acceptance was impossible. . . .

19th. Letter from Butt's Limerick committee, requesting my advice and assistance. I don't suppose anything I could write would be of the least service to Butt.

24th. Butt has been returned without opposition. . . .

27th. A minute and faithful diary of each day's existence in this secluded place would be a record of dull vegetation. Up in the morning at 7 or 8 o'clock— toilette sufficiently bucolic—post-boy (whose arrival is the great event of the day) with letters from political correspondents, or letters begging for pecuniary subscriptions—breakfast—answer letters if answers are required: if not, poke about the place making war on the thistles with a little instrument which, I am told, is called a 'spud'; read some old volumes in default of something new, Scott's novels, Grattan's speeches, odds and ends of other books — meditate on Home Government, and note the latest objections thereto for reply—communicate information on the subject to some friend who intends to write or speak about it—think suddenly of some old joke; here's one for instance:—Monteith of Carstairs and Richard Doyle's brother, Charles, were looking at a drawing representing a landscape in Holland. There were cows on one side of the picture and sheep on the other; "A scene in the *Low* Countries," said Monteith, pointing to the cows; "Yes, or in the *Pays baa-a-a*," replied Doyle, pointing to the sheep. Wander along the river banks looking at the inroads of the floods, and grumbling at the financial embarrassments which effectually debar me from fencing off the mischief—ramble through the woods and see with satisfaction the unusually vigorous growths the young oaks have made this year—presently ask myself why I should care much about the matter, as I cannot now have more than a few years to live; then the mind flashes back to long-past days, capriciously fastening for a few moments on events that have no connection with each other—thoughts of dead friends, relatives and enemies follow—accompanied in many cases by a prayer for their souls; a general sense of feebleness reminds me that I am no longer young — retire to my study — read newspapers, etc., down to supper—read, talk, till bed-time. So passes my monotonous life; the next day arrives without any marked variation in its course. . . .

October 17*th.* Accompanied my son and his gun to Barryroe, visiting on our way the old Abbey of Timoleague. The whole floor of the building is deeply encumbered with a vast accumulation of human remains and mouldering coffins, which choke up the pillars to the height, I should suppose, of six or seven feet.[1]

26*th.* This morning's paper announces the adhesion of Lord Garvagh to the Home Rule movement. . . .

27*th.* Spent last evening with Bechers and Somervilles. Mrs B. mentioned young T——, the son of a rich apothecary of patrician aspirings, who bought a commission in a fashionable dragoon regiment for young FitzGalen. The officers got their 'plebeian' associate to put his name to bills for £300, £500, and so forth, leaving him to settle accounts with the moneylenders at the maturity of the bills. At last the Colonel, from compassion, wrote to tell the apothecary that this process would beggar his son if he did not quickly sell out. This he did. The young officers, some of them sons of noblemen, who were scrupulously civil to him as long as they could fleece him, became impertinent when they could no longer turn him to account. His father became poorer, and allowed him £100 per annum to live on in Jersey, where he took to drinking, and finished his earthly career at the age of twenty-three. Here is another instance of foolish vanity. The Earl of B—— withdrew from a lawsuit on a threat from his opponent to exhibit in court a document in which his lordship's near relative, a

[1] These unsightly piles have now (1895) been removed, and the bones decently interred by the present P.P., Father Mulcahy, who takes great pride in this beautiful Franciscan Abbey.—ED.

clothier, was mentioned; the ignoble lord, whose earldom is a rascally Union bribe, shrinking from the public mention of his corduroy cousin. Akin to this trait of the Union peer, is the sensitive dislike of one of our attorneys, the now wealthy offspring of a publican, to have any reminder of his parent's business brought to light. A half-fool used to assail him in the street with reminiscences of his pothouse origin, on which he paid a stout blackguard five shillings to thrash the simpleton.

31*st.* Story of Mr D—— B——. He advertised for a wife; three ladies answered the advertisement; one of them stipulated for a carriage and four; another demanded a brougham and pair; the third only required a saddle horse. Mr B—— decided that the last was probably the best, because the cheapest, but he did not close the bargain until he could have an opportunity of feeling her head, and ascertaining whether her craniological developments harmonised with the economical tone of her reply to his advertisement. He fingered her bumps, found that of economy well developed, was satisfied, and married her. There is here (Glandore) an old English man-of-war's man named Pillman, formerly of the *Howe*, 120-gunship; they were taking out forty-five tons of gunpowder to distribute in the fleet; the gunner asked the captain for the key of the powder-room, and got it. A few minutes subsequently it was found that the gunner had committed suicide. The captain immediately proceeded to the powder-room and found a slow match burning, of which only two inches next the powder were unconsumed. A marvellously narrow escape! Pillman says the gunner was a good man, much liked and trusted by the sailors, but probably driven mad by the tyrannical conduct of the 'tartar' immediately commanding him. . . .

November 18*th.* Our English guest, Harrison, tells a story of the wife of Sir John B——, an English knight who rose from the lowest station to great wealth. Pressing a guest to partake of some *recherché* dish at her dinner-table, she would meet his refusal by saying, "Come now, *do* eat it; you don't know what a lot it's cost our Johnny!"

23*d.* Read Burton's interesting *Lives of Lord Lovat and Forbes of Culloden.* His stories of Scotch hard drinking could be matched in Ireland. P. V. Fitzpatrick told me of a monstrous drinking bout at Oxmantown, at which some seasoned heroes figured, including a certain Mr L. Waldron. They contrived to stumble into Dublin after their debauch, but one of them slipped into a deep aggregation of mud left by the scavenger, and was too drunk to get up. A brother convive, also very drunk, made some efforts to raise the fallen hero, but these proving ineffectual, he plumped down beside him in eight inches of filth, hiccuping, in a tone of maudlin affection, "Can't pull you out, Jack—but never mind—I'll never desert you, my poor fellow." . . .

CHAPTER XXVII

Social Economics—None so Deaf as Those Who will not
Hear—Decay of the Irish Language—Vicarious Valour—
Creditable Conduct of Orangemen—Dublin and the Aris-
tocracy—A Vice-Regal Caricaturist—Some Irish Viceroys
—Toby Glascock—Toby and the Undertaker.

1872.—January 11*th.* Received a presentation copy of
Lecky's *Leaders of Public Opinion in Ireland.* The
writer is in doubt whether O'Connell was a blessing
or a curse to Ireland. It used to be said of Rob
Roy that he was 'owre bad for blessing, and owre
gude for banning.' So far as O'Connell's public career
is concerned, he is certainly 'owre gude for banning;'
if it were only for his services in preserving emancipation from the drawbacks of the veto. . . .

February 7th. It is harder now for a man of small
income to live in this country than it was some years
ago. . . . Field labourers now work for about £20, 6s.
8d. per annum, instead of their old hire of ten guineas.
. . . We are also mulcted for the tenants' tithes, which,
in my father's time, no landlord had any concern with.
. . . Thirty years ago, a tradesman could support his
family better on half-a-crown a day than he now can
on four or five shillings. One cause of this is the increased price of certain kinds of food. Another cause is
the increased price of whisky, for it is a shameful fact

that larger wages in general mean more drunkenness, and the wretched propensity to drink strangely appears to have increased in proportion to the rise in the price of alcoholic drinks. . . .

March 3d. The death is announced of ' John Sobieski Stolberg Stuart, Count d'Albanie, who, with his brother, Count Charles, claimed to be the grandsons of Prince Charles Edward.' . . .

9th. Letter from Colonel Scott, who says there has been a long controversy in the *Standard* as to whether the deceased was or was not Prince Charlie's legitimate descendant. Scott was told by Mrs Fraser of Strichen, mother of the late Lord Lovat, that he exhibited documents proving his descent to the Chapter of the Order of Malta when he was received as knight. To be a Knight of Malta, the claimant, says Scott, must prove seven generations of nobility and legitimacy. Poor John Sobieski Stuart . . . was noted for discharging his pecuniary debts with honourable punctuality, a trait not always found among majesties, royal highnesses and other great people.

18th. Read Dean Ramsay's *Reminiscences of Scottish Character*—very lively and amusing. . . . The de'il figures here and there in proverb and in anecdote. At Kilcascan his sable majesty is used to illustrate speed, size, worthlessness, etc. An old woman, who saw my son on horseback, said he reminded her of his grandfather, 'the ould captain, mounted on Goldfinder, and riding, alea, like the divil!' This was meant as the climax of compliment. A fisherman boasted of having caught an unusually large salmon, 'a mighty big fish entirely, as big as the divil.' The same person, speaking of some worthless articles offered for sale, said, ' I

wouldn't give a divil for them." Dean Ramsay has a
story of a Marquis of Lothian who made successive
efforts to arrest the attention of a very deaf old countess,
to whom he repeatedly made offers of fish for dinner.
Feargus O'Connor used to mimic old parson Laird, re-
counting the several attempts of the Reverend Thomas
St Laurence to arrest the attention of his father, the
Bishop of Cork, at a large clerical dinner-party.
Loquitur Laird : "'Father,' says Tom, 'are you hearken-
ing to me?' Never a word from the Lord Bishop.
'My lord,' says Tom, 'are you hearkening to me?'
Not a word, upon my word, from the Lord Bishop.
'My Lord Bishop,' says Tom, 'are you listening to
me?' Dickens a word from the Lord Bishop. 'My
Lord Bishop of Cork, I'm speaking to you,' says Tom.
The Bishop kept eating away and never minded him.
'My Lord Bishop of Cork, Cloyne and Ross,' says
Tom, raising his voice, 'do you hear me?' 'Hould
your tongue, Tom,' says the Bishop. 'Pon my word
that was all Tom could get out of his lordship : 'Hould
your tongue, Tom!'" The story reads flatly enough,
but Feargus's exquisite mimicry of Laird made it very
amusing. Charlie Scott has an anecdote of someone
addicted to profane swearing, who was giving an account
of the anger of a Catholic Bishop, an amateur chemist,
on finding his chemical apparatus disturbed by a brother
prelate, who had come to visit him. The *raconteur* represented the episcopal chemist as furiously resenting
the disturbance with a profusion of horrifying blasts,
damns and curses at his visitor. "Surely the Bishop
cannot have used such language," exclaimed a listener.
"Oh, no, he didn't," answered the *raconteur*, airily ;
"that's only my way of telling the story." Within the

last few days the Editor of the *Cork Constitution*, the
leading Tory journal of Munster, has liberally printed
three letters of mine exposing the audacious swindle of
Irish revenue involved in the Legislative Union. . . .
My late cousin, Miss Macfarlane, was making a summer
tour in Scotland, before railways had become very
general, and in order to have full enjoyment of the
scenery, she occupied a seat on the top of a coach.
Next her, on one occasion, sat a Scotch gentleman of
elegant manners, general intelligence and much local
information, of which he was obligingly communicative
during the journey.   They had started at an early hour
in the morning, and the Scotchman applied himself from
time to time to the contents of a pocket flask of some
intoxicating drink.   For some hours the effect of this
beverage on his conversation was imperceptible.   But
at last his brain yielded to its influence ; he talked thick,
he talked nonsense, and finally he sank in a helpless
condition on his seat.   About two o'clock P.M., the
coach stopped at a stately gate, the entrance to a handsome domain ; an open carriage, well appointed and
containing two ladies, awaited the arrival of the inebriate, who was lifted from the coach in a state of
insensibility, and driven home in that condition to his
ancestral abode. . . .

April 22d. Achilles returned to-day from a visit of
some weeks to England.   The mention of an anecdote
he picked up from *Punch*, about an Irish labourer thinking his diminutive master would be "as hard to hit as a
jacksnipe," reminds me of the story of an Irish absentee
who lived in London, and who ordered his agent to
raise the rents of his estate.   The agent wrote to tell
his employer that he dared not comply with his man-

date, as the tenants had threatened to shoot him in the event of his raising their rents. The landlord wrote back from London in a strain of lofty heroism : " If the rascals think I am to be scared by their threats, they mistake their man. I defy their ruffianly vengeance ; so raise the rents as I have directed you, and show the fellows that I despise their menaces." I know not how far the agent, having to live in the midst of the tenants, felt his courage invigorated by this valorous exhortation from the landlord, who was 400 miles beyond the reach of gun-shot.

May 10*th*. Gardening and farming. . . . It is said that during the palmy days of Connorville a strange gentleman, who came to visit the family, saw a little man in the domain collecting horse droppings in a basket, and inquired of him whether Mr Conner was at home. " He is, sir," responded the collector of horse dung very respectfully. The stranger proceeded to the house, was received by such members of the family as chanced to be there, when, to his astonishment, the industrious little fellow who had borne the fragrant basket entered the drawing-room and announced himself to the visitor as Mr Conner. This eccentric personage was Roger, grandfather to Feargus, and brother-in-law of Lord Longueville. . . . One of the tenants, Tom Ahern, recounted a couple of anecdotes of the late Captain Bernard of Palace Anne. . . . He was a typical Orangeman of his day. One night, during the *régime* of one of the Insurrection Acts, he met two men driving carts on the high road, and shot one of them. He then jocosely said to the survivor : " Are you hungry, my good man ? " " No, plase, your honour," said the terrified peasant. " Well," rejoined the facetious captain, " if you aren't hungry now, you may be some other time, so take that fellow home with you" (pointing to the corpse) "and make broth of him." Another of this gentleman's exploits was the punishment he inflicted on a contumacious countryman, named Donovan, who refused to obey some behest of his worship. The captain tied Donovan to the tail of his horse, and galloped along the roads, dragging the unfortunate man after him until he was nearly dead. I expressed strong doubts that these outrages had been really committed; Ahern said they were the current talk of the country at the time. I suppose the stories are exaggerated, but they are by no means intrinsically impossible. Beaumont of Hyde Park, in the County Wexford, was perfectly capable of such atrocities. . . . But it must be added that the captain's principles underwent a salutary change before his death. He had spent some years in Belgium, and returned to Ireland an altered man. . . .

June 4th. George the Third's birthday. I remember the day being kept as a holiday in honour of his crazy old majesty, prior to 1820. . . .

August 19th. On the 12th of July the Orange celebrations took place as usual in the north. . . . The Catholics did not interrupt, relying on the reciprocal forbearance of the Orangemen when their own Home Rule celebration fixed for the 15th should take place. . . . The Derry Orangemen behaved extremely well. . . . The Grandmaster of the Monaghan Orangemen, Mr William Wolseley Madden, issued a notice to that body, counselling peace and forbearance. . . .

27th. Letter from L——, who mentions an odd case, in which a paralytic man and his rheumatic wife were struck by lightning, and their ailments cured by the electricity. This reminds me of old Nancy Beamish's story of her brother Adderley's nose. Nature had furnished him with a crooked nose; but he was flung from his horse against a stone, with which his nasal feature came in contact, and it was straightened by the collision.

September 7th. This month's *Liberator* . . . contains a most interesting detail extracted from the *British Quarterly Review,* showing how Mr Gladstone's pretended 'Disendowment' has given back the State Church property to the 'disendowed' clergy in a capitalised shape. (See Journal, 18th May 1868.) I was always afraid of this capitalisation scheme. I wanted to leave the tithe rentcharge with each rector for his life, and at his death to apply it to the support of the poor. But there was an outcry from some priests that this appropriation would be a boon to the landocracy, whom the objectors did not love. On the other hand, the Prime Minister was against it, because it would have lessened taxation, and withdrawn the tithe from the management of Government. We had simpletons of all sorts putting faith in Mr Gladstone and persuading themselves that he really meant Disendowment. The upshot is this, that the Protestant Church in Ireland has (according to the *British Quarterly*) got the whole property back again in another shape. . . .

November 28th. Sir B. Burke sends me his new volume, *The Rise of Great Families.* Among the chapters there is a pleasant gossip about the Viceregal Court of Dublin in past times. . . . Lord Townshend afforded more amusement, so far as I know, to the Dublin coteries by his eccentricities than any of his predecessors during the century. A contemporary

satire affirms that his lordship, who piqued himself on
his skill as a caricaturist, invited a young gentleman to
dine at the castle with the purpose of making prize of
his guest's face. He was not aware that his guest was
a first-rate master of the quizzical pencil, and that,
somehow suspecting the real object of the invitation,
he had come provided with the means to retaliate.
After dinner, when wine had circulated freely, his
Excellency fixed his eyes on the young man's countenance, and began to work away under the table.
The caricature was finished in a few minutes, during
which the young gentleman had been similarly occupied.
The Viceroy had been too intent on his guest's face to
observe the fingers that, unnoticed, finished a most
ludicrous caricature of his Excellency in the character
of a chimney sweep, with his broom, his scraper and
his bag. The Viceregal performance was handed round
the table and caused much mirth, until it reached the
original, who highly applauded the execution, and
laughed with malicious glee at the comic talent displayed by his noble host. He dexterously managed to
exchange the portraits, and when the substitute reached
Lord Townshend, that frolicsome personage was
astounded at beholding an incomparable likeness of
himself with his sooty accoutrements. The guest is
stated to have been a Mr T——l. Can this be Tisdall?
. . . Townshend is alleged to have been so inveterate
a caricaturist that, when visited by a wounded officer
who had an unusually long nose, he could not resist the
temptation of transferring his visitor's nasal peculiarity
to paper; this was immediately after the battle of
Quebec; and so proud was Lord Townshend of his
facetious performance, that he sent over the caricature

to his friends in England, along with his account of Wolfe's death. A note in my copy of *Baratariana* represents his Excellency as making an appointment to dine with the Hutchinsons at Palmerstown on a distant day. Hely Hutchinson invites all the officers of state; Mrs Hutchinson makes immense preparations for a splendid banquet, and after a fortnight's bustle, when dinner is half-spoiled, his Excellency sends an excuse, and dines with some casual acquaintance whom he has picked up that morning in the street. The same note states that the facetious Viceroy, in a state of post-prandial excitement at the castle, pretended to be so drunk as to mistake Hutchinson for Tisdall, and throwing his arms round Hutchinson's neck, exclaimed,—" My dear Tisdall—my sheet anchor—my whole dependence —don't let little Hutchinson come near me; keep him off, my dear friend, he's d—d tiresome, keep him off!"
. . . Townshend's successor was Lord Harcourt, who in 1777 was succeeded by the Earl of Buckinghamshire, and he in 1780 gave place to the Earl of Carlisle, who in his turn gave way to the trickish Duke of Portland.
. . . On the 24th of February 1784, the too convivial Duke of Rutland and his beautiful Duchess arrived in Dublin. Their social orgies turned night into day. But the Duchess had enough of maternal solicitude to send her daughters to bed at a seasonable hour, and to send them out to walk at six in the morning before retiring to bed herself. She used all sorts of artificial aids to preserve her beauty to a late period of life, only appearing by candle-light, as the glare of day would have been too trying to her made-up charms. The Irish officials affected great pomp. When Fitzgibbon was made Chancellor, he is recorded to have paid £4000

for a state coach. . . . In the time of Cornwallis and
Castlereagh, the old Viceregal palace was a nest of the
most flagitious corruption—so shameless, that it disgusted Cornwallis himself, whose position obliged him
to practise it. "How I long," he says, "to kick some of
those whom I am obliged to court." Castlereagh had
no such scruples. . . . In 1828 the Marquis of Anglesea
was Lord-Lieutenant, and his court was the most splendid,
and the best attended by the aristocracy, that had
enlivened Dublin since the Union. Among the most
admired beauties who frequented it was my early play-
mate, the lovely Letitia Stepney of Durrow in the King's
County. Her father was the Viceroy's first cousin.
There was a queer sort of person, generally known as
"Toby Glascock," expert in the pugilistic art, who had
been in the same regiment with one of Lord Anglesea's
sons, or, at anyrate, had been acquainted with him when
in the army. He called at the castle to visit
his former brother-officer, and presented his card to
Bartholomew, the huge state-porter, a glum and surly
Orson, requesting him to send it up to the individual
Paget he desired to see. Big Bartholomew looked
contemptuously at Toby, who was described to me as
a very little fellow, and not recognising him as one of
the castle *habitués*, refused to take up his card. "So you
won't take it up?" said Toby. "I won't," replied the
huge Jack-in-office. Instantly Toby squared at Bartholomew, struck out scientifically, and in a few moments
laid his big antagonist prostrate. He then triumphantly
marched up the grand staircase in search of his friend
with whom we may suppose he enjoyed a good laugh at
the lesson he had bestowed on the state-porter. Toby,
poor fellow, finally became a confirmed toper, and was

often visited by fearful attacks of *delirium tremens*. One day, while walking through Dublin with an acquaintance, Toby felt one of these terrible fits coming on him, and being pretty nearly penniless, he asked his companion for the price of a bottle of wine to satisfy the hideous craving for the vinous stimulant. Under such circumstances the artificial necessity for drink is, I believe, recognised by physicians, and as Toby's friend refused to lend him money to purchase it, Toby was driven to his wits to obtain wine by some other expedient. Looking across the street he saw the house of an undertaker, on which was displayed a signboard announcing the occupant's lugubrious profession. Toby crossed over to the undertaker's house, entered it, and passed into the parlour, where he seated himself, and rang a small hand-bell. The solemn proprietor instantly appeared, and inquired the commands of his visitor. Toby buried his face in his handkerchief, and enacted with eminent success the passionate sorrow of a man distracted by the loss of a beloved relative. His groans and sobs moved the pity of the undertaker. " Compose yourself, sir !—a severe loss, doubtless." " Oh, yes," blubbered Toby, " most severe and sudden," and forthwith he emitted a fresh series of appropriate sounds indicative of a grief that defied consolation and unnerved the sufferer, who seemed to be overwhelmed by the weight of his affliction. " If I could—have—a glass of wine," he faintly said, mingling sobs with his feeble accents. " Certainly, sir," said the sympathetic undertaker, and a tray with glasses and a decanter of sherry was promptly produced. As promptly Toby poured the contents of the decanter into a large tumbler, and thence down his throat. Reinvigorated by the wine, he rose, thanked the gracious undertaker, and was walking out of the house. " Sir," said the sable functionary, " you have forgotten to give any order ! " " Oh, did I," exclaimed Toby, relapsing into grief; " true, sir, but "—looking up the sign-board—" I think you furnish all requisites for funerals ? " " Yes," responded the man of coffins. " Then furnish the corpse also," said Toby, escaping briskly down the steps. . . .

CHAPTER XXVIII

Mr Daunt goes to Dublin—Discounting the Iron Duke—
A Short Shrift — Dinner-Table Anecdotes—Butt and the
Convention Act — Enthusiastic Meeting in Waterford —
Major O'Gorman's Story — Sir Bernard Burke on Lord
P—— — Mr Daunt invited to contest Waterford and
Tralee—'The Lion of the Fold of Juda'—The Cashel
Commoners—Important Conference in Dublin—Mr Daunt
invited to speak in Glasgow.

1873.—Letters from John Martin, Galbraith, A. M.
Sullivan, and Isaac Butt, strongly urging me to settle in
Dublin, and take personal charge of the Home Rule
movement. . . . The plain fact is, that these gentlemen vastly overrate my capacity for public business.
They seem to think that because I have made some
tolerable speeches, I must therefore possess executive
and administrative powers of which I know I am nearly,
if not quite, destitute. . . .

February 11*th.* Dublin. Met the Council in the Home
Government rooms.

12*th.* Heard a story of the Iron Duke. When asked
by a Father Flood to subscribe to the erection of the
Dominican Church in Dublin, his grace thus answered :
" F. M. the Duke of Wellington acknowledges Mr Flood's
application. The Duke knows nothing about the Dominicans, nor about the people who use their ministra-

tions, and as he takes no interest in the subject, he declines to comply with Mr Flood's request." The Dominicans held a bazaar to raise funds, and advertised as a separate prize, " holograph letter of his grace the Duke of Wellington." This brought £50 at sixpenny tickets. Butt drank tea with me at my hotel to discuss Home Rule. I told him that if I had my choice I would prefer Grattan's Constitution of 1782 to our present federal scheme. He said after a pause, " I am not sure that I would not prefer it myself." . . .

17th. Was chairman of Council. Read my address to the Irish people, which was approved of by the Council, with two added paragraphs by Waldron.

28th. . . . Vesey Foster Fitzgerald visited me, and presented me with a book he has written on Egypt, India and the Colonies. A good Council meeting in the evening. . . .

March 1st. Met the Bishop of Clonfert, and talked of nationality. He said that if an Irishman were brayed in a mortar, two principles would be found indestructible —love of Catholicity and hatred of England, which last, he said, was tolerably synonymous with attachment to Ireland. . . .

4th and 10th. Wrote to the Bishop of Clonfert and some priests, and to the Bishop of Meath, to enlist them in the cause of Home Rule.

12th. Wrote answers to English papers on international finance. The finance accounts mention a still existing relic of the Irish House of Lords, the housemaid, named Tomes, who gets £18 per annum, " compensation for losses by the Union."

14th. Visited Sir B. Burke, who told me he was at the play one night when Lambert the tallow chandler, then Lord Mayor, was enthroned in the corporation box in all civic state. A fellow in the gallery called out, "Three cheers for his Grace (grease) the Lord Mayor." "He isn't here at all," said another. "I saw him at the *Tallow* races." "You lie," cried a third, "he's gone to Kingstown for a *dip*." . . .

27th. Letter from Mr Mitchell Henry, M.P., enclosing his subscription of £50, and requesting to be enrolled as a member of the Home Rule Association.

April 8th. Dined with Mitchell Henry at Morrison's. Party were Shaw, Galbraith, Butt and myself. Talked politics and told stories till midnight.

13*th*. Spent the evening at Butt's. Butt told a story of a judge at Clonmel whose temper was ruffled by the howls of a prisoner who occupied a cell exactly under the court-house. "Crier," said his Lordship, "tell that fellow to stop his howling." Exit crier, who soon returned, saying, "My Lord, he won't stop." "Then I'll stop his howling," said the judge, "bring him up to me for trial." The howling prisoner was forthwith transferred to the dock, tried, found guilty, and sentenced to death, in about half an hour.

24*th*. Protestant Church Synod taking a great deal of superfluous pains to repudiate the presence of our Lord in their sacrament. Captain Macartney tells me it really was proposed to alter the creed to "I believe in the holy Protestant Church." . . .

May 1st. Story of a Cockney who had straggled over to the banquet at the opening of the Greenore Dock. Immense crowd ; tables marked alphabetically A B C, etc. The Cockney's ticket was marked K, but the corresponding table being fully occupied, and the neighbouring table L being much less crowded, our friend exclaimed to a group who, like himself, were looking for

seats, " Go to hell." This exclamation was at first mistaken for a burst of profane impatience, but next moment
the audience recollected the habitual misplacement of
the aspirate by Londoners, and acquitted the Cockney of
intending to give any worse advice than " Go to L."

15*th*. I have been drawing up my report on the
financial robbery of Ireland. A. M. Sullivan showed
me a letter from the President of Maynooth, affirming
that Cardinal Cullen has at last been converted to Home
Rule. I hear that the Cardinal's first cousins, wealthy
cattle-dealers, living at Liverpool, are as ruthless ex-
terminators as any in Ireland. They are said to have
swept large tracts of land in Meath clear of peasants,
whom they have replaced with bullocks to be fattened
for the English market. Father Lavelle calls this process the *Cullenization* of Ireland. . . .

June 23*d*. Frank Thorpe Porter pointed out an
equestrian figure in the engraving that hangs in the
council-room of the Association, representing the volunteers in College Green firing round the statue in 1777,
and he said, " That is my father." The present Duke of
Leinster's father is the principal figure in the foreground
of the picture. Wheatley's original painting is in the
National Gallery.

28*th*. Dined with Butt. Story of a child examined in a case before Chief Justice Lefroy. The
child was questioned concerning his knowledge of the
nature and obligation of an oath. " If you took a false
oath where would you go in the next world ? " " I
suppose," blubbered the child, " that I'd go where the
Protestants go." Another juvenile witness was asked
by the judge : " If you took a false oath what would
happen you ? " The child hesitated, and at last said,

" I suppose I wouldn't get my expinses." . . . Dr Shaw, F.T.C.D., mentioned two wealthy professional men who in early life had come to Dublin very poor, and were boasting to each other of their success. One of them said, " I had only half-a-crown when I first arrived in Dublin ; " " And I had only three-halfpence," rejoined his friend. " But I," said the first, " had to borrow the half-crown ; " " And I," replied the second, " had to steal the three-halfpence." The late Archbishop Whately was talked of. A barrister, named Webb, described his Grace's clerical *entourage* as the most shameless toadies, flattering him extravagantly to his face. As a sample, Webb mentioned that one of those gentlemen, in discussing some topic, would say, " I am borne out in my opinion by the following words of one of the greatest men and most profound thinkers this century has produced," then quoting something the Archbishop had written. Butt said that at a dinner in England, at which several Cabinet Ministers attended, Whately attracted notice by his eccentric questions. He called out to Lord John Russell, " Lord John, why is anybody ever hanged ? " " Because he cannot help it," answered his lordship ; " or, I should say, because he deserves it." " That's a statesman's answer," said Whately. " People have often been hanged who didn't deserve it ; but *I* will tell you why anybody is hanged, because the rope is too short." By-and-by his Grace asked, " Why do white sheep eat more than black sheep ? " There was a pause, and it seemed as if the frolicsome prelate would have the glory of the answer to himself. Butt, however, said, " Because the white sheep are more numerous than the black ; " and the Archbishop admitted that Butt had forestalled his answer. Butt has engravings in his hall, representing public buildings in Dublin. We were looking at the view of our House of Commons, now a bank, and I said, " Shall we ever get in there again ? " " Yes, certainly," said Butt. " Forty years ago," said I, " I was walking near it with Feargus O'Connor, and I said to him, ' When shall we get in there again ? ' ' Whenever you want to get change for a note,' answered Feargus," whereat Butt laughed heartily. Butt has in his drawing-room the organ on which Handel first played the " Messiah " in Dublin. . . . Butt talked as Captain Macartney had done of assembling 300 members in Dublin, returned by the old localities, notwithstanding the Convention Act. I said that O'Connell had failed to drive "a coach and six " through the Convention Act. " But I would drive the Irish nation through it," said Butt. . . .

July 4th. Meeting of our Association. Butt in the chair. I moved, and the Reverend J. Galbraith seconded a resolution, exhorting the northern Home Rulers to allow the Orange celebrations to pass un-molested. We had a lively-spirited meeting. Some-thing Galbraith said about William III. called up another Protestant clergyman, Mr Carroll, who abused his Majesty very comically, and this called up my Catholic friend, A. M. Sullivan, in defence of the said monarch. . . . The Orange newspapers announce, as a deputation from America, a Mohawk chief, named Ornhyateckha. Can their bond of alliance be a common sympathy with scalpers ?

12th. MacAlister tells the reply of a labourer to a question of the late Sir Benjamin Guinness, who was very bigoted. " What are you doing ? " he asked the man. " Digging the foundation of a Catholic Church, sir?" "I am sorry to hear it," said the baronet. "So is the devil," rejoined the labourer.

August 6th. Butt, Blunden and I have come to Waterford to address a great meeting of Home Rulers. When we changed trains at Maryborough, we were placed by the railway officials in a saloon carriage profusely decorated with green boughs. At Kilmacow, five miles from Waterford, we were met by a string of carriages and a band playing national airs. Two miles outside the city, we encountered the Trades of Waterford, who all bore handsome banners, which were lowered as they filed past the deputation. On entering the town, our escort had swelled to enormous proportions. The procession was conducted through all the principal streets at a slow pace. Frequent cheers greeted us; the houses displayed a profusion of laurel branches; there were triumphal arches and banners with national mottoes; women and girls, whose faces beamed with delight, crowded the windows, and waved handkerchiefs. The procession finally passed along the quay, where we saw the numerous vessels in the river dressed in bunting, and by the time we reached our quarters at the Mall, the concourse of people was computed by the Tory *Mail* at 20,000. Butt, Blunden and I addressed them. I have seen many great gatherings since 1832, and at none of them did I ever witness greater enthusiasm than at this one. . . We got a champagne supper in the evening, at which I drank water. . . . Butt told one or two ancedotes on the journey down. Travelling in France, his professional designation of Queen's Counsel was translated by the French officials, "Conseiller de la Reine," which they apparently took to mean Cabinet Minister. So to show

the *entente cordiale* between France and England, they
treated him with exceptional courtesy, placing him
in saloon carriages on the railways, and in every other
mode in which homage to his distinguished importance
could be exhibited. They supposed he was on a
diplomatic mission, and he afterwards found that he was
watched everywhere by detectives. He had a courier, an
Englishman, who professed to speak French well
enough for his business. Butt desired him at some
provincial hotel to procure him a private apartment.
The courier, whose knowledge of French was not as
good as he pretended, desired the servants to procure
un cabinet particulier for the *Conseiller de la Reine* of
Great Britain, whereupon the illustrious diplomatist
was ushered by a file of bowing servants into what is
politely called a lavatory. Major O'Gorman told me
that when Lord P—— was Mr P——, one of many
heirs presumptive to the peerage, and of course un-
certain whether he ever would inherit it, he ran a
very disreputable career, and became desperately embarrassed. When at last he succeeded to the peerage
and £20,000 a year, he was invited to dine with the
mess by the officers of O'Gorman's regiment, to which
his lordship had once belonged. Some talk about
horses and huntsmen elicited a difference of opinion,
and one of the disputants quoted Lord P—— as the
authority for his statement, a guest who knew of his
lordship's disgraceful history, but who did not know his
personal appearance, said, "Oh, don't mind any statement Lord P—— makes. He is a thorough scamp
and quite unworthy of credit," and the speaker branched
off into a narrative of the noble lord's misdeeds, notwithstanding admonitory kicks under the table from

his next neighbour, and ended by saying, " he wound up his adventures by marrying a woman of bad character." " Sir, I am your obliged humble servant. Will you take a glass of wine ? " said Lord P——, who sat opposite his biographer, apparently indifferent to the record of his evil exploits.

9th. Returned to town on the 7th. . . . Yesterday we had a Council meeting. I presided. . . . Visited Sir B. Burke. I asked him if he knew anything of Lord P——. " Certainly," said he. " He married to win a bet." He was in desperate difficulties, and he said he would marry any woman on earth if she brought him £5000. " I'll bet you £5000 you would not," said a brother officer. " Done ! " said Mr P——. The lady was easily had, being a mistress kept by the other, of whom he wanted to get rid. P—— married her, and was paid the £5000 he had won. She was in 'an interesting situation' at the time, and as a son was born shortly after her marriage, she got his name registered as the offspring of that marriage in the books of the church where he was christened. By-and-by P—— inherited the earldom, on which his wife's son assumed the style and title appertaining to the heir apparent. Sir Bernard inserted his name as such in an edition of the peerage ; whereupon Lord P—— wrote to Burke disclaiming the paternity, and desiring that the name of his *soi-disant* son should be expunged from the next edition. Burke has been the target for a cross-fire of letters from both parties. He believes that Lord P—— speaks the truth in this matter.

12th. Home Rule meeting at the Rotundo, convened by Butt, in order to refute some gross misrepresentations

of what he said at Waterford. . . . On our Waterford
trip I heard a story of Hymen's freaks. Mrs —— was
twice married ; in her youth to a man old enough to be
her father ; in her advanced age, to a man young enough
to be her son. She was a handsome barmaid. Her
first spouse was a gentleman who left her a pretty
domain and residence ; her second spouse married her
to obtain these possessions.

21st. To-day Butt meets two hundred Home Rule
delegates at Newcastle-on-Tyne.

27th. Visited by a Mr Hennessy from Waterford,
who inquires whether I would consent to stand for that
city at the next election. Declined.

September 1st. Tralee is in a mess. The O'Donoghue
is believed to have been offered a Government post,
which vacates his seat. . . . I have been asked very
pressingly (to stand), but of course I declined. . . .
Butt says that if I were too feeble or ill to stand the
turmoil, speechmaking, etc., he would go to Tralee to
represent me. . . . Visited Sir B. Burke, who was Lord
Lurgan's guest at the recent dedication of the Armagh
Catholic Cathedral. Lord Lurgan, a Protestant, liberally contributed to the building fund, and acted as one
of the collectors at the dedication. Burke accompanied
him to the cathedral, the Orangemen shouting, " Up
with Verner ! to h—l with Lurgan ! "

3d. Very urgent letter from Martin, entreating me to
consent to be put up for Tralee. . . . I am out of the
question. . . .

6th. Tuam. Arrived here this evening to visit the
Archbishop. . . . The line passes Woodlawn, a place of
infamous memory from the brazen rascality of its former
owner, Trench, M.P., who was purchased in market

overt by Castlereagh, and who, having spoken against the Union, voted against his own speech, Cooke having assured him during the interval that his terms of sale would be complied with. Those terms included a peerage, the title of Baron Ashtown.

7th. . . . Our noble Archbishop celebrated early Mass and preached. . . . More than eighty years old, his intellect is still strong, and his shrewd, sharp eye is as vigorous as ever. . . . He said he never had given a farthing to the Catholic University, not deeming its spirit national. He also said that the recent movement got up by Cardinal Cullen, under the name of the Catholic Union, was a scheme to take the wind out of the sails of Home Rule. I asked his Grace to sign our requisition calling a national conference. This he refused to do just now on some point of episcopal etiquette ; but he said that if I wrote him a letter inquiring his views on our agitation, he would answer it for publication in a way to do us good. . . . I dined with him. He said that when Lord Norbury, the hanging judge, was one of the visitors of Maynooth, Lord Chief Justice Bushe, who was also a visitor, engaged in conversation with the professors. They were all standing on a grass plot. Norbury came puffing up to the group, and addressing Bushe, said, " I never expected to see the Chief Justice engaged with Maynooth professors in a *plot*." Bushe turned aside muttering, " Norbury never can see anything without churning it in his mind to see how a pun can be made out of it." . . .

7th. Dined with Father Ulick Burke. . . . At his table was Mr Gannon, Chairman of the Town Commissioners. Speaking of the perpetual boasts of wholesale conversions from ' Popery,' by which the proselytisers swindle money out of gullible bigots in England, Mr G. said that during forty years that he knew Tuam, he never had known so much as one Catholic in the town converted to Protestantism. On one occasion a reverend gentleman, whose name, I think, was Seymour, wrote to England that all Tuam had become Protestant. . . .

15*th*. Enniskillen. Came here with Mr G. Swift MacNeill to address a Home Rule meeting. A fine sunny day ; crowds from distant places ; sixteen handsome green banners, fringed with white silk ; two or three bands. The number of persons present is stated in the *Mail* as 8000. Some Orangemen were on the ground ; a well-dressed, intelligent, appreciative peasantry, the *élite* on the platform being wealthy Enniskillen merchants.

17*th*. Dublin. Returned to-day from Enniskillen. In our carriage were reporters from the *Freeman's Journal* and the *Evening Mail.* The former told us that when Mr Hemphill was canvassing Cashel, he found that a party of the electors, locally known as ' commoners,' numbering some thirteen or fourteen, were notoriously corrupt, and always sold their vote to the highest bidder. Their usual price was £20 per vote. Hemphill requested the priest to preach a sermon on the sin of trafficking on the franchise, and the priest complied, and denounced corrupt traffic in votes as a mortal sin. Next day Hemphill met one of the commoners, and anxious to learn what effect the sermon had produced on these venal gentlemen, he asked the man whether he had been at Mass the previous day. " I was, your honour." " Was not that sermon against bribery excellent ? " " It was an elegant sermon entirely, your honour." " Will it do good, do you think?" "I think it will make the election run very close, your honour." "How so?" "Why, we always got £20 for a vote before we knew it was a sin, but as his reverence says we'll be damned for selling our votes we can't for the future take less than £40."

18*th.* Spent part of the evening with Butt. An Irish Protestant clergyman, named Coghlan, rector of a London parish, was one of the party. He told us that he encountered on all sides the most intense contempt for Ireland, and had many sharp battles with an English clergyman who habitually expressed that feeling. Coghlan tried to vindicate the intellectual fame of Ireland by naming her great men, such as Grattan, Burke, etc. The English parson said, "Why, those men were not Irish—they were *educated* men, and when a man is well educated I do not consider him an Irishman!" . . . Mr Smyth, M.P., comes to me accredited by the Home Rule electors of the city of Waterford, to accept my acceptance of their suffrages at the General Election. I of course declined to stand, thanking them, however, for their wish to return me as their representative. . . .

25*th.* Kilcascan. Got the Archbishop of Tuam's promised letter. . . .

29*th.* Got the *Belfast News Letter* of the 26th, containing a letter of mine vindicating the Irish Catholics from the scandalous charge of abetting the Union in 1800. Some of the prelates, cajoled by the Government, 'basely betrayed their flocks,' as Sir Jonah Barrington says ; but their guilt was not shared by the mass of the Catholic people.

November 6*th.* Went to Cork and met at Mr J. G. MacCarthy's four parish priests who desire to confer with me on Home Rule. Their advice is sound, sagacious and patriotic. They are the P.P.'s of Kanturk, Youghal, Middleton and Mallow. . . .

18*th*. Dublin. The Conference opened in the Rotundo, Mr Shaw, M.P., in the chair. . . . Dined with Sir Joseph M'Kenna, and had much talk on international finance.

19*th*. An excellent speech from Butt. Gladstone telegraphed for full reports of our proceedings. Dined at Mr Dodd's in York Street in company with Butt, who said he had been reading in an old newspaper a fierce attack I made on him some thirty years ago. I proposed to renew our fight. " No, no," said he ; " I should get the worst of it." . . .

20*th*. Conference resumed its sittings. . . . Spent the evening with Kenelm Digby. He said his father's conversion to the Catholic Church was caused by his study of Sts. Augustine and Chrysostom. He said that, so far as his experience went, he found the Catholic gentry in Ireland extremely ignorant of the grounds of their religion. They believe its teachings, but are incapable of defending them when attacked.

21*st*. Conference resumed its sittings at five o'clock P.M. . . . Visited Mrs Ffrench, O'Connell's daughter. . . . She is a person of genuine worth, and has a great dash of talent. . . .

22*d*. Kilcascan. A good deal tired with the journey and the week's excitement. Butt escaped from Dublin to Kingstown two days before the Conference, to prepare his speech undisturbed by visitors. He told me he did not sleep one moment the night previous to its delivery. Among the notables at the Conference was the O'Gorman Mahon, a fine, military-looking old fellow, who for the last twenty years has been in France. He at once introduced himself to me. We talked of past events, and I said, 'I believe you knew Tom Steele?' "Knew him? I should think I did; I paid £5000 for the knowledge. I was his second in the duel he fought with Smith O'Brien." . . .

December 31st. Butt has been announced for Home Rule meetings at Greenock, Glasgow and Edinburgh. . . . He told me lately that he knew, as a positive fact, that the great Sir Robert Peel was so afraid of the Federal agitation, which O'Connell seemed to recommend in 1884, that he actually suggested the composition and circulation of pamphlets and news-paper articles to be written in a furiously ultra-Irish spirit, attacking O'Connell for lowering the national claim from Repeal to Federalism, and thereby weakening O'Connell's influence.

CHAPTER XXIX

1874.—*January* 21*st*. Walter Holmes, who called here, mentioned the bankruptcy of young W——. His father was an industrious shopkeeper with flourishing shops in three provincial towns; he realised a large sum of money, with which he bought estates very cheaply at the time of the potato famine. . . . When times improved, the estates produced a rental of £5000 a year. His son . . . paid £600 to some person for introducing him to the Marchioness of Hastings; got among the swindlers on the Derby, and is ruined.

29th. . . . Telegram from Wexford inviting me to stand for that county against John Talbot Power. . . .

February 3*d*. Shaw, the late M.P. for Bandon, sends a messenger to beg I would propose him for the county. . . .

20th. The Irish elections result in sixty Home Rulers. . . . The English elections result in a Tory majority. Gladstone goes out, Disraeli goes in. *L'un vaut bien l'autre.* . . .

March 24*th*. A soft sunny day. One of the tenants said he remembered the way in which his brother-in-law, now a fat publican in Ballyneen, spent Christmas night a great many years ago. They were enjoying their festivities in one of the cottages occupied by the said relative, Robin Good by name. A snowstorm came on with such violence that the occupants feared their thatched roof would be blown off; whereupon Good sallied out, and got astride upon the ridge of the roof, where he remained for the night, in order to secure it by his weight and grip from being disturbed by the tempest. An original way of spending Christmas night, doubtless ! . . .

30*th.* Returning late last night from Brook Park, my horse started violently to the right, and when I had recovered my balance, he staggered off to the left and became unmanageable   I was flung into a dyke filled with water at the roadside. He seemed under the influence of terror. This happened at a spot which is deemed unchancy by the common people, and which they say is haunted by the ghost of a she-miscreant nicknamed Maura Gaelagh. It is at least an odd coincidence that at the same spot my old horse Monarch seemed nearly paralysed with terror one night some years ago. . . .

May 25*th.* . . . John Martin asks me to draw up the resolutions which Butt is to move in the House of Commons on the 23d June. . . .

July 20*th.* I have written my intended lecture on Grattan's Life and Times, but am undecided as to the time and place of its delivery. . . . *Apropos* of the penal laws and their enslaving effect on Catholic gentlemen, I recollect my grandmother mentioning a young Catholic gentleman of good family who visited at Moyle —his name, I think, was Barnewall, and that he was an officer—whose servile manners astonished the Wilsons.

26th. Visited my sister C——. Stories of queer parsons and queer laymen. *Eccentricities of Cupid.* The Reverend Mr S——, a widower and curate, attracted the regards of Mrs F——, a widow with four daughters. The enamoured curate was frequently her guest, and she enhanced her fascinations by an excellent *cuisine*, which Mr S—— very highly appreciated. Under the notion that the *recherché* dinner-table of the widow was a permanent institution, the reverend gentleman married her. But he soon discovered that the exquisite repasts which had ensnared the lover were deemed by his economical bride too expensive to bestow on the husband. He stormed, she retaliated. He swore that she should keep up the good cheer that had invariably rewarded his attentions in the days of their courtship; she replied that she could not afford it. Then followed a conjugal hurricane, which ended in his pulling her about the floor by her hair. She then referred the whole case to the rector, who exerted himself to make peace; but I don't think peace was permanent, as the disappointed *bon vivant* is said to have emigrated to London.

August 11*th.* I delivered my lecture on Grattan to-night in the Bandon Town Hall to a crowded and certainly intelligent audience; Mr Shaw, M.P., in the chair. . . .

24th. Letter from my cousin, Colonel Bushe, Grattan's grandnephew, reminding me of the old friendship between his mother and mine. . . . Bushe writes that he has ' every record of old Grattan.' . . .

September 10*th.* My son came home quite delighted with his Yorkshire trip. He met a Mr Hudson, who had joined a shooting-party in South Africa. Hudson told him of an Englishman who was shooting bucks in those

regions, and who, in mistake for a buck, shot a Kaffir. . . .
Afraid of Kaffir vengeance if the accident should be discovered by the tribe of the defunct, the English hunter
went straight to the native chief, told him what had
happened, expressed his sorrow, and offered to pay whatever sum the chief might demand as reparation. The
chief promptly named a pound of gunpowder ; the
Englishman generously gave him two pounds, which so
delighted the chief that he exclaimed, " White man, you
go shoot plenty more Kaffir at same price." . . .

18*th*. Heard with sincere grief of the sudden death
of my old friend, Lord Fermoy. . . . His ancient convictions that Home Rule is our right and our need never
deserted him. Last year he exchanged letters with
Gladstone, who said he did not know what the Home
Rulers required ; on which I sent him, for transmission
to Gladstone, the very explicit addresses drawn up by
Butt and myself. . . .

October 29th. Came to Cork on Monday. . . .
Attended a lecture delivered by A. M. Sullivan on
' Ireland under George the Fourth.' Sullivan exposed
the domestic profligacy and political falsehood of that
unfortunate monarch. The description of the old,
worn out debauchee's deathbed was impressively delivered. . . .

November 9th. Mr Gladstone has come out with an
elaborate attack on the Vatican Council, and the dogma
of Papal Infallibility. . . . The attack is a palpable hit
for English support at the next general election. . . .
As to the definition of Infallibility which Gladstone
thinks, or pretends to think, so dangerous, it is couched
in such studiously moderate language that John Henry
Newman told me that Cardinal Cullen was said to have

expressed his inability to see how the Pope could ever make use of it. . . .

26th. Scott writes to me from Caen that a portion of the French Protestant Synod represented to the Minister of Public Worship that many of their clergy were preaching heterodox doctrines, and begged that those reverend gentlemen might be deprived of their cures. The Minister replied that, as the leading principle of Protestantism was the right of private judgment, he failed to see how any doctrine could be consistently deemed heterodox by the applicants, and that consequently he, on the part of the Government, declined to interfere. . . .

CHAPTER XXX

The French Lady's Will—Examples of Fulsome Flattery—
Hartnett's Funeral—Lady Oxford and Sir F. Burdett—
Bonaparte and Ireland— Sir John Moore at Connorville.

1875.—*January*. . . . My Aunt Wilson picked up somewhere a story of a French lady who was attended in a fit of illness by a young surgeon. Bleeding was ordered. The surgeon, either from ignorance or awkwardness, opened an artery instead of a vein, and all efforts to stop the hæmorrhage were fruitless. The lady was bleeding to death, and in an *accés* of romantic generosity she dictated her will to an attendant, leaving her whole fortune to the surgeon. She had barely strength to sign the will, and faintly said that, as his maladroit performance on her artery would destroy his prospects professionally, she felt impelled to protect him from the consequences of his fatal mistake by a valuable legacy.

18*th*. . . . Looked through my old favourite *Waverley* and alighted on the passage where Charles Edward complains of the extravagant requests that his followers daily preferred to him. O'Connell often mentioned the multitude of strange requests he frequently received. A lady once asked him to get her a peerage ; a man at Rugby wrote to him to say that his wife had been

seduced by a parson, and the Great Agitator was requested to get Lord John Russell to punish the reverend
delinquent.   Again a priest asked to be admitted with
his sister (I think his two sisters) to the hospitality of
Dorrynane until his fortunes should improve.   "My
good sir," said O'Connell, "I have not the honour of your
acquaintance."   "Oh, yes," said the reverend gentleman,
"don't you remember I was introduced to you on board
a steamboat?"

29th. Heard of the death of the excellent Archbishop of Cashel, aged 69. . . .   His influence procured
the Sunday closing of public-houses in his diocese.   To
me his Grace was eminently useful in the Disestablishment campaign ; for it is more than doubtful whether I
could have effected a working union between the English Voluntaries and the Irish hierarchy unless he had
helped me. . . .

February 11*th*. Looked through a rare old folio
volume, *A Genealogical History of the Kings of England*,
by Francis Sandford, Lancaster Herald.   It is dedicated
to that most moral and religious monarch, Charles the
Second. . . .   He compliments the King on the splendour
of his royal progenitors, and then says, "Their virtues
are united in you as well as their blood.   Not to fetch
examples from darker antiquity, in you are daily beheld
the courage and magnanimity of King Edward the Third,
the prudence and policy of King Henry VII., the peaceable inclinations of your royal grandfather, King James,
and the *piety* and clemency of that blessed martyr, your
father.   Where should we find a centre to fix our obedi-
ence, but where Heaven has concentred all these advantages of blood and virtue?" . . .   This encomium
. . . is exceeded as a sample of flattery by the still

more complimentary record of celestial favour intimated to his Majesty on the day of his birth, 29th of May 1630. The auspicious event was commemorated by a medal, " bearing four oval shields in cross, their bases concentring, between which issue forth several Rayes, representing the Star which, at his birth, was seen at noonday by many thousands. *Such a remark of Heaven,*" says the loyal Francis Sandford, "*being never vouchsafed at any nativity besides that of our Saviour*,"—which adulation needs no comment. . . .

23d. George Harrison, who is here, mentions a man whose religion seems very comprehensive. He has a prayer - book in which are bound up the devotional services of various countries — the Catholic Mass, the Anglican services, Presbyterian hymns, Mahommedan liturgy, etc.; and he indifferently attends all, according to local convenience.

March 15th. Glasgow. . . .

17th. . . . Went to Airdrie, where some five thousand Irish turned out in procession—banners, scarves, etc. . . . Glasgow meeting in the City Hall, which was crammed, the people enthusiastic and orderly. I spoke at much length, and was well received. It is just thirty years since I addressed an Irish meeting in that same City Hall. . . .

19th. Reached Belfast at 5 A.M., and went on to Dublin in the afternoon. In the same carriage was Dr Hancock of Lurgan, brother to Dr Nielson Hancock, the Government statistician, whose official business it is to show that we are tremendously prosperous. . . .

30th. Returned home last week, and was shocked and grieved to learn that my dear friend, John Martin, was no more. . . . A purer, more unselfish patriot never lived. Himself an earnest Presbyterian, he had a gener-ous and loving confidence in his Catholic fellow-country-men. . . .

April 8th. Reverend J. O'Keefe arrives, deputed by Shaw to suggest to me the propriety of standing for Tipperary. ' No expense, no opposition,' etc. I am too old a bird to be caught with chaff.

11th, Sunday. The Bishop has forbidden the priests of this diocese to attend any funeral or celebrate Mass at any wake where whisky is distributed. Poor Sir John Gray is dead, aged sixty. . . .

May 31st. Mr Jenkins, M.P. for Dundee, brought on his motion for inquiry into the dexterous tricks by which the dignitaries of the State Church in Ireland contrived to secure an inordinate share of the ' compensation ' money for themselves and their subordinate clergy. Taking the diocese of Down as a sample, it appears that in 1868 the revenues of the clergy amounted to something over £12,000 a year. But, when their vested interests came to be valued in 1870, they succeeded in establishing claims to the extent of £17,000. In the town of Belfast, the increase as returned was so monstrous as to seem incredible—from between £800 and £900 a year to £6600, on which latter amount the clergy there obtained ' compensation.' To swell the number of appli-cants, and, by consequence, the amount of ' compensa-tion,' the Bishops, during 1870, ordained a large extra number of clergymen. . . .

June 23d. . . . Walked to Currabegs. Jerry Donovan told me of the queer funeral that Hartnett of Deelis had. I think this must have been the same Hartnett with whom my brother Tom and Feargus O'Connor once dined in 1832. He was a gentleman possessed of some property, but resided in a farmhouse not much better than a cabin. In this plebeian residence he gave his guests an excellent dinner, at which there was a fair display of plate. When death approached, he directed that he should be buried in Cork, and that his remains should be taken from Deelis at 6 o'clock P.M., in charge of two brothers named Hennigan, who, as he calculated, should reach Cork about 9 o'clock next morning. The Hennigans were great drunkards, and stopped to tipple at every public-house along the road. They at last became too drunk to attend to the hearse, and the horses, unguided, overturned it in a ditch. The coffin was broken by the fall, and the corpse was uncovered. Some persons passing fastened the broken coffin with ropes, and replaced it in the hearse. The bibulous indulgences of the Hennigans considerably retarded their progress, so that, instead of reaching Cork at 9 A.M., as the defunct had calculated, they did not arrive in that city till 6 P.M. The remains were then buried at St Finbarr's. When Counsellor Hartnett, son of the deceased, was informed of the misconduct of the drunken Hennigans, he only remarked that, as the poor fellows were thirsty, they went for refreshment to the public-houses, and that, as his father's corpse was inanimate, it incurred no pain from the accident that had befallen the coffin. . . .

July 27th. Got a card of invitation to the O'Connell Centenary ; wrote a polite refusal. . . .

28th. Letter from Scott. . . . He has been reading the Napoleon correspondence in the public library at Caen. . . . Roger O'Connor told the Palace Anne family that his reason for taking the Castle of Dangan from the Wellesleys was, that he might receive Bonaparte, whom he expected to invade Ireland, in a mansion of suitable magnificence. On the 23d June 1811, the Emperor wrote to the Duc de Feltre, Minister of War, that he intends to invade Ireland, in the October of that year, with 25,000 men. On the 4th July he writes to Feltre, directing him to consult with O'Connor and other Irishmen at Paris, and that, if there be a strong party of disaffected in Ireland, he (Napoleon) would send over in October 30,000 men of the line and 4000 cavalry ; that he would make with the Irish any conditions they pleased, as he attached great importance to the affair. On the 14th of July. . . . he says that he will send over 60,000 men, with 70,000 spare muskets. . . . On the 3d November he writes again to Feltre, expressing great impatience at not receiving Irish news; orders new agents to be sent to Ireland ; says that, if sure of a party in Ireland, he would invade it in February or March 1812, and directs the completion of the Irish regiments. . . . Scott tells me that his uncle, Lord Oxford, was arrested at Paris on the 14th October 1814, when about to start with letters for Murat, King of Naples. These letters were very important, and, says Scott, caused Castlereagh to take steps at the Congress of Vienna to have Murat dethroned. . . .

September 14*th.* Dublin. We have just had a really magnificent meeting in the Rotundo. . . . I took occasion to assail the bigoted impolicy of the O'Connell Centenary Committee, and was vigorously cheered by the meeting. . . .

16*th.* Met Father Ryan, P.P. of Headford, County Galway. . . . We talked of Souperism in the west. Ryan said that when, some years ago, Dr Wilberforce, the late Bishop of Oxford, came to Connaught to inquire into the reality of the alleged conversions to Protestantism, he, Ryan, requested his lordship to take down the names of a few of the children exhibited to him in schools, and to take great notice of their faces, adding, " I think, my Lord, you will recognise the very same children in some other schools paraded before you as a distinct batch of pupils." Wilberforce acted on the hint, and afterwards told Ryan that by doing so he was enabled to see through the deception. . . .

18th. Visited Sir B. Burke. . . . We talked of the odd position of the man who calls himself Viscount H——, and whose legitimacy is denied on very strong grounds by his mother's husband. " Butt thinks," said I, " that under the circumstances it would be very hard to prevent him from succeeding to the earldom." . . . " Ay," said Burke, " and I know of another such case in a more exalted rank than Lord P——." My sister mentioned a parson, Cotter, rector of Donoughmore, County Cork, who had married in succession three wives, of whom the first was extravagant, the second fat, and the third ill-tempered. The reverend gentleman called his three wives the World, the Flesh and the Devil. He had two sons, both clergymen, by one of whom, ' assisted,' as the phrase goes, by the other, he was married to the ' Devil.' When Lord William Lennox married Miss Paton, the actress, he seized on her professional earnings, and they quarrelled. In the dispute he said, " I gave you rank." " And I," retorted the lady, "gave you clothes, for you had scarcely a coat when I married you." They were shortly afterwards divorced. . . .

October 2d. Mr W. J. Fitzpatrick . . . sends me a letter from Mr Arthur Creagh Taylor, son of Captain John Taylor, aide-de-camp to Sir John Moore, who fell at Corunna, and with whom Captain Taylor was

associated in the search for Roger O'Connor at Connorville. . . . This was in 1798. Mr Taylor states that
on the arrival of his father and Sir John Moore at
Connorville, Mrs O'Connor invited them to breakfast,
an offer which was willingly accepted by Captain
Taylor, because he thought the delay would afford
Roger time to escape. . . . The search was merely
nominal, Sir John Moore taking no part in it. . . . He
adds that, when Captain Taylor was on his return down
the avenue, he observed a man in the shrubbery making
signs to him, and pointing to the out-offices, with the
apparent purpose of intimating that Roger was concealed there. Of this fellow's signs Taylor took no
notice. . . . The name of the rascal who tried to betray
Roger was Bob Joyce. . . .

November 11*th*. G. Harrison has just met in London
a very old Irish gentleman, General Minchin, who was a
schoolboy in Dublin . . . at the time the Union passed.
He saw Castlereagh on the steps of the House of
Commons; the street was crowded with soldiers to
overawe the enraged multitude, one of whom flung a
putrid cat that hit Castlereagh's face. Minchin saw
Castlereagh remove the stain with his handkerchief,
smile, doff his hat, and bow to the crowd, and enter the
House. . . .

CHAPTER XXXI

The Baronet's Story—Narrow Escape from Death—Exploits of Joseph Ady—The 'Infinitely Little'—Orange Fears of Cardinal Cullen—A Storm Warning—An Incident of 1798 —An Odd Fancy.

1876.[1]—*April 4th.* Visited by Sir —— ——, the ruined baronet, who is on a tour of visits to the 'charitable and humane.' This poor fellow leads a miserable life. His father squandered his estate in reckless living. Of him Feargus O'Connor said, when I asked him what Sir —— —— was like,—" Like a half-gutted codfish!" The present holder of the title . . ‚ once tried to get a situation of head clerk in a firm, with a salary of £300 a year, and had nearly succeeded, when the partners discovered he was a baronet, and declared that it would hurt their feelings to employ a man of his rank in a subordinate position. He spoke of the son of a rich merchant, whose nuptials were trumpeted in the newspapers some time ago by a pompous paragraph, headed, 'Marriage in High Life.' The grandfather of this person was a wandering 'poor scholar,' who chanced to pass by D—— on a day when Mr M—— of that place was setting off in his carriage for the races. A friend was looking at the arms on M——'s carriage, and asked

[1] In the commencement of the year Mr Daunt was ill.—ED.

326

him the meaning of the Latin motto.   M—— could not translate it, whereupon the 'poor scholar' modestly approached and asked their illiterate honours to permit him to construe the motto. . . .   "I am going to the races," said M——, "and I cannot be back for some days; but I'll give you a token to my steward to keep you at D—— until my return."   The poor scholar thankfully accepted the proffered hospitality.   He became a favourite attendant at M——'s shooting excursions, and at length rose so high in his good graces, that M—— conceived the idea of getting him married to his cook or housekeeper, who had saved money.   Mrs M—— demurred to this suggestion, thinking that the woman in question would not condescend to marry a 'poor scholar.' "Well," said M——, "we can try.   Do you sound the woman and I will take the lad in hand; the woman might do worse than marry him." . . .   The marriage took place.   M—— gave the bridegroom a farm for a very long term at a moderate rent.   He went into business as a butter merchant, and acquired considerable wealth.   It does not appear that he ever made himself ridiculous by aristocratic pretensions, but his descendants were less wise. . . .

   22*d*. Cork.   Breakfasted with Mr J. G. MacCarthy at Montenotte, where Lord Francis G. Osborne is his guest.   My intercourse with Lord Osborne originated in his having copiously quoted me as his authority for certain statements in a Home Rule speech he recently delivered at Liverpool. . . .   To-day I had a narrow escape of being run over by the train on the Dunmanway line.   To save time I incautiously got on the line near Manch station.   Providentially, the engine-driver had begun to slacken speed for the station when he saw me. He sounded the whistle, but the wind, blowing in my face, carried away the sound until he had whistled thrice. . . .

June 14*th.* . . . My thoughts ramble back to many unconnected reminiscences of long past years. . . . The peasantry have odd modes of expression. They will sometimes describe an awkward rider by saying, " I saw him going the road with a horse undher him." Of a long-legged man they say, " There's a dale of him split."
. . . An impudent London swindler, named Joseph Ady, was in the habit of sending letters to numerous persons, offering what he stated was valuable information on payment of a sovereign. He addressed one of these missives to the late John Gumbleton, who, as I was then in London, enclosed it to me for the purpose of inquiring about Ady from Sir William Heygate and Alderman Copeland, to whom Ady had referred him as vouchers for his respectability. . . . Mr Copeland answered that Ady was a thorough rascal. Sir W. Heygate wrote to the same effect, adding, that if I favoured him with a visit he would tell me much about Ady's unprincipled exploits. . . . One morning in the summer (I think) of 1824, we were informed at breakfast that a large crowd had gathered in the western end of this place to see Feargus O'Connor fight a duel with a Mr Good. We sent Feargus some hot, strong coffee to fortify him for the encounter. My brother Tom went to see the great event, and took his seat along with Feargus under a hedge that screened them from the expectant crowd. Half-an-hour passed, and Mr Good did not come. A young gentleman on the other side of the ditch expressed his impatience for the fight, saying it was a confounded bore to be kept waiting.

Feargus, who overheard him, exclaimed *sotto voce*, "The d—l crack your neck, what a hurry you are in! You wouldn't be in such haste if you had to fight the duel yourself." There was no duel after all, as Good did not appear. . . . Another time Feargus, driving through Cork, saw Robert Longfield on the trottoir, and summoned him into the carriage. Longfield jumped in and asked Feargus where he was going. "To fight a duel with a Mr Callaghan," said Feargus, "and I want your assistance as my second." Longfield demurred, but it seems he had once given Feargus a promise to act in that capacity if it should ever be found necessary, and F. now insisted on its performance. Away they drove to the scene of combat; pistols were courageously discharged in the air, there was no bloodshed; both belligerents emerged from the affair with the honours of war, and unscathed by its disasters. The mention of duels recalls Lord Norbury, who was said to have *shot* up to preferment; and the mention of Lord Norbury recalls the subject of punning, of which he had an inveterate habit. Seeing a crowd on the banks of the canal one evening, he inquired what had assembled them. He was told they were trying to rescue a man who had suddenly rushed out from his comfortable dinner of roast goose and plunged into the water. It was supposed he was mad. "Ay, mad indeed," said Norbury, "to exchange a hot goose for a cold duck." The Prussian Queen Sophia Charlotte complained of *l'infiniment petit*. If her majesty knew a certain Irish curate's English wife she might have discovered that there was something still less than her 'infinitely little.' The lady in question was a well-jointured widow whose thrifty habits harmonised with the economical disposition of her second husband. She produced some biscuits to a visitor, after whose departure she reckoned the remaining biscuits and fancied that more had disappeared than her visitor had eaten. She charged her servant with having purloined the invisible biscuits; the servant denied the accusation. Imagine a woman with several hundreds per annum addressing the following note to her friend : " My dear Miss M——, you will much oblige me by a few lines to say how many biscuits you ate when I had the pleasure of a visit from you yesterday. My object in making this inquiry is merely to ascertain whether the servant who placed them on the table abstracted any of them, as I did not find as many in the basket as I think you left there." Not bad this as a sample of *l'infiniment petit*. . . .

August 8th. Amused myself lately writing a historiette entitled *Kilgarvan*. . . . A Mr O'Hara had an illegitimate son for whom he asked the heir of entail to provide some support. This the heir refused to do, on which O'Hara 'married,' says my informant, 'a girl he met in a potato field,' and of course his son by this marriage excluded the contumacious heir of entail. *Episcopal eccentricity.* A certain Archbishop of Dublin had a violent temper, which occasionally thundered and lightened on his wife and children. But previously to these explosions, and while the passionate outburst was brewing, the prelate unconsciously gave notice of the coming hurricane by a series of snorts. His family soon learned to interpret these premonitory sounds as presaging the vituperative storm about to descend on their heads, and accordingly, whenever his Grace began to snort, they prudently scampered out of the room. . . .

September 30*th.* Letter from Colonel Scott, who mentions the mode in which an embarrassed lodger scared his landlady out of enforcing payment of rent, by threatening her with scarlet fever unless she allowed him, and a couple of infected children, to decamp without paying. She forgave the rent on the condition of the instant departure of the unwholesome lodgers. . . .

October 23*d.* Went to Bandon. . . . was introduced to Mr Berwick, who told me that his father, Reverend Mr Berwick, rector of Esker in 1798, found two peasants lying at the end of his lawn, where they had been shot by a gang of Orange yeomen. The charitable parson removed the sufferers into his house, where he procured medical aid for them. One poor fellow died, the other recovered, thanks to the clergyman's benevolent assistance. Shortly afterwards the reverend gentleman was met by Lord Carhampton, Commander of the Forces, who said to him, " I understand, sir, that you harbour rebels in your house ; if I hear any more of such conduct, I shall, without further notice, have you seized and put on board His Majesty's tender now lying at the Pigeon House." Mr Berwick, who personally knew the Viceroy, Lord Cornwallis, went at once to the Castle and complained to his Excellency of Lord Carhampton's threat. The Viceroy said he could not control Lord Carhampton, who, however, did not carry out his threat ; but he showed his hostility to the humane clergyman by quartering a whole company of militia on him. . . .

December 10*th.* Read in *Chambers' Journal* an amusing account of the family of Seton, by William Chambers. He says that George, fifth Earl of Wintoun, hired himself as bellows blower to a blacksmith. A queer fancy.

When my cousin, Robert Gumbleton, was at school at Bordeaux, a French lad who sat next him on the form had an odd fancy of feeling Robert's ear. The latter demurred to this practice ; but the French lad said it gave him so much pleasure that he trusted his Irish fellow-student would obligingly permit its continuance. Robert, with true Gumbletonian instinct, considered that his ear might be discounted, so he agreed to allow his friend to finger it on payment of a franc per week. The weekly franc was paid and the ear was fingered. . . .

CHAPTER XXXII

How the Diarist went a-Hunting—Decay of Irish Agriculture—How Royalty is flattered—A *Ruse de Guerre*—The
Rapparees Choice—Two Contrasting Pledges.

1877.—*January* 12*th*. Wrote to the *Nation* on the silly
fanaticism of certain Catholic enthusiasts who oppose
Home Rule on the ground that the want of self-government promotes emigration, and that the emigrants are
apostles of Catholicity wherever they settle abroad. I
showed that the loss of souls is greater than the gain,
and it just happens that Father Bannon, S.J., has more
than confirmed my statement ; for, in a lecture delivered
last Monday in Dublin, he says it is computed that there
are now in America fifteen millions of people of Irish
blood or Irish descent ; but of that number less than
five millions have retained the Catholic faith of their
ancestors. . . .

March 17*th*. This day fifty-six years ago I rode to a
foxhunt. The meet was near Palace Anne, now in a
ruinous state. I thence rode to Fortrobert, now also
a ruin, exchanged my mare with Feargus for Anne
Conner's horse, Gamecock, and followed the fox over
hedge and ditch. . . . When I descended to breakfast
on that morning, I found that my father and Tom had
gone off without telling me. My father rode Goldfinder,
a beautiful, bright bay, and Tom rode Alfred, a stout,

brown hunter. I felt vexed at being left behind, and as the servants were nowhere to be found, I went to the stables to get a horse for myself, when I found the doors locked and the key undiscoverable. Baffled in my attempts to get a good horse, I mounted a shabby old mare named Meg, and as decent bridles, etc., were inaccessible, I equipped her with an ancient cart bridle and blinkers. In that grotesque guise I rode to the cover near Palace Anne, which a number of keen sportsmen were drawing. My father did not relish the uncouth appearance of his eldest son and heir, and tried to coax me off the field. Finally I dashed off to Fortrobert. Feargus mounted Meg, probably for the joke's sake; Anne Conner's grey horse was saddled for me, and a very merry day we had. . . .

20th. Letters from Butt and Shaw on this new Valuation of Ireland Bill. Butt says he thinks if he had an hour's talk with me he could convert me into one of its supporters. Shaw condemns it as a Treasury scheme to rob Ireland. Shaw is right. . . .

June 8th. Mr Mitchell Henry sends me a *Morning Post* with the report on the debate and his resolutions. He clearly demonstrated that Ireland is shamelessly and ruinously fleeced by imperial taxation. . . . Of course Mr Henry's resolutions were defeated by a large majority. That was only to be expected in a hostile English Parliament, but what was *not* to be expected, and what is intolerably scandalous, only thirty-seven Home Rule members supported Mr Henry. . . .

18th. The Registrar-General's return has come out, bearing testimony to the annual progress of our national decay. The area under crops in 1876 shows a decrease of 125,000 acres below the quantity of land

under crops in 1875. . . .   In 1876 there were 3730 less
holdings in Ireland than there were in 1875.

23d. . . .   Heard an instance of *amphibologia*.   A
tippling scamp from Corrin was drinking in the house
of a Ballyneen publican during prohibited hours on a
Sunday.   An ominous knock was heard at the door.
Before it was opened, the scamp jumped into a cradle,
and got the publican to rock him a little.   The door
being opened, a policeman walked in, and was confronted
by the tippler. . . .   The constable threatened to sum-
mon him. . . .   When summoned to the court, the
magistrate asked what he had to say for himself.   The
delinquent being sworn, said, "I never drank a drop in
that same public-house since I was rocked in a cradle,"
which averment was literally true.

September 3d.   (Alluding to fulsome flattery of
Royalty, Mr Daunt writes :)   "Among the flatterers of
James I. was Joshua Sylvester, the poetical translator of
Du Bartes.   The poet, in one of his addresses, styles
His Majesty 'Scotland's bliss, England's wish, and
France and Ireland's terror.'   The translators of the
Bible were not ashamed to figure among His Majesty's
eulogists.   Queen Elizabeth had murdered his Majesty's
mother, and bought off his resentment with a round sum
of money. . . .   The royal murderess is referred to by
the translators as 'that bright, occidental star of happy
memory;' but King James is contrasted with the occidental star by the assurance that he comes forth 'as the sun
in its strength.'   This resplendent luminary had robbed the
northern Irish earls and their clans of 385,000 acres on a
pretext of treason that rested on no better foundation
than an anonymous letter dropped in the Council Chamber of Dublin Castle. . . .   His habitual language was

garnished with blasphemous oaths, as also had been the ordinary discourse of the occidental star of happy memory." . . . Sir Anthony Weldon informs us in his *Court of King James* that "Sir Edward Zouch, Sir George Goring, and Sir John Finit were the chiefe and master fooles, and surely their fooling got them more than any other's wisdome, farre above them in desert. Zouch, his part was to sing bawdy songs, and to tell bawdy tales ; Finit's, to compose these songs. Then was a set of fiddlers brought to court on purpose for this fooling, and Goring was master of the game for fooleries, sometimes presenting David Droman and Archie Armstrong, the King's fooles on the back of the other fooles to tilt at one another till they fell together by the ears." Such were his Majesty's actions and pastimes. Yet the crowned miscreant is praised by the reverend translators of the Bible, as " that sanctified person, who, under God, is the author of their (the people's) true happiness." . . .

7th. . . . I told Father F—— a story of St Lawrence, the late rector of Moragh . . . the same story, or similar ones, have often been told of other people. . . . St Lawrence's father, when Bishop of Cork, gave strict orders to the palace gatekeeper to exclude any of his lordship's sons who should not return before nine o'clock at night. Robert, disregarding this injunction, remained at some festive gathering till after midnight, and woke up the gatekeeper by violently ringing the bell. That functionary emerged from his bed, and in reply to Robert's request for admission, pleaded his lordship's commands, which he said he dared not disobey. Some chaffering followed, and the fellow was walking off, when Robert said, " Would this coax you to admit me ? " at the same time holding up a sovereign.

"Well, Mr Robert, I wouldn't like to disoblige your reverence," said Cerberus, relenting at the sight of the gold, "and if his lordship should not find it out, why—" So he opened the gate, and Robert, while entering, intentionally dropped his handkerchief on the road outside. "Please to pick up that for me," he said to the gatekeeper, who unsuspiciously stepped outside the gate, which Robert instantly locked. "Mr Robert," cried the man, "you aren't surely going to lock me out!" "Why, you know," returned the young gentleman, "that the Bishop has given strict orders not to let anybody in who is out after nine o'clock. I couldn't think of disobeying him. Good-night." And his reverence walked off. "Mr Robert," cried the man in accents of agony, "I'll lose my place through your means." Mr Robert returned to the gate. "Well," said he, "I wouldn't like to injure you, and if you give me a sovereign for letting you in I might stretch a point for once, though its against rules." The porter was obliged to refund the sovereign as the only condition of being admitted, and no doubt his appreciation of St Lawrence's facetious ingenuity was increased by the adventure. . . .

8th. I try to amuse myself by poking among some old books. . . . Lord Chesterfield's able, sagacious, profligate letters to his son. . . . Crébillon's tragedy, *Catiline.* . . . I know not if Lord C. . . . had heard a smart *mot* of Crébillon's son on that subject. "Il disait un jour en présence de son fils, 'Je me repens d'avoir fait deux choses, *Catiline* et mon fils.' 'Que celà ne vous inquiéte pas,' lui répondit le fils, 'on ne vous attribue ni l'un ni l'autre.'" I found this in the *Almanach Littéraire* for 1788, in which the French compiler ascribes to the Irish Judge Robinson a witticism commonly given to Curran. An officer had got into a jury box, and the judge ordered the sheriff's man to turn out " ce soldat. 'Je ne suis pas soldat,' repondit le militaire. ' Qu' êtes vous donc ? ' reprit le juge. ' Je suis un officier.' ' Eh bien, huissier, faites sortir cet officier qui dit qu'il n'est pas soldat.'" . . .

November 19*th*. Looked through Scott's *Tales of a Grandfather*. The story of Muckle-mouthed Meg has an Irish counterpart. . . . In the Irish case, a Rapparee, sentenced to death, was offered his life by a powerful chief, on condition of marrying the ill-favoured daughter of that personage. Before making his decision, the Rapparee requested to see the lady. On inspection of her ugliness, he decided to prefer the gallows to matrimony, and he cried out, " Crogh suas me ! Crogh suas me !" (Hang me up ! Hang me up !)

28*th*. A. M. Sullivan's generally excellent book has some defects. He is mistaken when he says O'Connell never defined the exact measure of Repeal which he demanded. . . . On the contrary, O'Connell published, on the 4th of May 1840, an elaborate detail of his proposed measure, giving an alphabetical list of the several constituencies that should return members to the restored Irish Parliament. . . . The general result was 173 members for counties and 127 for cities and towns. . . . Plowden, in his *Review of Ireland*, gives as follows the pledge of the United Irishmen, and the pledge of the Orangemen :—

PLEDGE OF THE UNITED IRISHMEN.

" I, A. B., in the awful presence of God, do voluntarily declare that I will persevere in endeavouring to form a brotherhood of affection among Irishmen of every religious persuasion, and that I will also persevere in my endeavours to obtain an equal, full and adequate representation of all the people of Ireland."

PLEDGE OF THE ORANGEMEN.

" In the awful presence of the Almighty God, I, A. B., do solemnly swear that I will, to the utmost of my power, support the King and the present Government, and I do further swear that I will use my utmost exertion to exterminate all the Catholics of the Kingdom of Ireland." . . .

CHAPTER XXXIII

Starting a Graveyard — Under Obligations to a Lion—A
Much Marrying Peer—A Grisly Tenant—Irish and Scotch
Morality—Eighteenth Century Morality—Genius in Rags
—Archbishop Whately's Prophecy.

1878.—*January 21st.* Mitchell Henry moved an Irish
Amendment to the Address to Her Majesty.
Brooks seconded it. A spirited debate in which A.
M. Sullivan delivered a brilliant castigation of Mr
David Plunkett. . . . Some of the Louth electors,
prior to his (Sullivan's) candidature, asked him whether
I could be induced to stand for their county. He knew
from my refusals to similar applications that I would
not undertake to represent them. They then invited
him. . . .

March 16th. There is a queer story of the graveyard
of Mabeg. The little Protestant church had been
erected for some years before any interments took
place in its tiny cemetery. The few Protestant parishioners were healthy and long-lived, and it was thought
that the cemetery had a comfortless, empty, untenanted
look. So the parochial Solons, resolving to terminate
the anomaly of a graveless graveyard, hired a corpse
or two, *pro tem.*, to start the graveyard respectably—
under covenant to return the said corpses to their legiti-

mate cemeteries as soon as a decent number of parishioners should be interred. . . . If this story is not true,
it deserves to be so.

April 2d. Letter from Colonel Scott, telling me
that, when in South Africa in 1839, he was placed under
obligations by a lion. One afternoon he rode out on
a very lazy horse, about six miles from Grahamstown,
where he was stationed. When he found it was time
to return to his quarters for dinner, he whipped and
spurred the horse in vain; no amount of whipping
and spurring could get the lazy beast to quicken his
pace. It was getting dark and Scott began to fear
he might lose his way, as well as his dinner, when
the roar of a lion was heard at no great distance, and
in an instant the horse started off at a furious gallop,
and brought his rider home in good time. . . .

13th. Two stories are recorded in the newspapers;
one of the abject poverty of the Vicountess Kingsland,
who has for years supported herself by the ill-paid
labour of her needle, supplemented by outdoor relief
of half-a-crown a week given by a London Board of
Guardians. . . . More than a century since, a certain
Lady Boyne supported herself in Tullamore as a school-
mistress. She had from one quarter an annuity of
(I think) £20 per annum, which was confided to the
agency of old Nicholas Crawford. . . . I recollect hearing of some Lord Frankfort who deserted his wife
and ran off with another woman, with whom he regularly went through the marriage ceremony once a
month, so that in case of his wife's death some of
her successor's offsprings might be legitimate. The
parson who performed his lordship's monthly nuptials
must have been a most accommodating ecclesiastic.

14*th*. Butt has really resigned the leadership of Home Rule, but not the representation of Limerick. Failing health is one of the causes he assigns. . . . Another cause is the insubordination of his troops. . . .

May 18*th*. Letter from my son. He and his wife are on a visit with Mr Campbell of Skerrington, in Edinburgh. They had a talk about ghosts the other night, and a gentleman mentioned a grisly apparition that inhabits an apartment in the ancient Castle of Glamis. This apartment is only known to three persons in each generation—the owner of the castle, his factor and the heir. When the heir reaches the age of 27, he is informed of the weird secret, and is under some infernal necessity of visiting the haunted room and beholding its mysteries; the necessity consisting in the fact that if the heir or his father should not visit the haunted room, the evil spirit would invade their apartments with unpropitious results. . . .

June 15*th*. My son has met a Mr Simon Fraser Campbell, recently returned from India. He has seen the English troops line the way and present arms when the car of Juggernaut passed, and he says that the ships that bring out Bibles to India from England, also bring out cargoes of idols of English manufacture for the idolatrous worship of the Hindoos.

19*th*. Read Lecky's *History of England in the Eighteenth Century*. On the whole, a very valuable and interesting work. . . . He has a good deal to say about the Irish Civil War of 1641. Here, as in other parts of his book, he effectively exposes the malignant falsehood of Froude. . . . Lecky's work is not only valuable for its matter, but attractive from its lively and elastic style. Lecky talks of the state of morality in

England and Scotland in the eighteenth century. . . .
In Ireland the position of the Protestant upper classes
was highly unfavourable to good morals.   The penal
laws placed a bounty upon crimes committed against
the remnants of Catholic property, and against the
domestic peace of Catholic families. . . .   There was
a feeling of insecurity in the landed titles derived from
confiscation.   All these causes produced a reckless,
dare-devil character in the Protestant aristocracy. . . .
In Scotland we have pictures the reverse of flattering
of the social morals of the century. . . .   In a paper
written by Mr Abercrombie in the Scotch periodical
entitled *The Lounger*, printed in 1785, there is the
following scene described as characteristic of fashionable manners at that period.   At a dinner in Edinburgh,
a father and son are of the company: 'The father
told us anecdotes of his son's debaucheries, and the
son amused us with stories of his father's licentiousness.
The old man got hold of the bottle, and filling a
bumper, asked leave to give a toast, and then roared
out a 'sentiment,' as he called it, in terms most shock-
ingly gross and indecent.   "Well done, my old boy!"
exclaimed the son, "here goes in a bumper, and may
we all at your age be as jolly and as wicked as you
are!"'   A respectable old Colonel is shocked and
leaves the room. (*Lounger*, No. 14.) . . .

August 5th. . . . A few evenings ago, my dairy-
man's son was overtaken by a miserable creature,
barefooted, dressed like a scarecrow and smelling
strongly of whisky, though not then drunk.   He accosted Tom with some remark on the weather, and
after a little chatter, inquired whether he would like
a sample of ventriloquism?   "Yes," said Tom.   The

genius then stooped, and called out as if to some person underground, "Come up out of that!" A response, as if from the bowels of the earth, was immediately heard. The scarecrow next threw off the ghost scene in 'Hamlet,' with, at least, great fluency. "Pray," said he, "did you ever hear Dr Butler, the Bishop of Limerick, preach?" Tom had heard his lordship. "Here's the Bishop for you," said the ragged mimic, and he thereupon gave a capital imitation of the prelate. He then diverged to the subject of music, and sang the *Gloria* from one of Mozart's Masses with taste and accuracy. . . . He had, he said, been once a thriving tailor in Limerick, and sang for four years in a choir; but he took to drink and was ruined. He then went to London and was engaged as an actor in some minor theatre. He drank himself out of that engagement, and returned to Ireland, ragged and penniless. He had often taken the temperance pledge, and as often broken it. . . .

November 21st. A Scotch field-officer, Major-General Robert Shaw, writes to the *Scotsman* of the 16th inst., condemning in unmeasured language the frantic wickedness of Disraeli's government in plunging the Empire into an unjust war with the Ameer of Afghanistan. . . . The General then quotes from the writings of Archbishop Whately the following very remarkable prophecy of the ultimate destruction of England: "There is," says Whately, "laid up for England a store of woes, the elements of a wider and more irreparable devastation than any which the history of man has yet recorded. Every year aggravates the danger, every alternation of commercial prosperity and depression brings to the reflecting mind fresh assurance of the approaching convulsion. The very glut and surfeit of national wealth in which we are now revelling; the unparalleled activity of all our manufactures; the growing demand for labour in all the branches of industry and in every field of speculation, while they do indeed protract the day, are only accumulating materials for a more deadly explosion." . . .

December 25th. Left the house at 8.30 A.M., intending to go to Mass at Ballinacarriga. I had scarcely gone a dozen steps, when, slipping on the frozen ground, I was thrown violently down, and my head coming in contact with the sharp corner of a wall, I was partially stunned. My hat saved me from worse injury. I was carried into the house, and, of course, was disabled from going to church.

CHAPTER XXXIV

Empress of Austria in County Meath—A Scriptural Dinner
—An Apt Retort—Ghostly Mysteries—Death of Isaac
Butt—'Slashing' of Butter—Letter from Mr Gladstone—
The Biter Bitten—Sir Robert Peel and the Scotchman—
Precedence—Upstairs and Downstairs.

1879.—*January* 16*th*. The Empress of Austria has taken Lord Longford's house at Summerhill, to enjoy the amusement of hunting in the County Meath. Lord Longford is only a Union peer; his title bears the ominous date of 1800. The equestrian movements of the august visitor will be free in a large district from the obstruction of enclosures—369,000 acres having been swept free of their human inhabitants to make way for cattle to be fattened for the English market. Of the excellent character and industrious habits of the peasants who were thus expelled. . . . I had the evidence of two very dissimilar witnesses, namely, Feargus O'Connor, who knew the people well when his father lived at Dangan, and, at a later period, Frederic Lucas, M.P. for Meath, who spoke with admiration of the 'heavenly religion' of the farming community. . . .

February 6*th*. Went last Saturday to Skibbereen. Slept at Hollybrook, a picturesque old seat of the Bechers, where the Bishop of Ross now resides. On Sunday afternoon I addressed a meeting of Home

Rulers, assembled to promote Colonel Colthurst's return
for the county. . . .   Yesterday I presided at a meeting
in Dunmanway, very largely attended by Colonel
Colthurst's supporters. . . .   His nephew, Sir George, is
his opponent.

25th. Read a Protestant publication entitled the
Christian Herald. . . .   Description in it of what is
called 'A BIBLE DINNER—every item of the meal
being ingeniously collected from various parts of scripture, given *verbatim* in the language of the text.' . . .

April 7th. William Glendonwyn tells me one or two
incidents of his litigation for a part of the Parton estate
with his cousin, Sir Robert Gordon of Letterfourie. . . .
William consulted three eminent lawyers on the prudence of appealing to the House of Lords.   These
gentlemen, to wit, Sir Roundell Palmer, Lord Advocate
Young and Mr Pearson, strongly advised the appeal.
Meanwhile, Sir Roundell was raised to the Woolsack
as Lord Selborne, and on hearing the appeal, gave
judgment against the appellant, and against his own
previous advice.   The Lord Advocate, who had concurred in advising the appeal, took a fee on the opposite
side. . . .   Mr Pearson was the only one who adhered
to his original opinion. . . .   Visited Lady Carbery,
and was surprised by her telling me that in her earlier
days she used to read my political speeches and letters
with great interest. . . .   In the evening we told ghost
stories.   William told of an extraordinary noise that
seemed to emanate from the portrait of his great-grandfather.   This was matched by my daughter-in-law, who,
when on a visit with a widow, Mrs N——, in East
Lothian, met in the house a gentleman who was paying
court to the widow.   Facing the enamoured pair was a

picture of the lady's first husband, and the hostility of the defunct to his widow's second marriage was evinced by a mysterious and ominous noise emitted by his picture, the sound of which passed close by the lady and her admirer. . . . By-and-by all the bells in the house, unstirred by human hands, began to ring continuous peals.

12*th*. Very pleasing letter from Mr Lecky, warmly thanking me for my review of his *England in the Eighteenth Century*. . . .

25*th*. Letter from Mitchell Henry, reporting some questions concerning the Irish Parliament proposed by Gladstone, whom he lately met at a dinner-party, and asking my opinion thereupon. . . .

May 6*th*. Much excitement in poetical circles about Tom Moore's centenary. . . . *Apropos* of poets and poetry, I remember a clever parody of Pope's lines :—

> ' If to her share some female errors fall,
> Look in her face and you'll forget them all.'

In the Repeal Association there was a clownish barrister, on whose uncouth face was stamped inveterate vulgarity. Commenting on a speech that had just been delivered by a rival orator, he censured it as being ' very vulgar.' " My speech has been criticised by Counsellor D—— as a vulgar effusion," replied the other ; " I should never have expected such an accusation from *him :*—

> ' If to *my* lot some vulgar errors fall,
> Look in *his* face and you'll forget them all.' "

It was a palpable hit and produced much amusement. The clever fellow who made it combined the incongruous professions of tailor and barrister. . . . This day's paper announces the sad news that Isaac Butt is dead. . . . Ireland in him has lost a son who loved her well.

June 9th. Many rural butter-makers have a rascally habit of what is called ' slashing' their butter. A copious infusion of scalding water, which is mixed through the butter, greatly increases its quantity, but horribly deteriorates the quality, and the article thus doctored does not keep. The result of this adulteration is that the Cork brand has lost its former reputation, and prices have fallen thirty to thirty-five per cent. . . .

16*th.* Loud demands continue for reduction of rent. . . . In numberless instances landlords are *not able* to make reductions consistently with their own solvency; their incomes being strained to the utmost to meet the inevitable calls of annuities, interest on debt, dishonest taxation, and the iniquitous tithe rentcharge.

18*th.* Reading to-day Sir W. Scott's *History of Scotland,* I was struck with a point of resemblance in the govermental management of the Scotch and Irish Unions. The million and half distributed as bribes in 1800, were raised off the Irish revenue, so that Ireland was forced to pay a monstrous price for the knife that cut her own throat. In the Scotch case a sum of about £400,000 was advanced by the English Treasury under the name of an 'equivalent' to Scotland, but England took care that it should be refunded to her out of the Scotch revenue. . . .

July 15*th.* St Swithin's Day ; fine and sunny. Lord Portarlington, who claims to be weather wise, has published a prediction that St Swithin's Day will be followed by fine weather.

16th. Extremely wet—the saint and the earl should have come to a better understanding. . . .

19th. Wet and stormy. The conjunction of Saturn and Mars seems more potent than the conjunction of St Swithin and Lord Portarlington. . . .

August 7th. Read a life of Dean Daunt by a Protestant clergyman named Wynne. . . . The name Wynne reminds me of an anecdote I heard from my grandmother. Many years ago a person of that name was High Sheriff of a western county. He was asked to dine with a nobleman, but did not arrive until the dinner-hour had passed. He apologised for the delay by saying that he had been unable to find anyone to hang a condemned prisoner ; the regular hangman had disappeared, and no offers of money availed to procure a substitute. " So," continued Mr Wynne, " I was under the necessity of hanging the rascal myself." " Sir," said the noble lord, " I do not dine at home to-day," a polite mode of telling Mr Wynne that, as his lordship did not wish to sit at table with a hangman, the High Sheriff should take his departure. . . .

8th. This morning's post brings me a reply from Mr Gladstone to a question I lately addressed to him, namely, whether the tithe rentcharge would be finally extinguished in fifty-two years from the date of his Church Act ? He answers that, so far as his recollection goes, it is certainly to the effect that the rentcharge paid at the rate fixed in the Act for fifty-two years, ' or some such term,' thereupon expires. But he adds that his remembrance is an inferior authority to speeches delivered at the time, and these again to the Act itself. One would think that Mr G., the author of the Act, could speak with more confidence of its provisions. I made the inquiry because some of our Poor Law Guardians seemed unconscious that any provision had been made for the final extinction of the impost. Without its extinction or its application to some really useful national purpose, Disestablishment would be worthless.

18th. Arrived, my little grandson, born in Cork last month ; a decidedly pretty child. . . . A deputation presented him with a pet donkey.

23d. Tenants' wives and daughter at a tea-party. . . .

29th. A dinner to the tenants. . . . Grace was said in Irish by a Maynooth student, speeches were made, and when they had dined, they danced and sang. . . .

September 6th. . . . My darling grandchild died. . . . The event was very sudden.

October 9th. Foxhunters beating up my covers ; two foxes found, earthed and baffled the hounds. Story of a rascal who manufactured potheen and who tried to inveigle a gentleman into concealing it, in order to get half the fine to which the gentleman would become liable if the potheen were discovered on his premises. The rascal brought his whisky to his intended victim, said the police were on his track, and begged permission to bury the kegs in his honour's garden, where nobody would ever dream of looking for it. The gentleman consented, and accompanied the fellow to a part of his garden, where, unseen by any others, they interred the potheen. In a couple of hours the rascal came back with some policemen, and conducted them to the spot where he had buried the potheen, volunteering his evidence against Mr —— as concealing illicit whisky on his premises. But that astute gentleman, suspecting the intentions of the fellow, had removed the whisky so that the intending informer and his escort were baffled. The police abused their conductor for giving them the trouble of a fruitless search on false information. When they were gone, the rascal had the effrontery to ask Mr —— to restore him the kegs. " What kegs? " asked Mr —— with an air of surprise; "you left no kegs here; I don't know what you mean. Get out of my house, you scoundrel!" Exit the scoundrel, crestfallen at having met his overmatch in craft, and who will say that he did not deserve it?

17th. Odd story from Tipperary of mingled ferocity and sentiment. Some ruffians agreed to shoot an unpopular agent. Lots were drawn to fix the perpetrator, and the lot fell on the only son of a widow. One of the conspirators chivalrously interposed, saying that if the widow's son were to be hanged for the intended murder, his poor mother would lose her only support. "But I," he continued, "am one of seven brothers, and if I'm caught and hanged, I won't be missed." Accordingly the shot was fired by this magnificently sentimental assassin, and he escaped the rope by quitting the country.

November 7th. My son had been reading an American tour by an Englishman who said his property was safer where lynch law prevailed, and where the ready revolver kept rogues in terror, than in places where the punishment of evil-doers was meted out by the more tedious judgments of civilised law-courts. Expatiating loosely on this, my young gentleman spoke of the moral and political purification of our social atmosphere that would result from a free fusillade at all rascals—from the scoundrel statesman down to the humble burglar. A bantering, country fellow said,

" Indeed, sir, you're right.   The divil a good will ever be done till some infernal law is passed to desthroy everybody ! "

9th. Read two lectures delivered in America by Dr Talmage. . . . He says that Scotchmen shake hands with peculiar vigour.   I remember an anecdote of the late Sir Robert Peel, who, shortly after he had carried the Repeal of the Corn Laws, encountered in the High Street of Edinburgh a big, burly Scotch farmer, who exceedingly disliked that measure.   The Scotchman extended his hand, which Sir Robert, thinking the action was the homage of an admirer, graciously accepted. But when he attempted to withdraw his hand, he found it closely grasped by his new friend, who said that as it was not every day he foregathered wi' a Prime Meenister, he wad keep him fast grippit till he tauld him a piece of his mind anent the Corn Laws.   Sir Robert struggled for some time vainly, while the Scotchman kept lecturing him on the mischievous impolicy of his legislation.   Sir Robert's predicament was ludicrous, and the incident must have rendered him cautious in thenceforth accepting a shake-hands from unknown Scotchmen.

13th. High life below stairs.   My daughter-in-law mentions having been told by Lord Lothian that his attention was once arrested by loud voices in contention, emanating from the kitchen apartments.   The dispute became so animated that curiosity induced him to ascertain its cause.   Descending the kitchen stairs, he found, much to his amusement, that the servants were quarrelling about the right of precedence in entering the servants' hall for dinner—dinner growing cold while the question of comparative dignity was hotly debated. Queen Victoria, according to Varnhagen, was very indignant with the Queen of Prussia for taking the arm of an Austrian prince preferably to that of Prince Albert at a *fête* in Berlin. She desired Baron Bunsen to inform the king of his wife's impropriety, and His Majesty humoured the Majesty of England to the extent of making an apology.

December 25th. Gladstone repudiates the imputation of favouring Home Rule. Ireland hangs crucified between him and Disraeli. . . .

CHAPTER XXXV

A Noble Lord's Carriage—Standing in her Mother's Shoes—
Result of a Caterpillar Race—Cure at Knock—Magisterial
Freaks—Dr Tisdall's Fair Friends—A Viceregal 'Spoon'
—Landlord and Tenant up to Date—Clerk of Eldin and
the Judge—'Dicky's Mamma'—A New Reading of 'Hia-
watha'—Boycotting.

1880.—*January 1st.* Popular resentment at the doings
of a defunct nobleman who some years ago was notorious for evictions, appears in the shape of a legend
concerning his illustrious ghost. Saith this legend, that
after his lordship's death his well-known carriage and
horses frequently astonished the neighbours by careering
about the country at night. A peasant who saw the
equipage remarked to a Wise Man that the noble lord
could not be in hell, as he was driven about upon earth.
"Did you touch his carriage?" inquired the Wise Man.
"I did not," was the answer. "Then touch it if you
should again see it." The peasant did so, but his hand
was fearfully scorched by contact with the weirdly
vehicle, which seemed to be heated to a white heat.
Tortured by the fiery touch, he repaired to the Wise
Man, who cooled and cured his scorched hand by clasp-
ing it in his own. . . . Some English journals are
indignant at the outcry in Ireland about famine. They
remind me of the fishmonger whom Dr Johnson heard

cursing an eel he was skinning alive because the fish would not lie still.

20th. Arrived Major Glendonwyn and his Spanish wife. . . .

26th. Major G. tells a story of the mode in which full houses were obtained for a play at Drury Lane which had no great success on its first representation. The play was quite correct on the score of morality, but as the public did not seem to appreciate its merits, the manager, or the author, or somebody in their interests, got a letter into the newspapers attacking it on the score of its thinly-veiled indecency, and calling on the Lord Chamberlain to suppress the performance of a piece so calculated to corrupt public morals. Next night the. house was crammed to suffocation. The flavour of imputed immorality was irresistible, crowds were obliged to go away, the manager rejoiced in full pockets, and we may suppose the audience were exerting their wits to discover prurient meanings where the author had never meant any. . . .

March 16*th.* The distress is very severe in numerous places. Among the instances of destitution given by a Cork reporter for the *Examiner,* is the sale of all the shoes of a starving family to make up their rent. This is stated to have happened in an island near Skull, which the reporter visited. That the family had shoes to sell indicates a somewhat better previous position than that of a bare-footed family with whom some tradesmen from this locality were lodged when building a Catholic church at Sherkin a good many years ago. In that family there was only one pair of shoes, at least for the temale members. They were an heirloom, had belonged of the *vanithee's* mother, and were only worn on great occasions. The *vanithee's* daughter was married during the sojourn of our informants, and as it would have been undignified to be married in bare feet, the bride wore the hereditary shoes during the performance of the nuptial ceremony, while her mother stood barefooted among the spectators.

17th . . . When the late Mr Conner's uncle, old Roger O'Connor, was dying, he was visited by Father Crolly, P.P. of the Ovens, and shook hands with his reverence. The interview, or the shake-hands, was interpreted by the servants to imply the conversion of Roger to the Catholic Church. But if the shake-hands had any efficacy it was in the opposite direction, for shortly after Roger's death, the reverend gentleman became a Protestant, obtained a parish from the Protestant Archbishop of Dublin, and married on the strength of the tithes. . . .

April 11*th*. After last Mass at Dunmanway, I addressed a large meeting in support of the candidature of Shaw and Colthurst. A Mr Kettle also addressed the constituency, promising to support a project of making every man his own landlord. . . .

18th. Shaw and Colthurst are returned. . . .

29th. To-day a poor man, named Patrick Willis, came here with his son, a young lad, who had accompanied him from their home in Skibbereen to Knock, in the County Mayo, where the Blessed Virgin is said to have appeared some months ago, and where many cures are reported to have since then blessed the faith of visitors. Willis was a soldier discharged from the army for blindness. He walked the whole way from Skibbereen to Knock, his son attending as guide. He had been barely able to distinguish light from darkness objects seemed clouded by a dense mist or fog. At Knock he performed the prescribed devotions, and is now able to read small print. Some who go there are cured, others are less fortunate. Willis says there are many cures, but also much exaggeration. . . .

May 3*d*. That there was nothing new under the sun was true enough in Solomon's day. This month's *Liberator* gives extracts from the evidence before the Royal Commission on Church Patronage. Solomon could hardly have anticipated the following statement of Mr Herford, the Coroner for Manchester : " It is stated that when the living of Astbury was about to become vacant, one of the ladies of the Crewe family was allowed to stake it on a bet with one of the ladies of the Egerton family, the decision being made to depend on a race between two caterpillars." This, I think, is something new under the sun. . . .

18*th*. Lunched at Phale with Lady Carbery, who introduced me to a half-Scotch gentleman, her agent, named Bogue. He told a story of 1822, the Whiteboy year, when magistrates were signing warrants by wholesale for the deportation of delinquents. Mr Henley, of Mount Rivers, had included a batch of unfortunates in his warrant, when one of his employés told him there was a drunken man singing seditious songs near the house, and inquired how the disloyal melodist should be dealt with. " Oh, we'll give him seven years," replied Henley, and forthwith the poor fellow's name was interlined in the list of persons destined to exile. When his drunken fit passed off he found himself *en route* to the port of departure in company with a party of real or suspected Whiteboys doomed to exportation. He remonstrated in vain ; his name was included in the

awful warrant, from which there could be no appeal. . . .
Lady Carbery said she was glad that the Carbery
peerage had no connection with the Union, and that she
derived a more ancient descent from the very old Irish
race of MacCarthy of Togher than the date of the
peerage—1715. . . . *Story of a lucky snuff-box.* More
than fifty years ago my cousin, Tom Roberts, was
travelling in England in a mail coach, *vis-à-vis* to an old
gentleman whom he had never previously seen. While
conversing with the stranger, Tom R. took a pinch
of snuff from an old silver snuff-box, which he courteously tendered to his neighbour. On the lid was
engraved a coat of arms which arrested the attention of
the stranger, who said, " Sir, may I take the liberty of
asking if your name is Roberts ? " " It is," replied the
person interrogated. " I at once recognised the arms,"
said the stranger, who proceeded very courteously to
inquire the particulars of the ancestry, settlement in
Ireland, and so forth, of the owner of the box. It turned
out that the querist was an old bachelor named Roberts,
owner of an estate (I think in Kent) named Glassenbury. He had no ascertainable relations in England,
and, on being satisfied that Mr Tom Roberts was a
genuine descendant of the ancient stock, he made him
his heir. It is half a century since I heard this story
but I well remember that Roberts showed me a drawing
of the Manor House of Glassenbury, a long, venerable,
old brick mansion, moated, and backed by trees. . . .

June 11th. Left home for Dublin. . . . Story of a
lady who had tried to captivate the Reverend Dr Tisdall.
When the affair cooled she asked the doctor to return a lock of her hair which she had given him in a
moment of enthusiasm. He opened a drawer filled with

locks of hair and desired her to select her own from a
vast number of similar tributes of regard his fair
admirers had given him, as he could not distinguish the
gift of each enthusiast among so many. What a sentimental wig he could have made of all these hirsute
pledges of affection !

14*th*. Visited Sir B. Burke, who said he had met Mr
Gladstone at Lord Annaly's, where G. said that Dublin
surprised him; he had been told that the Union had
ruined it, but instead of ruin he saw great crowds,
good carriages, etc. I went to the Home Rule League
rooms and arranged with the secretary to meet the
council on Saturday next.

18*th*. Visited Sir B. Burke, who told a few *mots* of
that unlucky joker, Corry Connellan. Dr Tyghe, Dean
of the Chapel Royal, who was in embarrassed circumstances, had expectations from a Mrs Deverell, living in
England. The lady died, and left Tyghe the expected
legacy, which he went to England to receive. On
returning to Dublin he met Mr Connellan, and deemed
it decorous to assume an appearance of grief, spoke
feelingly of his late dear friend, and actually shed tears.
Connellan, who doubted the sincerity of his woe,
adroitly quoted the lines:—

> ' Keep tears for those who know you less,
>   But keep your smiles for me.'

Lord Carlisle, when Viceroy, told Connellan that he
deemed it impolitic to treat convicts returned on tickets-
of-leave as if they were hopeless criminals. "They may,"
he said, "have thoroughly repented, and I try to make
them respect themselves by taking them into my employment. Several of the fellows you see in my livery

are ticket-of-leave men.   What think you of my plan ? "
" I think, my lord," said Connellan, " that some morning,
on awaking, you will find yourself the only *spoon* in
Dublin Castle."

    19*th*. Went to the Home Rule League rooms.   I op-
posed the compulsory expropriation of the landlords. . . .

    July 8th. Dined with my sister L——.   Story of a
gentleman who wanted his son to marry a gigantic lady
who had money.   The son was appalled by her stupendous magnitude, and declined to comply with the
paternal wish.   The father persisted in urging the
match. . . .   " Oh, sir," said the son, pointing to the
human mountain, " how could you expect me to marry
all that ? "

    10*th*. Meeting of Home Rule League. . . .   I spoke
at some length, and as usual was much dissatisfied with
my speech. . . .

    24*th*. I have been strolling about Kilcascan for the
past week.   Maxwell Gumbelton has been telling my
son some of his experiences of the land agitation.
Max goes about with a rifle. . . .   He has got some
threatening notices.   A tenant came to ask him for
reduction of rent, when the following dialogue occurred :
—*Maxwell :* " How are your potatoes coming on ? "
Tenant : " Thanks be to God, they're looking elegant."
Maxwell : " How about your oats ? "   *Tenant :* " Oh,
very good entirely, your honour."   *Maxwell :* " Have
you been getting good prices for your pigs, butter
and stock ? "   *Tenant :* " Bedad, sir, I can't complain ;
the prices were good enough."   *Maxwell :* " But why
do you want a reduction then ?   You say your crops
are excellent, and that you have been getting good
prices for everything.   I don't see that you are en-

titled to any reduction on your own showing." *Tenant :* " If I don't get a reduction I'll pay no rent. Public opinion will force your honour to give me a reduction this year, though I don't need it. I have every half-penny of rent in my pocket this minute, but I don't care a d—n, I'll not pay if you don't give me a re-duction. Next year, or the year after, maybe, when I'd be in difficulties, and if the times wouldn't be bad, you wouldn't allow me anything, but as reductions are going this year, 'a bird in the hand is worth two in the bush,' and begor I must get it." Maxwell did not say if he gave the reduction.

28th. Found among my letters of forty years back one or two stories of that queer old Scotch lawyer, John Clerk of Eldin. He began a speech in court by saying, " As I was coming over the Earthmound this morning I thocht within mysell—" " Come now, Mr Clerk," said a judge who loved to snub him, " give us nane of your thochts on the Earthmound." Clerk began again, " As I was coming over the Earthmound this morning I thocht within mysell—" " Weel, sir," in-terrupted the judge, " what have your thochts on the Earthmound to do with the case ? Pray go on wi' the business before us." A third time Clerk began, " As I was coming over the Earthmound this morning I thocht within mysell that I should not finish a sentence before your lordship would interrupt me." When Clerk was promoted to the bench by the title of Lord Eldin, he said, " The difference between me and the Lord Chancellor of England (Eld*o*n) is all in my *i.*"

August 6th. Strolled through Phale, on which poor old dismantled Fortrobert looks down from its

desolate hill.   The sight of it reminded me of old
Bob Conner, whose literary acquirements were never
very great, and were not increased by the defective
vision of old age.   A newspaper which Bob was reading chronicled the misfortune of a gardener who was
cutting *creepers* on the roof of a garden-house, from
which he fell down and broke his leg.   Bob blundered
the passage thus, "A grenadier cutting capers on the
roof of a guard-house fell down and broke his leg."
Bob, who commanded the Ballyneen Yeomanry, was
indignant at this specimen of military eccentricity, and
demanded, "What the d—l the fellow had to do in
such an irregular position."   Something Lady Carbery
said about Irish and English miles reminded me of
the notion of a country girl whom, some fifty years
ago, I met on the road to Skibbereen, to which town
I was riding.   The milestones had just then been
recently changed to substitute the English for the
Irish measure.   "How far to Skibbereen?" I asked
the girl.   "A thrifle over five miles," was the answer.
"I think you mistake," said I ; "it isn't so long since
I passed a milestone marked seven."   "Oh, never mind
that stone," rejoined the collieen, "it isn't there six
weeks."   She seemed to think the stone had not been
there sufficiently long to acquire accurate knowledge
of local distances. . . .

September 1*st*.   Mr Gladstone, in the course of a sea
trip ran into Dublin on Sunday, and said his prayers
in Christ Church.   He was enthusiastically cheered by
crowds. . . .   Gladstone . . . must have formed Lord
Stafford's opinion of Irish gullibility when cheered by
crowds on whose country he had imposed between 50
and 60 millions of taxes since 1853 *in excess* of the

just quota which Ireland should pay to the Imperial Exchequer. . . . Letter from Mr Lecky, who is now in Switzerland. He thinks the immense popularity of some of the 'compulsory expropriation' advocates furnishes a presumption against Irish capacity for self-government; but those people could not gather half-a-dozen followers if it were not for the strength they derive from bad landlordism. Lecky says, "that any mischief to Ireland that Froude's writings can do is infinitesimal compared to the damage inflicted on our national character and cause by the vicious and idiotic gibberings of the extreme land leaguers."

15*th.* Story of Lady M—— and her son, Sir R—— M——, who fell in love with a bouncing country lass, and proposed marriage to her. Lady M—— was indignant at the intended *mésalliance*, and remonstrated in vain with her son. Finding him immovable, she sent for the girl in the hope of inducing her to give up the enamoured baronet. Lady M——, handsome and stately, was seated in her drawing-room when the girl was announced. "Show her in," said her ladyship. The damsel accordingly entered, and her air was so confident and self-possessed that Lady M——, in order to imply reproof, said, in her stateliest manner, "Young woman, do you know who I am?" "To be sure I do," was the unabashed reply; "sure, you're Dicky's mamma." How the dialogue proceeded after that I have not heard, but finally 'Dicky' married one more suited to his station. The scene must have been dramatic. . . .

October 2*d.* Looked into a volume of Longfellow's poems. I am no judge of poetry, and dislike it; I am therefore probably wrong in expressing disgust at the queer style of 'Hiawatha' Rhymes are, I think, a

nuisance ; but, bad as it is, rhymeless octosyllables
are worse.   They run somewhat thus :—

> ' The pigs are rooting up the barley,
> Heard ye not their grunt defiant ?
> Those old sows make fearful havoc ;
> Go, gossoon, and turn them out, or
> Else I'll scourge your lazy carcase,
> Raising welts as thick as fingers.'

Now, in my opinion, this sort of metre is enough to
destroy the most interesting narrative, or the descrip
tion of the most interesting scenery. . . .

November 2d. Wrote to John Bright explaining how
the inevitable operation of the Union is to dislocate,
ulcerate and permanently disorganise the social and
political condition of Ireland. . . .

December 17th. My acquaintance, Mr Bence Jones,
has been boycotted, and his labourers were frightened
into leaving him, although he always treated them well.
. . . It is said that when his milkmaids deserted his
dairy, application was made at the military barracks to
know if any of the soldiers could milk cows. . . . The
incident reminds me of the occupation of a regiment of
hussars, who were employed to drive twelve geese seized
for tithe in the tithe war of 1832. . . .

CHAPTER XXXVI

1881.—*January 1st.* I was told a story of a man who after potations of strength at the shebeen at Fanlobbus, boasted in his cups that if all the dead in the adjacent old graveyard rose in his presence, he would feel no alarm at the sight. One of the convives wagered him five pounds that, notwithstanding his boasted valour, he would not stand on one of the old tombs and cry, ' Arise ye dead.' . . . Instantly a figure slowly arose from the end of the tomb and announced in a sepulchral voice that he answered the summons. The tipsy braggart, stunned with terror, fell back on the gravestone, cutting his head so severely . . . that he was laid up for many weeks.

16*th.* . . . Dan Conner said to me a few days since, " When I was in Trinity College some thirty years ago, a standing toast at the students' supper-parties was, ' To h—l with the Pope ! ' Now any man giving that toast would be deemed mad." . . .

21*st.* Letter from M. Leonard, who is making

arrangements for the publication of my statement of the Irish question in a French translation for a Parisian paper. . . .

March 1st. Story of a Scotchman to whom some unlucky debtor owed sixpence. The debtor fell into such distress that a subscription was raised on his behalf. . . . The Scotch creditor was applied to, and, after some consideration, answered, "Weel, maybe I'll forgie him the saxpence." A story certainly not characteristic of the kindly, generous Scotch friends I am fortunate enough to know. . . .

11th. Received the French journal *La Civilisation*, containing my letter explanatory of the Irish question. . . . Story of two commercial travellers, a Scotchman and an Irishman, who disputed the pre-eminence of their respective nationalities over their whisky toddy in a Cork hotel. Each maintained the superiority of his own country in every particular ; the beauty of the women, the valour of the men, every subject of national rivalship was contested. When most of the disputable matters had passed in review, and the toddy had inflamed the spirit of rivalry, the Irishman boasted that Cork could produce greater blackguards than any town in Scotland. The Scotchman answered, with an air of lofty scorn, "Your Cork blackguards may be vera weel for Irish blackguards, but they are no to compare wi' our black-guards in the Saut Market of Glasgow." This pretty little anecdote suggests a more extended series of comparisons between Scotland and Ireland.'[1]

[1] Here Mr Daunt goes into an exhaustive and interesting parallel of the treatment meted out to each of these countries by England from the demand made by Henry I. of sovereignty over Scotland, and Henry II. of sovereignty over Ireland to the final absorption of

April 28th. . . . Father P. Hurley told us that when marrying a woman to a widower, the latter seemed dull and silent. To the question, " Will you take this woman for your wife ? " he made no reply. " Yerra, Bill, spake up," said the lady, " one would think you had never been married before." Thus encouraged, the bridegroom announced his assent.

May 9th. Left home for Glanatore. . . . Story of a Land League banner at one of the meetings, on which Adam was depicted in primitive nudity, with the motto in big letters, ' Who was Adam's landlord ? ' " *Adam was evicted,*" said an anti-Land Leaguer.

11*th.* . . . Maxwell Gumbleton, when travelling many years ago in Scotland, looking out for a moor, had as *vis-à-vis* on a mail coach a seedy-looking old man. Their talk was about the Crimean war then in progress, and Maxwell observed to his companion that the best thing he had seen on the subject was a letter in a Scotch paper signed ' D.' The *vis-à-vis* seemed gratified, and asked Max where he was going. " To look for a shooting at Thurso." " Oh, ye needna gang sae far. I can get ye plenty of shooting about Wick." . . . D——n (he revealed his name to Maxwell) became very gracious, and bade him a friendly adieu at the inn at Wick, promising to show him good shooting next day. Max

the Parliaments of both kingdoms in that of England. The methods of government in Ireland, consisting of violent repression, massacres, outrages, etc., were paralleled in Scotland. In each country great patriots arose from time to time, who struggled bravely to regain lost liberty. Charles I. tried to force Protestantism on the Irish, and Episcopacy on the Scotch. The Irish, notwithstanding, remained true to his cause, while the Scotch betrayed him. Cromwell impartially sold Scotch and Irish prisoners taken in their respective battles to the West Indian slave-drivers. So history continued to repeat itself through many generations.—ED.

went into the commercial room, not being aware that it
was exclusively appropriated to commercial travellers.
On the following morning a handsome carriage and
pair appeared at the door, with Mr D——n's compliments
to Mr Gumbleton, who, entering the vehicle, was driven
to D——n's excellent house, and introduced to some
good shooting. D——n, it appeared, had risen from
a humble grade to be a wealthy banker, and a man of
much local influence. His carriage usually deposited
Maxwell at the inn at night, and took him thence in the
morning. The 'commercials' were mystified, and one
of them begged an explanation. " Excuse my curiosity,
sir, but we cannot make you out. Mr D——n will
hardly look at any of us, and he pays you the greatest
attention. Pray, sir, what line are you in ? " " In
feathers," answered Max, whose business in the north
was an onslaught on the feathered creation. . . . D——n
told Maxwell he could put him into Parliament for that
district of burghs. . . . He intimated that in case Max
adopted his suggestion, he could neutralise hostility by
employing *in terrorem* the mortgages he held on the
estates of many landed magnates of the district. Pat-
ting the head of a red-haired lassie, he said significantly,
" I can gie this lassie £200,000." Maxwell had then
neither matrimonial nor Parliamentary ambitions, so he
took no hints. . . . Maxwell pays £300 a year in
tithes ; a tremendous mulct.

14*th*. Youghal. Drove here *en route* home. Passing
the ruined Castle of Mogeely, Mrs Gumbleton said that
a wedding festivity having lasted three weeks within its
walls, and no sign of departure being given by the numerous guests, Lord Desmond burned the castle in order
to get rid of them. The version of the story that I

heard was that Desmond, when out hunting, heard that a great number of visitors were on their way to the castle, and as he knew there was no adequate provision for their entertainment, he sent orders to set fire to the castle as the most convenient excuse for excluding them.

24th. Wrote a statement of English hostility to Irish manufacture from the reign of Charles the Second downwards, at the request of the secretary of a Cork society instituted to revive, if possible, some portion of our manufacturing industry. . . .

June 15*th.* The United Trades Committee of Cork invite me to a meeting to be held on the 19th for the revival of Irish manufacture. . . . I see that Charles Edward Stuart, brother of my old correspondent, John Sobieski, has died, leaving a will in which he constitutes Lord Lovat his executor, and bequeaths to his lordship some Stuart relics. The interesting part of the will is the testator's assertion that he is the ' Young Pretender's ' grandson. If so, his grandmother was probably Miss Walkinshaw, and his mother the lady whom Prince Charles Edward legitimised, and entitled ' Countess of Albany.'

27th. A Protestant gentleman, Mr Marmion, living at Rineen, writes to the *Cork Examiner* to repudiate the suspicion of his being an Orangeman. He says he heard the following toast given by an Orangeman : " May our churches be built with the bones of Catholics, thatched with the skins of priests, with the Pope's head for a weather-cock." . . . Story of the disreputable Duke of M——, whom old Scott knew. His Grace had an illegitimate daughter to whom a millionaire brewer proposed matrimony. The Duke said that if the brewer gave him £20,000 he would permit the marriage. The brewer assented, and marriage articles were drawn up by an attorney. But the brewer's relatives conceived that their interests would be seriously compromised by a bargain involving the diversion of so much money into the ducal pocket, and prevailed upon the brewer to recede from the affair. But the articles were drawn by his authority, and an expensive action for breach of promise was an ugly probability. He finally obtained an arrangement by which the young lady undertook to release him from his promise on payment of one thousand pounds. Walking through the streets of W—— with a £1000 note in his greatcoat pocket, he stopped to stare into the window of a print shop which had already attracted some spectators. He then proceeded to the house of the attorney to conclude the transaction by paying down the money. But on feeling in his pocket for the £1000 note, he discovered that it was gone, stolen probably by some pickpocket. All he had for it was to furnish a second sum of £1000; and doubtless the result of his romance, if it left him a sadder, left him also a wiser man. On being asked his motive for proposing marriage to the young lady, he said, " I wanted a bit of blood !"

August 5*th*. Maxwell Gumbleton has received an anonymous letter threatening him with death if he speaks to a neighbour who has been boycotted by the Land Leaguers. Among recent items of the land war is this. A farmer who complained that he was too poor to pay his rent, suddenly appeared as complainant against someone who, he said, had robbed him of a purse containing £410. . . .

September 23*d*. . . . Much indignation expressed at land meetings against the Government for continuing the incarceration of 175 Land League agitators who were imprisoned under the recent Coercion Act. One of the incarcerated heroes was tenant of a farm not far from Maxwell Gumbleton's residence. He had not then joined the Land League. Talking of the state of the country to Maxwell, he deplored the agitation, saying :—"All would go right if six men I could name were hanged." "Whom would you hang first?" asked Maxwell. "Parnell," was the answer. This individual was recently let out of jail, and his restoration to freedom has been celebrated with manifestations of popular delight. . . .

October 21st. The Viceroy has proclaimed down the Land League as an illegal and criminal conspiracy. . . . But it must never be forgotton that if Parnell and his followers have raised a tremendous flame in Ireland, the anti-Irish landlords have supplied all the fuel for the conflagration. . . .

31st. I would back my old friend Feargus O'Connor for good bouncing invention against a host of hesitating story-tellers. A writer in the *St James' Gazette* gives us, with apparently undoubting credulity, the following delicious *morceau*, '" Napoleon's intention," wrote Feargus O'Connor, "was not to invade Ireland. Upon hearing this announcement, my uncle (Arthur O'Connor) started for Paris *and threw his commission in Napoleon's face.*" Napoleon, with amazing softness, thereupon offered him the command of the army which was to invade Spain. "My uncle, however," wrote Feargus, "refused the commission. He afterwards proposed for Napoleon's sister, who married Murat. *Napoleon gave his consent.*"' Just fancy a journalist so exquisitely unsophisticated as to believe that Napoleon would reward a man for throwing his commission in his face, by offering him the command of an army, and consenting to his marriage with Mademoiselle Bonaparte! . . .

November 3*d.* Lunched with the Carberys. The agent, a Scotchman, remarked that twenty years ago you could not have found an Irish congregation walking out of the church as a protest against their pastor's exhortation to act honestly. The present exhibitions of anti-clerical insubordination he ascribed to the march of infidelity. . . .

10*th.* A meeting of the Home Rule Council was held in Dublin on the 8th. I was invited to attend it, but could not. . . . The English notion of continuing their grasp on a nation that their grasp has avowedly tortured and injured permeates all classes. Many years ago I was amused at a trumpery instance of it exhibited by a shopman in the Strand. Public attention was then excited by some Irish question in the House of Commons. I entered a shop in the Strand to make some small purchase. The shopman was very loquacious, dashed into the Irish topic while getting what I wanted, and concluded his chattering by saying, with imperial emphasis, " Sir, I would RULE Ireland."

17*th.* . . . Mr Penrose Fitzgerald of Corkbeg suggests a landlord agitation to obtain the extinction of tithe rentcharge. . . . Nearly fifty years ago I was introduced to old Mr Fitzgerald of Corkbeg, who, I believe, was the person whom the Government bribed to support the Union by promising to double the value of his property by the construction of a Royal Dockyard at Cork Harbour, which promise, of course, has never been performed. . . .

CHAPTER XXXVII

Stage Stories—County Cork Grand Jurors and Tithe—Carlyle's Tour in Ireland—Ghosts and Cobras—A Laudable Ambition.

1882.—*January 9th.* Land League anecdotes diversify existence in the absence of anything better. Father Foley, P.P. of Kilmichael, sent his horse to a gow to be shod. The gow shod the horse, and the priest's boy was leading him home when some busybody told the smith that the priest had contravened the laws of the Land League; I believe by employing a boycotted labourer. On receiving this information the gow called back the boy, saying he had something else to do to the horse. The unsuspecting lad returned, and the gow unshod the horse, which was sent back shoeless to its owner. . . .

February 7th. Read over some of Molière's plays. . . . *Apropos* of plays, here is a Dublin story of the last century. Foote brought George Faulkner on the stage in the character of Peter Paragraph; the make-up was perfect, the mimicry admirable, and Faulkner was paraded before the laughter-loving Dublin public in the most ludicrous light possible. Angry at being thus held up to public ridicule, he sent a large number of his own employés, compositors, clerks, etc., to the theatre, with instructions to hiss Foote vigorously when appearing as his representative. To enjoy unseen the expected discomfiture of Foote, he ensconced himself in a recondite corner of the gallery, expecting that the appearance on the stage of Peter Paragraph would be greeted with a storm of hissing and groaning. Peter Paragraph came forth in due time, but instead of being hissed or groaned by Faulkner's troops, they received him with applause, which continued throughout the representation. Faulkner on the following day scolded his men for disobeying his orders. 'Sure, sir, it was yourself that was there,' was the answer, 'and how could we hiss our worthy master?' Among the remarkable stars on the Dublin stage was Peg Woffington, of whom Provost Andrews of Trinity College was an ardent admirer. It is not, I believe, generally known that Peg was a convert to Protestantism from the Catholic Church. In a *History of the Theatres of London and Dublin*, by Mr Benjamin Victor, it is stated that Sheridan, when manager of the Dublin theatre, conveyed Peg to his country seat at Quilen, County Cavan, where a parson called the Primate of the Mountains received her recantation of Popery. . . . Says Victor : ' An estate of £200 a year in Ireland had been lately left her by her old friend and admirer, the famous Owen M'Swiney, Esq., which she is now in the possession of by virtue of that recantation.'

28*th.* I have forwarded to Colonel Shuldham a form of petition to the English Parliament for the extinction of that oppressive swindle, the tithe rentcharge. He writes to me that Sir George Colthurst, Sir Augustus Warren, Lord Bandon and other landlords whom he had met at the County Club, warmly approved of the extinction, and ordered a number of copies of the petition to be circulated in order to get numerous signatures. . . .

March 20th. Went to Cork at Colonel Shuldham's instance to confer with the Grand Jurors on a movement against the tithe rentcharge. At the Bandon station Lady Carbery met me, having kindly brought me the promised *Edinburgh Review*, which also contains an adverse criticism of my *Catechism of the History of Ireland.* Met the Grand Jury. . . . All agreed that the tithe rentcharge is an oppressive grievance and should be got rid of. The case is comprised in a nutshell. The law exacts the impost from the landlord, while the law, by reducing the rent, prevents him from getting it from the tenant. The law says to him: You must make bricks without straw ; you must pay what you don't receive. . . .

May 3d. Read over Duffy's clever *Bird's Eye View of Irish History.* Among other items noted by him is the degrading fact that in great numbers of Irish schools Irish history is *not* taught, and English history *is* taught. How English writers, even those who intend to be fair, treat Irish history is curiously exemplified by the mode in which Hallam treats the scandalous confirmation of Cromwellian confiscations by Charles II. . . . So faithful had they (the Irish 'insurgents') been to Charles's father, that Ormonde declared that many of the Irish soldiers had starved by their arms in his Majesty's cause, and that he could have persuaded half the army to starve outright. Cromwell robbed the Irish proprietors of their estates to punish their fidelity to Charles, and Hallam holds that when the son of the king whom Cromwell had murdered succeeded eventually to the sovereignty, he acted rightly in confirming the robbery of his own and his father's loyal adherents, because "as chief of England, he stood in place of"—the robber. . . .

June 24th. Read in the *Nation* extracts from Carlyle's *Diary of an Irish Tour.* The hospitalities the atrabilarious creature received he repays with ingratitude and insolence. . . . Triumphant brutality was the ideal of his adoration. His naturally savage mind was incapable of sympathy with the gallant, though unsuccessful struggle of an oppressed people to recover their liberties. Yet one reads with some interest the ebullitions of his odious mental nature, the same sort of interest a medical student might take in examining the symptoms of a loathsome disease. . . .

July 10th. . . . Story of a party of 'converts' in the County Waterford when Souperism was rampant They had been supplied with clothes to wear when confirmed by the Protestant Bishop. They accordingly accepted the clothes, and passed under the Episcopal hands. Next Sunday, however, they all went back to Mass, and on being reproached by the donors of the clothes for accepting them, they said they thought they had given sufficient value for them in allowing the Protestant Bishop to confirm them. The donors took a different view of the matter, and demanded back the garments, alleging that they were meant to cover Protestants, not Papists. Whether the clothes were restored I do not know.

August 3d. Arrived Colonel and Mrs Gordon ; the Colonel was twenty-eight years in India. . . .

11th. My daughter-in-law has a ghost story of an

old woman who appears in a haunted room at Lord Strathmore's. His lordship's house was so full of visitors on one occasion that the only spare bedroom was the haunted chamber, into which two of his lordship's guests, the Misses Davidson, were ushered without being told of its ghostly reputation. After midnight one of the young ladies was wakened by some noise, and shrieked at seeing a hideous old woman in an antiquated dress leaning over her, grinning fiendishly, and bringing her loathly visage into close conformity to that of Miss D. Recovering her courage, and suspecting that the ghost was flesh and blood, the girl sprang out of bed to repulse the intruder. The phantom retreated and disappeared at a door, to the astonishment of both ladies, who still thought it might be a living human being. Next morning they related their nocturnal adventure to the company at breakfast, on which the Earl's family exchanged significant glances, but gave no explanation.

15*th*. Mrs Gordon describes an interview with a cobra in India, which called forth her heroism. She was reading in a room of her bungalow in the hill country, when she heard a hiss. This she did not mind, and continued to read, when the hiss was repeated. Looking up, she saw the hideous snake advancing through the doorway, tongue vibrating rapidly, eyes glaring, hood expanded. She flung her book at the cobra and missed it, merely exasperating the reptile, which moved forward rapidly, its total length being eight or nine feet. Mrs G. then hurled a chair at her visitor and struck it. The snake then retreated into the outer apartment. Mrs Gordon sprang out of a window and called her attendants, who tracked it through the grass to an old Brahminical temple, where it probably entered its hole, as it could not be found.

18*th*. Colonel Gordon says that when he was in India a soldier on his deathbed made a dying confession to the doctor in attendance, that he was guilty of the memorable murder of Lord Norbury at Durrow in 1834. That Lord Norbury was son of the hanging judge, and a mild, generous, benevolent man, spending an ample income at Durrow. Dr Wallace believed that the murder had been committed by a man named Gill, an ill-conducted tenant who lived near the gate of the domain. Lord Norbury's agent, Garvey, had served notice to quit on Gill for non-payment of rent. Gill told Lord N., and begged for time to pay, which his lordship promised to give him. When Garvey discovered this he insisted on Lord Norbury retracting his concession, which his lordship unfortunately authorised Garvey to do. "They will murder Garvey for this," said Lady N. "I shall take care they don't," said the vacillating lord, "for I shall tell Gill it was all my doing." He did so, and was murdered next day.—*Strange hymeneals*. Mrs Gordon mentions a wealthy Miss P—— of Shropshire, who, in rather advanced life, was anxious to be married. The family solicitor proposed, was accepted, and prevailed on the lady to settle her whole fortune on him. As they left the altar, the bridegroom shook hands with his wife and bade her a final farewell. He enjoyed her wealth, and allowed her a small pittance for her support in a convent in Brittany. . . .

October 6th. . . . My son visited our Bishop, who deplores the havoc of our national morals effected by the turmoil of the land war.

18*th.* Arrived, quite unannounced, my old friend
Charles G. Scott and his son. . . . Story of a gentleman
who was late for the funeral of his friend's fourth wife,
and asked a servant which road the procession had
taken. " I don't know the road, sir, but his *habit is* to
bury his wives in Glasnevin." Wife interment had become a habit.

November 5*th.* . . . I found a cavalcade of huntsmen at the hall door. One gentleman . . . who ex-
haled a strong odour of whisky, greeted me with an
assurance that he was somehow related to me. . . .

22*d.* How various are the objects of ambition. One
man courts fame as a statesman, another as a novelist,
and so on. The whisky - smelling gentleman commemorated in my journal of the 5th inst., places his
ambition in blowing the horn at foxhunts. He complained of the grievance, the indignity of having the
duty of horn-blower entrusted to another person; he
had, he said, blown his horn for twenty-five years, and
could blow it as well as any man. It was treating him
extremely ill to confer on anybody else the distinction of
blowing the horn. It was impossible to withhold our
sympathy from the ill-used gentleman, whose noble
ambition was so cruelly disappointed. . . .

December 31*st.* This day ends the centenary of
glorious 1782. The year now ending has been blackened
by most abominable murders and crimes. Parnell and
his followers acquired vast popularity by denouncing
the evictors, the extortioners, the rackrenters. Had
they stopped there they would have merited praise.
But in attacking all landlords, bad and good indiscriminately, they fatally widened that severance of classes
which has always been the curse of Ireland.

CHAPTER XXXVIII

Lady F. Dixie—The *Dynamite Evangelist*—Mr Penrose Fitzgerald on Irish Landlords—Carlyle and Cromwell—Henry VIII., after Carlyle—Value of a Coronet—Hiring Royalty—Yankee Intrepidity—Estcourt and the 'Proud Duke'—Mr Parnell gets £40,000.

1883.—*January* 10*th*. Letter from my daughter. . . . On board was an officer who described to her a ball which his regiment had given, and at which six ladies, sisters, each six feet high and massive in proportion, were among the guests. "I thought I should have fainted," said Captain N——, "when I saw them all filing into the ballroom." Lady F. Dixie has collected £2000, with which she has preserved a hundred poor families from eviction. A noble deed! . . .

March 24*th*. Letter from Mr Penrose Fitzgerald soliciting information on the rascally tithe rentcharge tax, which, of course, I am very glad to give. . . . *Making the most of it.* An old man in our neighbourhood, an inveterate devotee of tobacco, first chews it, then dries and smokes it, then picks the ashes out of his pipe and inhales them as snuff. . . .

31*st*. My son went to Cork to-day and entered the anti-tithe meeting while the audience were cheering my letter, which Mr Penrose Fitzgerald had just read to them. . . .

April 28*th.* External events are *bizarre* enough. A
speaker at one of the meetings of the anti-Irish Church
(which, by way of a grim joke, calls itself the Church of
Ireland) expressed his opinion that the Land League
murders were caused by the absence of Bibles. There
comes forth a student of the Bible, a Mr P. M'Gill,
M.A.C.E., with a pamphlet styled the *Irish Avenger*, or
Dynamite Evangelist, in which, by an interpretation of
scripture of a rather Cromwellian type, he exhorts his
Irish readers to wrap London in flames, and to look for
God's blessing on the conflagration. "The Lord said to
Saul," quotes Mr M'Gill, "'Go and utterly destroy the
Amalekites, and fight against them until they be consumed. And he gathered a host, and smote the Amalek-
ites, and delivered Israel out of the hands of them that
spoiled them. And the Lord approved.'" . . .

May 7*th.* Lunched with Lord Carbery. Lady C.
speaks rather hopefully of the anti-tithe rentcharge
movement, although Penrose Fitzgerald, who has been
acting vigorously in the cause, writes to me that he
finds the Irish landlords, even where their own interests are concerned, "are as hard to drive as Spanish
mules." . . .

June 1*st.* Read again—I believe at the end of forty
years—Carlyle's queer tract on 'Hero Worship.' . . . Of
Cromwell he says, "Everywhere we have to note the decisive, practical *eye* of this man ; how he drives towards
the practical and practicable ; has a genuine insight into
what is Fact." This practical man was also pious. . . .
We can imagine Carlyle's pious hero, who commenced
his great enterprise with prayer, assembling his officers
to preface his enterprise at Drogheda with vehement
supplications for Divine light. Carte, Lord Ormonde's

biographer, describes the result : " All the officers and
soldiers of Cromwell's army promised quarter to such as
would lay down their arms, and performed it as long as
the place held out, which encouraged others to yield. But
when once they had all in their power, and feared no hurt
that could be done them, Cromwell, being told by Jones
that he had now all the flower of the Irish army in his
hands, gave orders that no quarter should be given, so
that his soldiers were forced, many of them against their
will, to kill their prisoners." . . . Cromwell, with profound humility, thanked God for what he called " the
marvellous great mercy of the massacre at Drogheda."
Carlyle speaks of the " depth and tenderness of his wild
affections."   It is a loss to lovers of grotesque absurdity
that Carlyle omitted to include Henry VIII. in his catalogue of heroes.   He might have said, " We will not
praise Henry's actions as always of the superficial sort ;
there it can be said there is always a tendency to good
in them ; that they are the true dictates of a heart aim-
ing at what is just and true.   We have everywhere to
note the decisive, practical Eye of this man ; how he
drives straight for the practical and practicable ; sees
into Fact ; has a genuine insight into what is Fact.
Consider him ! Look at his quarrel with the Black,
Spectral Nightmare seated on Seven Hills ! He had a
priceless, divine message struggling within him for utterance. He stood there, the strongest soul in England,
the indisputablist Hero of England.   The common
speech of him has a rugged nobleness, idiomatic, ex-
pressive, genuine.   ' If you pass not my Bill by to-
morrow, your heads shall not rest on your shoulders ! '
The speech this of a man who could see into Fact, whose
eye could discern the inner harmony of things.   Tender,

scrupulous of conscience, he recoiled from a continuance of conjugal union with Katherine of Arragon. He asked the Pope to dissolve it, which the obstinate pontiff refused to do. The Hero-soul of Henry could not brook the insult. How indeed could *He*, charged with sacred, stupendous message, submit to be thwarted by the Three-Hatted Italian Chimera? There was a depth and tenderness in his wild affections, of which Anna Boleyne had now become the object. Here we note the decisive, practical nature of the man, how he sees into Fact; sees that by longer pottering with diplomatic papal shams he will still endure the conjugal encumbrance of Katherine. Intolerable this! The weight of his life's meaning, the terror and splendour as of heaven itself, now flamed out on England and on the world in dazzlingest effulgence. 'Thou Pope of Rome,' he said, 'art no true ruler of the English conscience. I am England's Pope.' And he was so; and by him was England set free from the Italian Nightmare. This royal reformer is to me no hateful man. If the gibbet and the faggot were employed by him, let it be remembered that . . . Henry's new pontificate needed strongest measures to support it. Yet, in his rugged exterior was enshrined a heart of tenderest charity; a most gentle heart withal, full of pity and love, as, indeed, the truly valiant heart ever is. However provoked by Katherine's contumacious resistance to the divorce, he would not shed her blood. No, he permitted her to retire, undecapitated, to the towers of Ampthill. But when conscience, or it may be the impulse of a divine instinct, impels him to sacrifice his softer instincts to the call of stern duty, he brings Anna Boleyne to the block. H'm! Here, I think, we have

an authentic ruler of men—and of women also, the diffi-
cultest problem of sovereignty." . . .

July 1st. C. G. Duffy sends me his book entitled
Four Years of Irish History. To me this book is most
interesting. . . .

26th. There is a report that Lord Mountcashel, at
the age of ninety-one, is about to marry a young English
lady possessed of £5000 a year. What utilitarian
democrat can allege that coronets are worthless when
this ancient gentleman, tottering on the verge of the
grave, can discount his coronet at such a splendid
premium. Many years have elapsed since Tom Moore
inquired,—

> " Who the devil, except his nurse,
> For Lord Mountcashel cares a curse ? "

His lordship has now discovered somebody who cares
for him, or for his title, and will affectionately ' rock the
cradle of declining age.' . . .

August 29th. A—— arrived from Wales. . . . She
heard the Welsh language spoken everywhere ; in the
streets, the markets, the shops. . . . Compare their
noble attachment to their ancient national language and
their persistency in preserving it, with the wretched,
servile, contemptible indifference to the preservation
of the Irish language that characterises our people at
home. Forty years ago the Irish language was spoken
by at least ninety per cent. of the inhabitants of the
County Cork. At present it appears by a recent return
that only 350 persons in every thousand can speak it,
and its decline is progressive. . . .

September 12th. H. C—— called. Story of Captain
R——, who, when exasperated by some blundering

mismanagement of his hounds at a foxhunt, exclaimed solemnly, with uplifted hat, " I would take it as a personal favour if the devil were to fly away with you all ! "

13*th*. Story in the newspapers of the American millionaire, Mackay, *se non e vero e ben trovato.* He is credited with £7000 a day . . . gives balls and dinners of fabulous magnificence—has catered to the aristocratic ambition of his American lady guests by hiring the King of Sweden to dance with them at the rate of a thousand dollars per hour. This is better than sending round the hat to the taxpayers. A Frenchman once said to me, " Your Queen is a hereditary President." I am a Monarchist, not a Republican, and I prefer a hereditary President to the periodical scramble for the Presidental office by which America is convulsed every four or five years. . . .

18*th*. . . . Penrose Fitzgerald has great pluck. He writes to tell me he has organised sixteen counties against the tithe swindle. . . .

24*th*. Letter on the tithe rentcharge question from Mr Robert Staples of Dunmore, Queen's County, lamenting the spiritless conduct and intellectual weakness of the gentry who recently had an anti-tithe meeting at Kilkenny. . . . Writing to Mr Fitzgerald, he designates me ' that grand old rebel '—rebel to the Union certainly, but as certainly not to the Crown. . . .

29*th*. . . . J. G. Lockhart tells us that in Sir Walter's time two Yankee tourists, dressed in Highland costume, invaded Abbotsford and asked Lady Scott how old she was. My daughter-in-law records a somewhat similar incident of Yankee intrepidity. She, Mr Hope Scott and Lady Victoria (his second wife) were once walking in a private part of the grounds, when an

American tourist entered the reserved precincts. Hope Scott informed him that while he was welcome to walk through the other parts of the domain, *this* enclosure was reserved for the exclusive use of the family. The unabashed intruder looked at him, saying, "Well, stranger, as I'm here I guess I'll stay." Hope Scott laughed, and the Yankee, having satisfied his curiosity by inspecting the parterres, quietly departed. . . .

October 15*th*. Old Lord Mountcashel's death in his 92d year is announced. . . . Here are two stories of Estcourt, the actor, which my grandmother told me. The proud Duke of Somerset was rigidly exclusive and could not endure any sort of contact with social inferiors. Estcourt made a bet that he would dine with the Duke by invitation from his Grace. Accordingly he drove to the Duke's door in a handsome chariot at the ducal dinner-hour, and sent in a letter informing his Grace that he, Estcourt, could, if admitted to the honour of an interview, show his Grace how he could save 10,000 guineas. The idea of so large a saving overcame the Duke's usual repugnance to plebeian company, and he sent a polite message to the effect that he was now at dinner, and that if Mr Estcourt would join the party, they could afterwards speak on the business affair referred to in that gentleman's letter. When dinner was over, the Duke requested his visitor's presence in another apartment, and begged to know the mode in which he could effect the saving of 10,000 guineas. "It can be easily done, my lord," said the actor ; "it is well known that your Grace gives to each of your daughters on her marriage a fortune of £20,000. Now I am quite ready, with your Grace's permission, to marry one of them with a fortune of £10,000, thus enabling your Grace to keep the other £10,000 in your pocket.' Estcourt then bowed and vanished, leaving the irate Duke to consider the obliging proposal he had made. The other story is this. Estcourt was travelling in a stage coach which was attacked by armed high-waymen. "Your money or your life," cried a robber, presenting a pistol at him. Estcourt assumed an expression of vacant idiocy, and gazing with lacklustre eyes and hanging jaws at the robber, pointed to a fellow-traveller, saying, " Nuncle always payshe for me." The deception was perfect ; the robber took him for a fool in the care of his uncle, of course unprovided with cash, and not worth the trouble of having his pockets examined. He thus saved a large sum of money. . . .

December 14*th.* Parnell had a grand display at his banquet in Dublin last Tuesday. Cash flows rapidly into his tribute. He has now got not far from £40,000, and I presume that amount will be finally reached. . . .

CHAPTER XXXIX

Lynch Law—Mail Coach Travelling—Arrest of a Chartist Leader—Demand for Impossible Tithe—Dishonesty of the Church Act—The Domvile Bodyguard—H.R.H. Prince of Wales and Mr Daunt—Lady F. Dixie and the Prince of Wales—A Lump of a Rat—Weasels and their Prototypes—How the Church Act works—A Schoolgirl's Trick—Mr Parnell's Home Rule Scheme.

1884.—*February* 11*th*. Professor Baldwin calls notice to the fact that between 1871 and 1881 more than half a million acres in Ireland had gone out of tillage; the labourers having been banished, the land lies untilled. . . .

23*d*. Messrs T—— of B——, *père et fils*, were fishing here and came to lunch. The son is a very handsome fellow. The father has rambled over much of the world, and tells of his adventures in California, the Rocky Mountains, etc. He was the younger son of an embarrassed landlord, and when less than fourteen set out to seek his fortune. In California he was one of a party of fifteen who were tortured with thirst under a broiling sun. They went to a tavern where the only drink was rum, much adulterated by the publican. There was not enough of doctored rum at the bar to supply the applicants; the publican withdrew to an inner apartment to get more, and was followed by some of T——'s party, who caught him in the act of adulterating the rum with vitriol. They made short work of his punishment—hanged him on the nearest tree and left him suspended until he was half dead. When the party were digging for gold, their nuggets were pilfered by thieves, whose ears they docked to punish their roguery. The thieves allowed their hair to grow long enough to hide their mutilated ears, so that long hair became suggestive of dishonesty. T—— made money enough to buy back the family estate. . . .

June 1st. . . . Parnell's tribute . . . recalls the days of the O'Connell tribute, which was generally collected on a Sunday in November, on which day the great Dan used modestly to hear Mass in private at Maynooth, or perhaps at Darrynane. P. V. Fitzpatrick, who was agent to the tribute, had quite a genius for compliment-ary mention of the priests who collected it. ' The Rev-erend and truly Apostolic pastor of So-and-so ' ; ' the respected and patriotic gentleman who so worthily guides the consciences of the simple and virtuous people of Ballywhack ' ; ' the exemplary pastor of ' (some other parish), ' whose fervid zeal for our legislative independence is only exceeded by his earnest anxiety for the spiritual welfare of his flock,' etc., etc. I remember a ' Mrs Hill ' forwarding the earliest subscription of a certain Nov-ember. The amount was £100. ' Mrs Hill ' was an assumed name. There was a contribution of £1000 from an English cotton lord, who was said to have wished for O'Connell's advocacy in some question in which he was interested. . . .

13th. Drove to Bandon. . . . Here are two Scotch stories. A Presbyterian with whom St Peter presum-ably was not a favourite (perhaps because he had been Bishop of Rome), disparaged that apostle's declaration to our Lord : ' Behold, we have left all things to follow

Thee!' "A braw thing to mak' a boast of!" said this
censor. "What had he to leave? A wheen auld nets, and
an auld rickle of a boat!" The other story is of an old
lady who was scandalised at Her Majesty's taking a
drive on Sunday afternoons, and who considered such
excursions a sad breach of the Sabbath. "Don't you
know," said a neighbour, "that Christ walked out on the
Sabbath?" "I ken weel that He did,'' replied the old
lady, "an' I dinna think the better o' Him for it." . . .

23*d.* Baal fires lighted on the hills for St John's Eve.
A policeman came here to-day to make up the agricultural census. One of my labourers addressed him in
Irish, which he did not understand. "A shame for you,"
said another, "not to know our country's language."
"Oh, d—n it," returned the policeman, bitterly, "it isn't
our country; it belongs to England." . . . "Why don't
you say that in Irish?" I said to a man who was giving
some directions to his little son. "Oh," said he, "we
always spakes English to the childher." Addressing a
young man or woman in Irish, I am pretty sure to be
met with some such answer as this, "I don't ondherstand
Irish,' or, "I has no Irish." This is disgusting and
humiliating. Nobody denies the utility of being acquainted with English. But there is no reason why our
people should not, like the Welsh, be bilingual. . . .

July 10*th.* Amateur coachmen have revived coaching
trips for the season's amusement. . . . The perquisites
to coachmen and guards at each change of these func-
tionaries was a heavy tax on passengers. Old Noble
Seward, a rich County Cork attorney, used to counter-
feit sleep on his journeys when he knew that the demand, 'Coachman and guard, sir,' was coming. The
old gentleman was very fast asleep, apparently and

insensible to the first application. The applicant would then rouse him with a tap on the knee, on which Seward would start up as if suddenly wakened, exclaiming that he would give nothing to a fellow who had disturbed the pleasantest sleep he ever had. On a journey from Dublin to Cork, three outside passengers, when within a few miles of Clonmel, descended from the coach to take a short cut through the fields to that town. But before they could reach it, their short cut emerged on the road where the coach just met them. " Ah," said the coach-man, Jemmy Reilly, "you thought you'd escape the coachman, but it won't do, young gentlemen." Jemmy got his perquisite, which, perhaps, the youths could badly spare. Bianconi's cars were at that time running over the greater part of Ireland. Speaking of some new publication, I asked Bianconi whether he had read it. " No," said he, " I can read no book that is not composed of waybills." I remember 24 hours in winter, and 20 hours in summer, were deemed excellent speed by the mail between Dublin and Cork. I have heard O'Connell speak of 48 hours on that line before 1797 or '98. . . .

August 5*th*. Ballybuy fair. Two horses were killed at the fair in an extraordinary manner. Their riders were galloping them at right angles to the same point, where the horses' heads dashed against each other, and both animals were instantly killed by the collision. . . .

19*th*. This morning, at an early hour, died my valued friend, Lady Carbery . . . one whose residence was a blessing to her poor neighbours, many of whom she has kept out of the poorhouse by giving them employment at good wages. . . .

September 1*st*. Came to Glanatore to spend a few days with Maxwell Gumbleton, and revive old recollec-

tions. . . . Maxwell once met the police officer whom
the Government employed to arrest Feargus O'Connor
on a charge of sedition.   He found Feargus in the midst
of a vast crowd of Chartists, whom he was haranguiug
with vehement volubility.   The policeman's first difficulty was to get near him through the dense crowd.
He had five assistants, all dressed like himself in plain
clothes. . . .   The police conceived that their best plan
was to pass as Chartists, cheering vigorously for every
seditious hit made by their intended prisoner.   In this
mode they wriggled their way through the crowd till
their leader came quite close to Feargus.   During a
burst of cheering, he whispered in the ear of that personage, " I arrest you by a warrant from the Home
Office.   If your followers here knew my errand they
would murder me, but *you*, Mr O'Connor, should go
first.   I have a loaded pistol at your back which I discharge into you at once.   So, sir, if you value your life,
keep spouting away, and walk before me to my cab."
Feargus valued his life, and obeyed his captor, whom
the crowd supposed to be one of Feargus's disciples.   It
was from the police officer concerned that Maxwell got
the story.   There is in the neighbouring town of Tallow
a Miss A——, who has a craze for litigation.   She now
threatens to bring an action against the parish priest for
refusing to give her Holy Communion—damages laid at
£200. . . .

20th. H. Conner sends me an old pamphlet containing two trials, one of Roger O'Connor robbing the mail
in 1812.   The trial did not take place till 1817, and he
was acquitted. . . .   The second trial is for the alleged
perjury of Michael Owens, one of the gang who robbed
the coach and murdered the guard.   Owens had been

King's evidence and was the chief witness against Roger, who now prosecuted him for giving false evidence. The jury acquitted Owens of the charge of perjury, which verdict was morally equivalent to convicting Roger of the robbery.

26th. Apropos of robbery, the tithe rentcharge commissioners announce that unless an impossible amount of arrears be paid up before the 31st of October they will put me into the hands of their attorney. This Church Act is truly characteristic of its author. . . . Tom Moore tells a story that Lord Llandaff used to spend £1000 a year in bribing bailiffs not to serve writs on him ; and a writer who describes Santry Court, the seat of the Domvile family near Dublin, says that an embarrassed Domvile protected himself from bailiffs by a bodyguard of fierce, well-trained bull-dogs, that accompanied him in his walks, and would fly at the throat of any bailiff that approached suspiciously near their master. I prefer the Domvile tactics to Lord Llandaff's. . . .

October 24th. The papers give copious extracts from Froude's life of the quack philosopher, Thomas Carlyle. Carlyle disparages Mr Gladstone, calls him a man without true insight into the reality of things, and contemptuously says, " Poor Phantasm ! " This is really too bad. Mr Gladstone fulfils two conditions that should awake the sympathetic praise of his censor, who applauds Cromwell because ' he drives straight at Fact.' Mr G. drives straight at our pockets for the benefit of England. Surely *that* is driving straight at fact. Again the quack philosopher tests merit by success. " Await the issue," he says. Now, the issue of Mr Gladstone's financial operations is largely to help the other agencies of the Union in expelling the Irish people from their country, and this ought to have secured for him the approval of a philosopher who hated the Irish as heartily as Carlyle's published *Tour in Ireland* shows him to have done. . . .

December 12*th.* Wrote to Mr Gladstone representing the mischief inflicted on the payers of tithe rentcharge by his Disestablishment Bill, which does not authorise the septennial revision of the impost—thus depriving us of the benefit we should have derived from the great fall in the market price of corn.

18*th.* Letter from Mr Gladstone's secretary, Mr Horace Seymour, saying that G. had forwarded, or would forward, my statement to the Chancellor of the Exchequer, but could give no pledge as to the result. . . .

1885.—*January* 26*th.* Wrote to ask Parnell here to have a conversation upon Irish affairs. . . .

February 2*d.* Parnell writes to say that he got my letter when sitting in a railway carriage, *en route*, I believe, for the County Clare. He expresses willingness to correspond—but after all, *cui bono ?* . . .

April 6*th.* An Englishman named Jephson advocates in the press the abolition of the Viceroyalty as a means of completing and consolidating the Union. I wrote to the papers . . . that any scheme for further consolidating such a hideous national curse should encounter the opposition of every Irish patriot. There is here a Colonel Gillman, who sometimes rides with our hunt club, and whose estimate of the Irish country gentleman's intellect is not flattering. He said to my son that they have not an idea beyond, ' This is a fine day,' or, ' that is a good dog,' or, ' will you have a drink ? ' . . .

16*th.* Letter from Lady Florence Dixie saying that

she has sent the report of my recent political interview with Potter, editor of the local paper, the *West Cork Eagle*, to the Prince of Wales, with a request that H.R.H. will read it, and an assurance that she concurs in my views. The Prince is godfather to one of her children. . . .

22d. Letter from Lady F. Dixie saying that the Prince of Wales begs her to inform me that he has read with interest my views on the Irish question. Much royal civility is added. . . .

May 9th. St Stephen's Review sent me by Lady F. Dixie, containing her letter to the Prince of Wales, and one of my letters to her ladyship, which she forwarded to H.R.H. Now, how did those things get into print? Lady F. declares she doesn't know. Has anybody meddled with her writing-desk?

12th. M. Leonard sends me the *Soleil*, a Paris journal, which has a notice of the aforesaid correspondence.

19th. Letter from Parnell thanking me for information I had given him on the Union robbery of Ireland. . .

June 11th. Discussions going on about the probable appointment to the Archdiocese of Dublin. If the Pope should appoint a man stamped with the recommendation of the English Government, it would be worse than the *veto* which Rome formerly sanctioned, and which O'Connell defeated. The name of O'Connell reminds me of some of his characteristic sayings. On one occasion he had offended the whole corps of reporters at the Corn Exchange, and they mutinied against him. He commenced a speech, and they all laid down their pens. They were all Catholics, except one who was said to have abandoned the Catholic Church and become a Protestant. When O'Connell saw that they meant to leave him unreported, he indignantly exclaimed, "Am I to be put down by a set of mice?" The reputed convert to Protestantism, a stout, portly fellow, defiantly asked, "Do you call *me* a mouse?" "Indeed I don't," replied O'Connell, "I call you a good lump of a rat." This hit disarmed the wrath of the other mutineers— they all laughed and plied their pens as usual, the convert joining in the merriment.

15*th*. . . . The following letter from Lady F. Dixie to the Prince of Wales acknowledges one in which H.R.H. courteously requested she might assure me of the interest with which he had perused the statement of my political sentiments :—

> "THE FISHERY, WINDSOR,
> *April* 25*th*.

"SIR,—I duly forwarded your Royal Highness's reply to Mr O'Neill Daunt, and have to-day received the enclosed letter, which, being more addressed to your Royal Highness than to myself, I venture to forward on. It expresses my own opinions, and those of many thousands of subjects of the Queen as loyal as myself; opinions, the neglect of which by the British Government has brought into existence the vile communistic and revolutionary party. Such a party could not have been born in Ireland had the opinions of such true patriots as Grattan and O'Connell prevailed with England. They, unfortunately, failed to prevail, and revolution has in consequence been sown. Mr O'Neill Daunt's letter deserves careful perusal and consideration as that of a true Irish landlord patriot, who does not find landlordism inconsistent with patriotism, or patriotism inconsistent with loyalty. His letter speaks the minds of thousands, and advocates the only remedy against discontent and revolution.—I have the honour to be, sir, Your Royal Highness's most obedient servant,

"FLORENCE DIXIE."

Here is the letter which she transmitted to the Prince.

"KILCASCAN, BALLYNEEN,
COUNTY CORK, IRELAND,
April 23*d*, 1885.

"DEAR LADY FLORENCE,—I am extremely obliged to you for having transmitted my 'interview' to the Prince of Wales, and I am much gratified that he has read it with interest. When you next correspond with His Royal Highness, may I ask you to tell him, with assurances of my profound respect, that I only express what millions feel when I say that never did monarch or patriot receive a more enthusiastic welcome than would await him, when opening, on the part of his royal mother, the first session of the restored Irish Parliament. I know no act more certain to promote loyalty to the Crown than the re-establishment of the Irish Constitution of 1782; and I know no act more fraught with all the elements of evil than the act which destroyed the Irish legislature. Let an Englishman imagine his country governed by any foreign power, say by France—(and Macaulay tells us that such a fate was on the cards in the time of the Plantagenets)—and let him then ask himself whether he would not feel hatred of the Power that had suppressed their exercise? There is much silly talk about the 'dismemberment' of the Empire by repealing the Union, just as if the Empire was dismembered before the year 1800, or if it was now dismembered by the legislative independence of Australia and of Canada! In like manner the enemies of Home Rule calumniate the Home Rulers as 'separatists,' whereas there were never more determined friends of the Imperial connection than Grattan, Ponsonby, Foster and the other opponents of the Union in the Irish Parliament. . . . Men would be returned to Parliament, heartily desirous to preserve the connection with England on such terms as would not compromise our honour, embitter the international relations, strip us of our revenues, public and private, and banish our people.—Believe me to be, dear Lady Florence, most truly yours,

" W. J. O'NEILL DAUNT."

. . . I took care to impress on my correspondent that the Parnellite agitation was all the fault of the landlords. . . .

July 14*th*. Saw a rabbit pursued by a weasel near the western gate. The weasel pounced on the rabbit's neck and began to suck its blood. Thought the rabbit on this occasion typified Ireland, and the weasel represented the Chancellor of the Exchequer, who, in matters financial, is an effective blood-sucker. . . .

15*th*. Collapse of the Munster Bank. . . . The directors appear to have made off with large amounts of the bank capital. A neighbouring farmer who had saved £15 for his own funeral and lodged it in the bank, philosophically says that he will forgive the rascals, provided they will give him a coffin, a pound of tobacco and a few bottles of whisky to be consumed at his wake. . . .

26*th*. Achilles and I dined to-day at Father Delay's to meet our good old Bishop, who is returning to Cork after his last visitation. . . . He said that about a hundred converts were annually received into the Church in Cork at the present time. . . .

October 20th. H. Conner came; a pleasant, intelligent fellow, whom I cordially esteem. Story of Roger O'Connor's daughter, Mrs Wilhelmina Smithwick. In her young and sportive days she played off a trick on a Mr Llewellen Nash. There were two gentlemen, father and son, of the same name. Wilhelmina addressed a letter to 'L. Nash, Esq.,' purposely omitting 'junr.,' enclosing a young lady's portrait, and breathing the most fervid assurances of passionate attachment. The letter, of course, fell into the hands of Nash, senior, who naturally believed that he had discovered a secret love affair of his son, whom he rated soundly for engaging in a matrimonial project without the paternal sanction or knowledge. Nash, junior, had great difficulty in persuading his father that he knew nothing of the writer of the amorous epistle, and in short that it was a mischievous trick. A Mr Frederick Cavendish was accused of burning his house, was tried for arson, and although he was acquitted, yet a suspicion of guilt still adhered to him. He was significantly nicknamed 'Moscow Cavendish.' Meeting Lord Norbury shortly after his acquittal, he acquainted his lordship with the news of his marriage. "I am happy to hear it," said Norbury; "you know that St Paul says 'it is better to marry than *burn*.'"

November 8th. . . . Lady F. Dixie. . . . asks me to address to herself such a letter as she may submit, together with my article (on the Irish Difficulty), to the Prince of Wales. . . .

17th. Parnell is said to have drafted a bill for Home Rule, of which the provisions are, firstly, an Irish

Parliament, consisting of a single Chamber; secondly, the control by England of all imperial matters ; thirdly, the abolition of the Viceroy.   Wrote to him. . . . that a bi-cameral Parliament is better than one with only a single Chamber, as the second one, which might be elective, would interpose a check on precipitate or crude legislation; secondly, that if England had sole control of all imperial matters, we should be mercilessly robbed, as at present. . . . and thirdly, that the Viceroyalty, cleansed of its errors by reform, is the very best mode of an executive government for Ireland.

CHAPTER XL

Tories turned Out—A Survivor of '98—Mr Gladstone's Home
Rule Bill—More Ghosts—Substitute for Brickbats—Mr
Gladstone to Mr Daunt—Mr Gladstone on the Landlords'
Claims—Daniel O'Connell's 'One Word'—Mr Gladstone
and the Landlords' Claims—Mr Daunt and Mgr. Persico—
The Castellan of Lisfinny—Mr Gladstone's Confession—
Mr Gladstone and Irish Finance—Conclusion.

1886.—*January* 24*th*. Letter from Lady F. Dixie,
announcing the gracious reception by the Prince of
Wales of my article on *The Irish Difficulty*.

30*th*. Parnell and his party have turned out the Tory
Government. . . .

February 16*th*. Accompanied my son to Dunmanway,
where he, as a magistrate, had to register claims to vote
for Poor Law Guardians. One of the claimants was
a fine old relic of the last century, aged 97 ; he remem-
bers the French fleet in Bantry Bay. . . .

April 12*th*. On the 8th Gladstone made his speech,
introducing the measure of Home Rule for Ireland ; a
speech of splendid eloquence. It occupied three hours
and twenty-five minutes. He deserves gratitude for
this attempt to solve the old international quarrel. . . .

28*th*. My 79th birthday. . . . Here are some
weirdly memoranda, believe them or not who pleases.
A Ballyneen mason, George Farr, returning home one
night, saw a woman's ghost, with a light in her hand,

gliding through the fields to the Bandon river below the village, until she reached a part of the river where a woman had been drowned. The apparition then disappeared, and until that moment he had taken it to be a woman of flesh and blood. When poor Mary —— a suicide, was carried to her grave at B——, a noise proceeded from the coffin, so like the mewing of a cat that the persons next the coffin imagined that the cat must somehow have been shut in with her mistress's corpse ; but on returning home, the funeral party found the defunct lady's cat in her accustomed quarters. When my wife and I for some time occupied the old house, we heard a nocturnal noise exactly resembling the sound of people walking in heavy shoes up and down stairs and past our bed, but we never could see anyone. This happened several times. One night, before we had been long in bed, our feet were violently pulled — simultaneously—by some invisible intruder. We both called out, 'Who's there?' but received no answer. That it was no human intruder I am quite certain. After the death of my grand-aunt, Miss Crawford, in 1821, my grandmother, her sister, saw a clear, bright flame ascending from the bed which had been occupied by the deceased. . . .

June 5th. I am invited by the Protestant Home Rulers of Cork to become their president. It seems they think I am a Protestant. Wrote to thank them for their patriotism, but a Protestant president would be preferable.

8th. Gladstone's Home Rule Bill lost by a majority of thirty. . . . O'Connell was defeated (on the Repeal question) by a majority of 485 ; Gladstone, by a majority of only 30. This contrast shows progress. . . .

19th. It appears that some clergymen in Ulster represent the majority against the Home Rule Bill as an answer from Heaven to their prayers. If they think that their prayers have this efficacy, they would do well to induce their Orange followers to substitute prayers for the brickbats, cudgels, dead cats, stones, and fire-arms with which they at present manifest their love for peace, law, religion and order. . . . I am told that Mrs ——, who is undergoing a year's imprisonment for trying to burn her house, thereby to recover compensation from the county for ' malicious injury,' has improved in health and spirits while in jail. She is exempt from the worry of domestic miseries that tormented her at home ; the authorities are kind to her, and she gets enough to eat ; this last is a change for the better, as the domestic larder was so scantily provided that it is believed her abortive attempt at conflagration was undertaken in the hope that the county rates might be made contributory to the food supply. What a wretched condition when a half-starved lady, a magistrate's wife, adopt such wild means to get something to eat. . . .

July 5th. Wrote to Mr Gladstone on this Home Rule question, stating the disparity between the real rights of Ireland and the concessions proposed in the Government scheme. . . .

12th. Letter from Gladstone's secretary, Mr Lyttleton, saying that Mr G. has read my statement on the Irish question with 'singular interest.' I had quoted Lecky's description of the Union, ' a crime of the deepest turpitude,' and Mr Gladstone records his agreement with it. . . .

August 13th. Lady F. Dixie has written a review of my *Eighty-Five Years of Irish History*, which will appear in the *Liberal Home Ruler*. This is very kind. . .

23d. . . . My son and his wife have just returned from Scotland. They bring Chambers's *Traditions of Edinburgh.* . . . *Inter alia,* Chambers records the discontinuance of sedan chairs. I remember two stands of sedan chairs in Dublin, one at the north-east corner of Rutland Square . . . the other at the corner of Clare Street. . . .

October 15*th.* A civil review of my book appears in the *Times ;* marvellously favourable when the anti-Irish politics of that paper are considered. I was also sent favourable reviews in the *New York Times* and the *New York Tribune.* . . .

December 27th. Extracts from the late Lord Shaftesbury's diary. . . . record that people were in the habit of ascribing to him influence which he did not possess. This reminds me of O'Connell's complaint to the same effect. " One word from *you* will get all we want." " Oh, how sick I am of that one word ! " he used to say. . . . He once had a pathetic request from a love-sick youth to obtain for him a situation which would enable him to get married and support a family. O'C. had no knowledge of the inamorato who relied on the sympathetic benevolence of the great Dan to employ the ' one word ' in his favour. That one word was not spoken. . . .

1887.—*February* 24*th.* Notice from the tithe banditti that if the arrears, with costs added, be not paid within ten days, they will place a receiver over the rents. Now they know perfectly well that the means of paying this demand no longer exists. It has been swept off by the Land Act of 1881, and by the fall in all landed values. . . .

April 11*th.* Harry and Mrs Conner called. H. says the Tithe Commissioners are placing receivers on rents right and left.

28th. My eightieth birthday. I might have hoped. . . . to be allowed to spend my few remaining days in peace, instead of being beggared by these Tithe Commissioners. We read in Scripture, that in the process of exorcism the evil spirit tears and rends the person from whom he is expelled. We have been trying, hitherto unsuccessfully, to drive out the evil spirit called tithe rentcharge ; like its prototype in the Gospel, the said fiend lacerates and rends us in our struggle to expel him from among us. A hotelkeeper at Castleisland, Kerry, has been summoned before the magistrates for the disloyal offence of setting up before his door the disloyal words, ' God save Ireland.' He has been fined £2 for this prayer. . . .

June 17*th.* Wrote this day to the Pope, to place before his Holiness my views of the extreme danger to the Catholic religion in Ireland, of allowing the English Government any voice or influence in the appointment of Irish Bishops. [1]

August 9*th.* Letter from Mr Gladstone telling me that he thinks the financial management of Ireland requires readjustment, and that the landlords, as a class, have as strong claims for consideration, notwithstanding their misdeeds, as the W. India planters had in 1833. . . . The Reverend Henry Stuart Fagan, rector of Great Cressingham, Norfolk, has been in Derry, and gives the *Guardian* some notes of his visit. He met a young Orangeman, to whom he recommended unity among Irishmen of all creeds. The reply was, " We won't knock under to those brutes." Mr Fagan protested against these words, on which the Orange youth retorted, " Yes,

---

[1] This letter made a considerable impression at the Vatican. It delayed, and nearly prevented, Mgr. Persico's mission.—ED.

they've proved themselves brutes, and will again; and that's my Christianity." . . .

September 14th. Went to-day to meet Mgr. Persico, the Pope's envoy, at Ballyneen station. The train to Skibbereen could only wait a few minutes, which I tried to utilise by impressing on his Excellency that the principles of Irish Catholicity and Irish nationality were so indissolubly interfused that any attempt to dissociate them would be very dangerous to religion. . . . He seems to be about seventy, and has courteous, gentle manners. I asked him to visit me, but he said the time at his disposal was too limited to allow him to accept my invitation. . . . There is a Mr R——, handsome, eccentric, of solitary habits, with (reputed) £6000 a year, and unmarried, who thinks himself ill-used because no lady has proposed to marry him.

October 9th. The Coercion Act has developed a romantic episode. Under this Act it was intended to arrest Mr Jasper Douglas Pyne, M.P. for one of the County Waterford divisions. Mr Pyne does not choose to be arrested, and accordingly he entrenches himself in the strong old Castle of Lisfinny, near Tallow, fortifies the ancient edifice . . . provisions it for a three months' siege, and bids defiance to any attempt to arrest him in his fortress, of which the walls are eighteen feet thick. . . .

December 3d. Yesterday the Lord Mayor of Dublin, T. D. Sullivan, was imprisoned in Richmond Penitentiary under the new Act for creating crime.

1888.—*January 4th.* Mr Gladstone has been justly and ably denouncing the Union in the *Westminster Review* and other periodicals. He has given many unanswerable arguments against it. He might add, however: 'If you want to appreciate the evils of the

Union, look at me, W. E. G. When Ireland lay crushed and prostrate beneath the miseries of a seven years' famine, when multitudes had perished by starvation, and when all who could obtain the passage money were flying to America, I, W. E. G., seized the propitious moment to give a spur to the exodus by adding 52 per cent. to the previous taxation of Ireland, and pleaded the terms of the Union as my justification for inflicting this scourge on the suffering people.' . . .

February 5th. The landlords have had an audience of Lord Salisbury, stated their sufferings, decreased incomes, charges, either stationary or augmented. Lord S—— was civil, expressed sympathy with the applicants, said he would examine their statements one by one, and —dismissed them.

March 9th. . . . Mr Purcell dined here. He amused us by an account of his relative, the late Mr Cotter, rector of Donoughmore, in this county, an anti-Catholic controvertist — married three times — had twenty-two children—spent £2000 bequeathed to him by one of his wives in a ramble on the Continent. When the money was gone he returned to his parish. The tithes were £1500 per annum, and the congregation consisted almost wholly of his own family. Facetious Catholic peasants amused themselves with his controversial propensities, by knocking him up after midnight, pretending they were in a hurry to be converted.

15th. Postcard from Mr Gladstone saying that he deems the financial question needs scrutiny—glad he has my 'approval,' which, in fact, applied only to his admission of wrong—

CONCLUSION

HERE the diary so faithfully kept for more than forty long years (and of which a much-abridged transcript is presented to the reader) ends abruptly. Mr Daunt lived for six years longer, growing more feeble bodily year by year, but losing nothing of his keen interest in Irish politics, or in anything that concerned the welfare of the country so dear to his heart. He frequently addressed letters to the newspapers bearing on Irish taxation; for the fiscal relations of the two countries he had at his fingers' ends. Therefore it was that the prospect of a new and heavy impost filled him with indignation. The mental agitation into which Sir William Harcourt's Budget proposals threw him, actually hastened his end. The very last letter addressed to a newspaper, *The Wexford People*, a page of which that journal reproduced in *fac-simile* after his death, was on this theme, imploring the Irish members to pause ere they helped in heaping a fresh tax on their country. His words were of no avail. The succession duties passed into law, and a new bitterness was added to dying beds. Mr Daunt's character stands pretty well revealed through the pages of his diary. He was upright and honourable, unalterably true to his political and religious principles, and to his private friendships. His simplicity was that of a child ; he could scarcely be brought to believe evil of anyone, without at least overwhelming proofs. His estimation of himself was a very humble one, and therefore he was quite free from those petty jealousies and spites that sometimes disfigure the career of public men. His urbanity and gentleness were charming, his sweetness of character and manner increasing the more helpless, physically, he grew. Latterly he became very lame and feeble, and moved with difficulty, although he came downstairs daily about two o'clock. The end came very unexpectedly. On Friday, June 29th, 1894, he complained in the morning of feeling unwell. His indisposition, which seemed of small account at first, increased as the day went on, and his heart was attacked. In intervals of sickness and pain he prayed fervently. Yet what might have been the peace of this deathbed was disturbed cruelly from time to time by thoughts of the new and crushing tax which he feared would ruin his family. Towards three o'clock he became unconscious, and without a struggle the soul of this truest of Irish patriots winged its flight to a happier land. Emphatically it must be said, Ireland was the poorer by his death, for never had she a son who loved her from youth to age with a more single-hearted devotion.

By his own express desire his funeral was not publicly announced, so that crowds of admirers and sympathisers from Cork, Macroom and elsewhere, who would gladly have followed this ' Nestor of Irish politics ' to his last resting-place, were unable to do so. Almost all the papers, daily and weekly, and of all shades of politics, had appreciative articles upon his career, for even those most opposed to him, politically, had come to recognise and reverence his perfect honesty of purpose, and his stainless life.

THE END

INDEX

A

ABDUCTION of heiress, 6
Aberdeen, 46, 68
Abbotsford, 111
Abercorn, Marquis of, 169
Abercrombie, *The Lounger*, 343
Acquittance in full, 183
Advowsons sold, 181
Adams, Dr Maxwell, 37
Adventure, A priest's, 481
—— A lawyer's, 85
Admiralty orders, 125
Ady, Joseph, 328
Afghanistan, Ameer of, 344
Allen, Bog of, 1
Alison's *History*, 146
Algeria, Irish colonisation of, 263, 264, 273
Albany, Count of, 287
—— Countess of, 370
Amphibologia, 335
Amory, 86
Amusing falsehoods, 198
American gambling, Amenities of, 206
Amendment to Address, 340
Amateur coachmen, 391
Ancestry, Mr Daunt's, 1, 2, 3
Anti-State Church meeting, 91
Anjou, Margaret of, 2
Anecdote, Law student's, 49
Anderson, Miss, 68
Anglesea, Marquis of, 295
Andrews, Provost, 375
Apparition, 9
Arab steamer, 33, 34
Ardee, Member for, 43
Ardagh, Bishop of, 16, 17, 75, 280
Arbroath, 45

Ardrossan, 90
Arran, Earl of, 170
Archie Armstrong, 336
Assassination in County Tipperary, 22
Astbury, Living of, 358
Assizes, 156
Athlone, Meeting at, 17
Attorney's trick, 77
Airdrie, Meeting at, 36, 320
Aitchison, Mr, 91
Auckland, Lord, 138
Autun, Bishop of, 163
Azrael, Angel of Death, 197

B

BARRY, Philip ōge, 3
—— Garrett Standish, 142
—— Mr, 214, 217
—— Serjeant, 253
Barrington, Sir Jonah, 310
Barnard, Major-General Sir Andrew, 6
Baronet's story, 326
Ballymahon, 16
Ballinakill, 30
Banagher, Meeting at, 18
Ballyneen, 52
—— Relief meetings at, 53, 62
Ballymoney, 62, 64
Ballyward, Old castle of, 141, 200
Ballinacarriga, 51, 200, 204
Baltinglass, Lord, 231
Bartholomew, State porter, 205
Baldwin, Professor, 289
Baal fires, 391
Ballybuy fair, 148, 392
Banner, Land League, 368

411

Colston & Coy. Limited, Printers, Edinburgh.